TO DIE OR NOT TO DIE?

TO DIE OR NOT TO DIE?

CROSS-DISCIPLINARY, CULTURAL,
AND LEGAL PERSPECTIVES ON
THE RIGHT TO CHOOSE DEATH

EDITED BY
Arthur S. Berger
AND
Joyce Berger

New York
Westport, Connecticut
London

Library of Congress Cataloging-in-Publication Data

To die or not to die? : cross-disciplinary, cultural, and legal
  perspectives on the right to choose death / edited by Arthur S.
  Berger and Joyce Berger.
       p.   cm.
  Includes bibliographical references.
  ISBN 0-275-93585-X (alk. paper)
  1. Right to die.   2. Euthanasia.   I. Berger, Arthur S., 1920- .
  II. Berger, Joyce.
  R726.T6   1990
  179'.7—dc20   90-34370

Library of Congress Catalog Card Number: 90-34370
ISBN: 0-275-93585-X

First published in 1990

Praeger Publishers, One Madison Avenue, New York, NY 10010
An imprint of Greenwood Publishing Group, Inc.

Printed in the United States of America

The paper used in this book complies with the
Permanent Paper Standard issued by the National
Information Standards Organization (Z39.48-1984).

10 9 8 7 6 5 4 3 2 1

Copyright Acknowledgments

The author and publisher are grateful for permission to reprint from the following sources:

Statement on Uniform Rights of the Terminally Ill Act, Copyright © 1986 by the United States Catholic Conference, Washington, D.C., is used with permission. All rights reserved.

American Medical Association. "Withholding or Withdrawing Life-Prolonging Medical Treatment," *Journal of the American Medical Association,* 1986, 256(4):471, Copyright © 1986, American Medical Association, is reprinted by permission.

Society for the Right to Die. Excerpts from the leaflet "Society for the Right to Die in Support of Dying with Dignity" are reprinted with permission.

World Federation of Doctors Who Respect Human Life. Excerpts from "Euthanasia in Holland, Part Two," 1988, 99:4, are reprinted with permission.

National Hemlock Society and Derek Humphry. Excerpts from "Derek Humphry: Author, Journalist, Communicator, Campaigner" are reprinted with permission.

World Federation of Right to Die Societies. "Submission to the United Nations Organisation Regarding the Right to Die with Dignity as Agreed to by the 7th Biennial Conference in San Francisco, California, USA, April 7, 10, 1988". Reprinted by permission.

Contents

Preface

The history of a people or nation is the product of the event-shaping lives of powerful and commanding figures—an Einstein, a Lincoln, a Napoleon, yes, even a Hitler. But the history of the subject of helping or allowing a person to die is very different. It is a special kind of history because it is the product of the lives and deaths of little and inconspicuous people—Paul Brophy, a firefighter; Elizabeth Bouvia, a quadriplegic; Joseph Saikewicz, a retarded man; Claire Conroy, a nursing home resident.

This special history began in 1976 with a 22-year-old woman no one had even heard of—Karen Ann Quinlan—who, after ingesting drugs and alcohol, passed into a persistent vegetative state. She came to personify a medical technology whose advances had finally made it possible, with its machines and techniques, to keep people alive even after life had ceased to be a precious gift. Karen's case made headlines when, after her family tried in vain to get a hospital and the attending physician to disconnect her from a respirator, a court authorized her parents in 1976 to remove it and to let her die. Since then, the subject of helping or letting someone die has been the focus of attention in the media, by pro-life and right-to-die advocates, and in recent court decisions in the cases of Brophy, Bouvia, Saikewicz, Conroy, and others. Interest in the subject has spread and soared.

In spite of this interest, the problems raised when people choose to end their lives and, when necessary, request others to help them do so remain among the hardest nuts we have ever had to crack.

CROSS-DISCIPLINARY, CULTURAL, AND LEGAL PERSPECTIVES

Part of the difficulty may be that the Karen Quinlan case forced us for the first time to take a hard look at our attitudes toward death, the dying process, and medical technology. Among health care professionals, the members of a patient's family, lawyers, ethicists, and clergy, conflict erupted concerning just what was the "right" answer or thing to do. But another part of the difficulty may be that most of the books written by philosophers, ethicists, lawyers, physicians, and the clergy to address the problems examined them only through the narrow slits of the authors' specialties and their Western culture. Such authors are like bishops on a chessboard, forever traveling along diagonal lines that can never meet. They can never have a dialogue with others who are also examining the problems through other cultures and specialties.

To Die or Not to Die? was assembled to meet the need for a fresh approach to these medical, ethical, and legal issues. It is the first attempt to provide cross-disciplinary, cross-cultural, and cross-legal guidelines on the issues. It takes three steps to help us broaden our insights.

The first step is to make an interdisciplinary dialogue possible by breaking down the barriers that have isolated disciplines. No single discipline offers an insight that alone will solve the problems caused by medical technology. On the contrary, specialization in the context of these problems may have contributed to confusion and conflict.

The second step is to globalize the subject and allow us to view it in a comprehensive manner by gathering and presenting the perspectives of cultures and traditions outside our own.

The furor over the issues does not only transcend specialties and cultures. It cuts across the legal systems of many countries. The importance of these systems cannot be overstated. Everywhere the courts and legislators have been the ones to assume the principal role as mediator between patients and their families on the one side and physicians and hospitals on the other. Jurisprudence—not medicine, philosophy, ethics, or religion—is the real life-death decision maker and it is legislation and case law that patients and health care professionals depend on for guidance. A knowledge of U.S. law is indispensable, but knowledge of how the issues are addressed under the legal systems of other civilized countries may be highly instructive and have legal and ethical implications for us. Thus the third step is to break down the barriers that have insulated legal systems and to integrate the legal concepts of countries other than our own. Besides furnishing multidisciplinary and cross-cultural views, the editors have included chapters on the ways the law in England, the Netherlands, and India as well as in the United States has focused on the issues.

The fundamental aim of *To Die or Not to Die?* is to use an approach that permits and stimulates many disciplines, cultures, and legal concepts to relate to, learn from, and cross-fertilize one another so as to broaden insights. It brings together the ideas and experiences of a distinguished group of authorities from different disciplines, cultures, and legal systems who have been involved in the problem of whether or not to assist or permit the death of another. This group includes a physician, a clergyman, an ethicist, scholars, and lawyers. Their contributions deal with such questions as: What are the views of the terminally ill patient, the patient's family, and the physician? What are the philosophical, moral, and ethical considerations? What are the responses from the Catholic and Jewish communities? What are the perspectives of the African, Islamic, and Japanese traditions? What legal concepts relevant to the problem have been formulated in England, India, the Netherlands, and the United States?

The Appendices, with references to statutes and key judicial decisions as well as forms for several kinds of advance directives, provide valuable guidance and practical tools for greater insights and more detailed consideration and handling of the problems. Appendix A contains the names and addresses of right-to-die and right-to-life organizations; and Appendix B, the guidelines, principles, opinions, and statements issued publicly by important and influential groups or institutions such as the American Medical Association and the Vatican.

The growth in recent years of a body of case law relevant to the right to refuse medical treatment has prompted us to prepare Appendix C, containing some judicial decisions selected for their significance. Although the material might have been divided by states and the case law in each state given, we have found it more convenient and desirable to prepare a digest of these cases classified by subject-matter headings. Points and cases bearing on these points have been arranged under each heading. Appendix C is not meant to provide legal advice. For specific and authoritative answers to questions, readers should consult the statutes, case law, and attorneys in the states in which they reside or pursue their professions.

Living will (also called "natural death," "right-to-die," or "death-with-dignity") statutes have now been enacted in thirty-eight states and the District of Columbia. The statutes differ, yet have similarities. A Table of the states that have adopted these statutes, with citations to them, is found in Appendix D. Also in this Appendix is a comparison of the similarities and differences among the statutes concerning some key features.

Living will, proxy, and durable power of attorney forms are found in Appendices E, F, and G, respectively. One must take care, however, before using the forms in a particular state since the validity of an instrument may be determined by the statute of the state in which it is executed. The statute may require that that instrument conform to its provisions.

A bibliography on various aspects of the subject including major sources of information follows the Appendices.

The wide assortment of material contained in this book and the resources it offers should appeal to a variety of readers and their different needs. It is our belief that this book builds a new foundation for thinking or rethinking about the issues associated with the subject of helping or allowing a person to die, because it provides readers with the opportunity to consider new and diverse perspectives side by side for the first time. The book should be useful as a college text; challenging for professionals in medicine, nursing, theology, law, public health, and the disciplines of philosophy, ethics, psychology, and sociology; and helpful as well to seriously ill patients and their families.

I Cross-Disciplinary Views

1   The Right to Die: Perspectives of the Patient, the Family, and the Health Care Provider

David V. Schapira

Possibly the most neglected aspect of patient care is the medical and psychological management of a patient's death. The existence of a deficiency may seem surprising. One would think that either patients would have reached a conclusion regarding their deaths and resuscitative measures prior to serious illness, or a discussion by the physician with the patient and family would result in a decision on how to handle resuscitation.

When addressing how aggressively to manage and treat serious illness, implications that lie outside the boundaries of human rights and a person's quality of life should be considered. Approximately two million Americans die each year and, because of an increase in the population and particularly an increase in the number of elderly citizens, the annual number of deaths is rising. Eighty percent of the health care dollar is spent on people who survive less than one year. The care of nonsurvivors is approximately double that of survivors (Scotto and Chiazze, 1974). Only 10 percent of patients who require admission to an intensive care unit because of complications of their disease or treatment leave the hospital. In the past fifteen years the cost of health care has risen from 8 percent to over 13 percent of the gross national product—more than a 50 percent increase. These statistics should encourage health care providers to address the issue of resuscitation and aggressive management of life-threatening or terminal illnesses.

By addressing such issues at an appropriate time, the use of expensive medical care in the pursuit of prolonging a patient's life would be averted. It is particularly important that the decision of whether or not to implement heroic measures be resolved at a time when the patient is able to make a decision.

Despite our best intentions to grapple with and resolve the issues of a patient's right to die, there are obstacles that can render arriving at a solution difficult, if not impossible. I would like to describe these obstacles from the perspective of the patient, family, and health care provider.

THE PATIENT'S PERSPECTIVE

Patients may not wish to decide how aggressively their illness should be managed; they may wish to relinquish the decision to the physician. The severity of the illness can affect a patient's desire to participate in active decision making. Increasing severity of illness increases a patient's dependence on the physician. As the severity of illness increases, the fear of dying may alter a patient's decision whether or not to be resuscitated. The reality may be too overwhelming. Additionally, medications such as potent analgesics may alter a patient's mental state and reduce his or her capacity for judgment.

Although the physician may attempt to inform patients about the severity of their illnesses, patients may employ an appreciable amount of denial. In a study of 315 cancer patients (Eidinger and Schapira, 1984) being treated with chemotherapy or radiation therapy for advanced cancer, only 50 percent of the patients correctly responded that their cancer had spread and was in an advanced stage. All the patients had been informed of their condition prior to the study. This lack of knowledge was not due to an unwillingness to seek information, as over 90 percent of the participants wished to learn all information regarding their disease, irrespective of whether the information was pleasant or unpleasant. We asked the participants what they felt their prognosis was. The majority of patients felt they would live at least three years or longer, and an appreciable percentage felt they would "beat the cancer." In fact, over 75 percent of the patients expired within a year of participating in the study. If patients have a very optimistic view of their prognosis, discussions regarding resuscitation may seem incongruous.

If patients deny the severity of their condition, they may not make a rational and realistic decision about how the process of dying should be medically managed. Patients may also feel that making a decision not to be resuscitated may result in abandonment by the health care team and enhance a feeling of hopelessness. It is of interest that only 14 percent of patients who had a "do not resuscitate" order on their chart left the hospital alive at the end of the admission.

Factors other than denial may affect the patient's decision regarding resuscitation. A patient may make a decision not to be resuscitated based on erroneous information, emotion, or mood. A patient may become depressed with the side affects associated with the disease and feel that "life is not worth living." If, however, the symptoms can be alleviated, the patient's quality of life may be markedly improved and the desire to be aggressive with medical management may change.

Patients who feel they have not received a desired amount of attention and emotional support from spouse, family members, or friends may express a desire not to be resuscitated in an attempt to engender sympathy and emotional support from these individuals. Patients may even go so far as to attempt suicide to achieve the desired outcome.

Patients may have preconceived unpleasant illusions about the aspects of resuscitation. They may fear the trauma of intensive care units, tubes and intravenous lines inserted into the body, respirators, or the cardiac arrest procedure. Impressions of these traumatic measures may lead patients to decide to make a more passive decision.

These feelings of depression or fear that lead to a decision not to be resuscitated may be implemented by the health care team unless the reasons underlying the decision are examined. The situation can arise in which the patient's quality of life and desire for life is not dealt with appropriately. This is exemplified when an elderly patient with a terminal disease is admitted to an intensive care unit. The medical staff may view the admission and intensity of care to be inappropriate. They may be unaware that the patient wishes to remain alive for a few more weeks or months to see the birth of a grandchild or wedding of a child.

A somewhat similar philosophical decision was presented to a Massachusetts court (*Brophy vs. New England Mt. Sinai Hospital*). The court authorized the withdrawal of nutrition from an adult in a chronic vegetative state. While healthy, he had stated that he would not want his life sustained if he were permanently unconscious. The court rejected the view that a decision to withdraw life-supporting measures could be made on the basis of a quality of life that was determined by individuals other than the patient. The decision should not be perceived as a step toward euthanasia for those patients who lack the capacity to satisfy someone else's vision of a satisfactory quality of life or are deemed to be a social burden.

THE FAMILY'S PERSPECTIVE

For reasons of grief or guilt, the family may press for disproportionately aggressive management. One can observe this phenomenon in patients undergoing treatment for advanced cancer. When all conventional treatments, usually chemotherapeutic drugs, have been exhausted and the patient and family have been told that nothing more can be done to prolong survival significantly, the family may persuade the patient to turn to unconventional therapies as a last resort. These therapies may not have demonstrated objective tumor shrinkage, but guilt or grief may drive the patient to try these treatments in desperation. Unfortunately, this decision can have disastrous economic results as the travel to the clinics and treatments are not covered by insurance. Thus the surviving family may expend an appreciable amount of its savings.

Families are placed in a similarly uncomfortable position when the patients are gravely ill and unable to make their wishes known due to decreased consciousness. Families may express a desire for inappropriately aggressive management because of guilt. A physician may attempt to educate a family with an objective presentation of the medical facts surrounding the case. Many families are uncomfortable with this amount of education and participation. They may not understand and assimilate the information at such an emotional time and may lack the objectivity to make such an important decision concerning a loved one. In order to avoid the responsibility and guilt associated with adopting a passive approach, they choose a safe course of action and request that "everything be done" for the patient. This situation can be rectified by the physician's explaining why a passive approach is in the patient's best interest; this can alleviate the family's guilt when they agree with the physician's decision.

Cultural or ethnic factors can make a decision regarding resuscitation almost impossible. Hispanic families prefer to shield the patient from unnecessary anxiety and depression and may ask the physician not to tell the patient anxiety-provoking information such as a diagnosis of cancer. Throughout the patient's course, the family protects the patient from any depressing information; therefore a discussion about dying and resuscitative measures between the physician and the patient is obstructed.

Although the situation of not informing the patient may seem inconceivable, one must be careful not to impose one's belief system as regards health, disease, treatment, and death on patients from a different ethnic or cultural background. If one attempts to impose one's wishes and values on patients, the response is often denial, resistance, and decreased compliance. In fact, although we feel that we are open in telling patients their prognoses, physicians often collude with patients in not correcting optimistic misconceptions of prognoses.

Because of their cultural or religious beliefs, and indeed their personality, some patients may wish to take a passive role in the decision making regarding the circumstances of their deaths. To disregard the wishes and beliefs of the family and to confront the patient with the decision will probably not be fruitful, and indeed may lack understanding and not be in the patient's best interest. Such a confrontation may impair the patient's quality of life and future communication with the physician.

Although such an approach may still seem untenable, I would like to illustrate how the traditional approach of Western medicine can be unsuccessful. A Haitian man may present to an emergency room with palpitations. This is usually a benign condition called paraxysmal atrial tachycardia, and can be aborted by stimulating the vagus nerve, whether by manually massaging the carotid body in the neck or by having the patient swallow ice or attempt to blow air out of the mouth with the mouth closed. The condition can be precipitated by drinking excessive amounts of coffee, tea, or alcohol. Having corrected the abnormal rhythm, the physician could warn the patient not to consume the stimulants that precipitate the condition, teach the patient the cardiac-slowing maneuvers, and possibly prescribe a B-blocker, a medication that slows the heart. Such an approach would most likely be ineffective and the patient would not take the medication. The reason is that the Haitians call this condition *battement de coeur*, or beating of the heart, and believe it to be due to weak blood. They would expect to receive a liquid tonic to build up the blood. If a Haitian did not receive a tonic, it is unlikely that the patient would return to a practitioner of traditional Western medicine. Lest this example seem too primitive and far-fetched, one only has to remember that almost half of the population of the United States takes at least one vitamin pill per day for no justifiable reason—certainly not to avoid vitamin deficiency. A study I made (with others) revealed that over 90 percent of vitamin takers are unaware of the recommended daily allowance of any of the vitamins. Indeed, attempting to persuade the members of this sophisticated population to stop taking a vitamin has, in my experience, been extremely difficult.

Unfortunately, medical anthropology and thanatology are not part of the curriculum of most medical schools. Without a knowledge of these areas, physicians may lack awareness and sensitivity toward alternate belief systems relating to health, disease, and death. The physician can only be left to impose his or her belief system and values on the patient, the result being an unsatisfactory outcome.

THE PHYSICIAN'S PERSPECTIVE

Dealing with ill patients exacts a toll on physicians, particularly if they deal with chronic diseases in which dramatic improvement is not often seen. A physician may have a tendency to equate a patient's death with professional failure, or unrealistic expectations. Having to impart unfavorable information to patients on a continual basis tends to lead to a feeling of being "burned out." The physician finds that it is easier not to become engaged in a discussion with the patient over topics that will be emotionally draining and time consuming. Thus physicians may avoid discussing topics such as prognosis or resuscitation unless approached directly by the patient or the family.

Apart from their desire to avoid discussing emotionally laden issues, physicians vary in their communication skills. Some may lack directness or honesty or may use technical language that is beyond the understanding of the patient and family. In this situation a facilitator, such as a psychiatrist attached to the health care team, nurse, social worker, or chaplain, can act as an intermediary and resolve any difficulties in understanding the issues. I find this approach very effective as patients and families may not want to ask physicians questions for fear of interrupting their busy schedules or for fear that certain questions are too simple or inappropriate. Members of a psychological team may be able to discuss and allay a patient's or family's fears because of their training and the fact that patients may find them less intimidating than the physician. In a study by Bedell et al. (1983), 95 percent of physicians felt it was appropriate to discuss the patient's wishes regarding resuscitation, yet in only 19 percent of cases did the physician discuss the subject of resuscitation with the patient, and in only 33 percent of cases did the physician discuss resuscitation with the family.

Fear of legal liability may interfere with a physician's ability to make the best choice for the patient. A physician may have a primary objective of minimizing liability, real or imagined. This strategy may be at the expense of humane treatment and may be at odds with the family's wishes. There is only one case (as of 1984) in which two physicians were charged with murder for withholding life support from a comatose patient. The charges were dropped by the California Court of Appeals. The fear of litigation following the withholding of life support is grossly exaggerated by physicians. If the conversation with, and wishes of, the patient and family are documented in the hospital records, it is extremely unlikely that a physician will be sued. In spite of legal uncertainties, appropriate and compassionate care should have priority over undue fear of liability.

WHAT CONSTITUTES RESUSCITATION?

It appears that most members of the public understand resuscitation to involve cardiopulmonary arrest maneuvers. They may be aware that these maneuvers involve the mechanical stimulation of the heart by manual compression of the chest, ventilation by a small ventilatory bag, and the insertion of intravenous fluids and cardiac stimulus. Although this is certainly a valid impression of the scenario that surrounds the final event of a cardiac arrest, there are other interventions in medical management that, if withheld, would lead to the death of the patient. These more subtle areas of medical management that the public is often not aware of lead to problems of interpretation when a patient has written a living will. These subtler areas of "resuscitation" are frequently not included in the conditions or scenarios of a living will; they include the withholding of antibiotics from a patient with a terminal disease who has a life-threatening infection; the withholding of steroids for patients with cerebral metastases; withholding of intravenous fluids or hyperalimentation; and not performing laboratory tests to correct electrolyte disorders. All of these instances obviously assume that patients are unable to transmit their wishes because of decreased consciousness. Although these situations do not directly involve the saving of life, they can, when implemented, appreciably prolong a patient's life. If patients are not conscious and cannot make their wishes known, implementing these interventions would seem to be uneconomical and contrary to the patients' interests.

The living will is a document, distributed nationally, that outlines patients' wishes regarding medical management should they subsequently become incompetent to decide (Society for the Right to Die, Living Will, New York, 1985). This document is not binding in some states, but it does clearly outline a patient's desires and expectations. At the present, thirty-eight states have enacted living will or "natural death" legislation (Jonsen, 1978).

CONCLUSION

There are no simple solutions when attempting to elicit a patient's request for withholding resuscitation and granting that request. The most important point to be made is that the patient has the ultimate right to control all aspects of medical care and resuscitation, and the family and health care team must abide by the patient's wishes. If patients are unable to make a decision, their spouse or close family may decide what course should be taken. It is hoped that their decisions would be based on prior discussion with patients regarding their opinions and wishes concerning resuscitation.

The medical team in a hospital is often faced with a situation in which a patient has a life-threatening episode such as cardiac arrhythmia or cardiac arrest, and there is no statement in the patient's chart regarding resuscitation. Under these circumstances the medical team has to make every effort to resuscitate the patient, even though resuscitation seems inappropriate and would have been against the patient's wishes. This not uncommon situation can be frequently averted if the attending physician discusses resuscitation measures with the patient either before admission or on the first day of admission to the hospital. This discussion should not be held with every patient, but only with those patients deemed to have limited survival or a serious life-threatening condition.

I doubt that this practice will become widespread, as it involves many emotionally draining and time-consuming discussions. I do not state this opinion with any degree of cynicism because I realize the very appreciable increased amount of time and emotion that physicians would have to give to engage in such discussions on almost a daily basis.

Another approach would be to educate patients regarding their rights to make a living will, and to make the drawing up of such a will a relatively simple and inexpensive exercise. Living wills drawn up by patients attempt to extend patients' authority to decline certain therapeutic measures that may be involved in their death. This attempt would be made at a time when the patient was capable of entering into decision making. A standardized document could be obtained from a doctor's office or hospital that would describe the various levels of resuscitative measures with explanations. Patients could then make informed decisions as to the level of resuscitative procedures that they would want to have invoked should they become critically ill.

A third approach would be to have certain criteria for the entry of patients with terminal illness into intensive care units. There is considerable evidence (Cullen et al., 1974) that an appreciable portion of the cost of caring for terminally ill patients is associated with treatment in intensive care units. There are standards that cover the admission of patients to intensive care units. The bill for such an admission may not be totally covered by the insurance company and the surviving family may be left having to pay a considerable amount of money. A more stringent application of admission guidelines would reduce expenditures for the health care system and family, which is important when the admission of a patient to such a unit is inappropriate and unsuccessful.

A very reasonable alternative in caring for terminal patients who do not wish an aggressive approach to their management is the hospice movement. Hospices provide an alternative form of care for the dying. They allow terminally ill patients a choice of dying at home or in facilities other than the hospital. Hospices are often a more appropriate form of care, as they are designed for palliation and caring rather than curing. Patient autonomy and dignity are enhanced.

In 1982 Congress ensured that hospice care would be covered by Medicare. It is not clear that hospice care will reduce the cost of health care, but the system allows terminal illness to be more bearable for the patient and family if a decision has been made not to follow an aggressive course.

I feel strongly that patients, their families, and physicians must collaborate and deal with the fearful subject of the patient's potentially impending death. Apart from the needless suffering for the patient and family generated by the inappropriate and unwanted prolongation of life, an appreciable percentage of health care costs could be saved and,

I hope, diverted to research, care, and the prolongation of the lives of patients who would be able to enjoy a better quality of the additional life gained.

REFERENCES

Bedell, S. E., Delbanco, T. L., Cook, E. F., et al. 1983. "Survival after Cardiopulmonary Resuscitation in the Hospital." *New England Journal of Medicine* 309:569–76.

Cullen, D. J., Civetta, J. M., Briggs, B. A., et al. 1974. "Therapeutic Intervention Scoring System." *Internal Care Medicine* 2:57–60.

Eidinger, R. N., and Schapira, D. V. 1984. "Cancer Patients' Insight into Their Treatment, Prognosis, and Unconventional Therapies." *Cancer* 53:2736–40.

Jonsen, A. R. 1978. "Dying Right in California: The Natural Death Act." *Clinical Research* 26:55–60.

Scotto, J., and Chiazze, L. 1974. *Third National Cancer Survey*. National Institute of Health 76–1094.

2 The Right to Die: Perspectives from the Catholic and Jewish Traditions

James J. McCartney

At the present time, a "right to die" has been proclaimed by many organizations and individuals. There is a Society for the Right to Die, many states have so-called "right-to-die" or "death-with-dignity" statutes, and increasing numbers of individuals have filled out advance directives for health care, so-called "living wills," outlining, sometimes in great detail, ways in which their right to die should be honored when they are terminally ill or irreversibly comatose. In fact, supporters of California's proposed Humane and Dignified Death Act are attempting by referendum to transmute the "right to die" into a "right to be killed by a physician" if a person is terminally ill.

What is the attitude of religious communities to this alleged right to die? Can the Christian and Jewish ethical traditions support death with dignity? What is the response of these communities of faith to the ethical dilemmas raised by modern medical technology that can stave off death without restoring health for days, weeks, months, and even years? In this chapter I shall examine Roman Catholic and Jewish perspectives on the right to die. I do so as one trained formally in philosophy and Catholic moral theology and who has learned a great deal about the Jewish tradition from three Miami rabbis—Solomon Schiff, Warren Kasztl, and Rex Perlmeter. Any wisdom from the Jewish tradition contained herein can be attributed to them; any mistakes should be attributed to me.

Because I know it best, I will begin with the Catholic tradition in Part 1. Part 2 will deal with Jewish perspectives and Part 3 will conclude with a reflection on Florida's right-to-die statute, The Life-Prolonging Procedures Act, and its relationship with the religious principles elucidated above.

THE CATHOLIC TRADITION

In examining the Catholic tradition we must first consider whether it recognizes a right to die as such. If not, are there any other rights or limitations of duty that would be the functional equivalent of the right to die? Following St. Paul, the Catholic tradition sees death as a great evil—the wages of sin—but even death is relativized by the raising of Jesus of Nazareth from the dead by God. As the preface to the Eucharistic Prayer in Masses for the Dead puts it so succinctly, at death "life is changed, not ended." Thus death, an unnatural evil brought into the world by sin, is itself redeemed by the death and resurrection of Jesus. Catholics believe that they will be co-sharers of the resurrection of Jesus at the last day when their own mortal bodies will be raised again in glory if they have tried to make the Kingdom of God a reality in their lives. In the Catholic tradition, spiritual death, in which a human being rejects the offer of God's self-disclosure and cuts himself or herself off from the source of supernatural life, is worse than physical death.

Since the Catholic tradition sees death as an unnatural state brought about by sin, even though death itself has been redeemed and given a new meaning through the glorification of Jesus, it is reluctant to speak of a right to die. Catholicism sees the Christian as having an obligation to prepare for death so that, when death does come, the Christian may be able to live with Christ in God. Thus the Catholic tradition sees death as a negativity and not as something one has a "right" to; however, it also sees this negativity relativized in the light of the human's spiritual end—union with God.

If Catholic teaching does not admit to a right to die, must it therefore be concluded that Catholics are obliged to preserve biological life at all costs? To answer this question, we must examine Catholic views on the dignity and value of human life. First, Catholic belief holds that God is the source and author of all life and that human life is a precious gift from God. In the Catholic tradition, as in the Jewish, God gives life and only God may legitimately take it away. Thus, to directly take the life of an innocent person is not only wrong because of the harm done to the other party, but, for Catholics, it is also wrong because it is an act of appropriating to oneself an activity reserved to God alone.

Human biological life is seen by the Catholic tradition as a great value and, in fact, the source of all human values; without biological life none of our other spiritual activities, our true likeness with God, would be possible. Thus Catholic theology holds that we have an obligation to promote and preserve our lives and health because it is in precisely this way that we can both grow spiritually and render due thanks to the Creator for the gift of life. But how strong is this obligation? Are Catholics called to "vitalism," an approach that sees biological life as an almost absolute value and believes that anything and everything must be done to preserve and prolong our living? The clear and almost unanimous answer throughout the Catholic tradition to this question is no, not-withstanding contemporary vitalists who are attempting to interpret the tradition more conservatively today and whose position will be considered in Part 3. In the Catholic tradition, we are not obligated to preserve life or health at any cost; we do have a right to refuse medical treatment, and we do have a right to a dignified death, especially when all that is being prolonged is physiological existence without the cognitive-affective functions that make us truly able to pursue spiritual ends.

I will now review classical and contemporary Catholic moral teaching to show how the religious and ethical principles presented above have been developed and have found application in concrete settings. In an article written several years ago, Gary Atkinson reviewed the positions of several classical Catholic theologians on the issue of prolonging life. Here he points out that St. Thomas Aquinas holds that "the test (for temporal goods, including biological life) is whether their pursuit or avoidance is useful in serving the final end of knowing, loving, and serving God" (Atkinson 1981:97). Applying this teaching of Aquinas to the use of food by the sick, the sixteenth-century Dominican Vitoria holds that "if the patient is so depressed or has lost his appetite so that it is only with the greatest effort that he can eat food, this right away ought to be reckoned as creating a kind of impossibility and the patient is excused, . . . especially if there is little or no hope of life." He continues by holding that "to fulfill the obligation to protect life, it is sufficient that a person perform 'that by which ordinarily a man can live,' " and "if a person 'uses foods which man commonly use and in the quantity which customarily suffices for the conservation of strength,' then the person does not sin even if his life is notably shortened thereby" (Atkinson 1981:98).

I have also discussed elsewhere (McCartney 1980) the views of other classical moralists and pointed out that Bañez in 1595 stated that

while it is reasonable to hold that a human being must conserve his or her life, one is not bound to employ extraordinary means, but only to preserve life by nourishment and clothing common to all, by medicine common to all, and even through some ordinary and common pain or anguish, but not through any extraordinary or horrible pain or anguish, nor by any undertakings extraordinarily disproportionate to one's state in life. (McCartney 1980:216)

Several commentators have shown that there was not much change or development over the centuries until very recently regarding this teaching since the art of medicine itself was not radically changing during this time. Thus in his *Theologiae Moralis Institutiones* (1902), Edward Génicot discusses care of one's own life in the following way. First, he points out that each person is responsible for conserving his or her own life using ordinary means (i.e., means fitting to one's state in life). Not to do so is the moral equivalent of suicide. The same responsibility pertains to preserving one's health and functional integrity. However, no one is bound to use means that are extremely difficult (i.e., extraordinary) to preserve life, health, or functional integrity, since positive laws do not command such means universally. Hence:

1. Even the most wealthy are not obligated to move to a more healthful climate, or to travel a long distance for mineral baths, even if this is the only way of prolonging life.

2. No one has to undergo major surgery accompanied by profound suffering even if one could not otherwise prolong one's life. Even if profound suffering can be prevented, however, as it usually can be nowadays, we should not think someone to be obliged to undergo that same type of major surgery if he or she really cannot cope with the thought of undergoing this operation or is horrified at the prospect of it. For this very horror itself should be considered a grave burden. (Génicot 1902:346–47; my translation)

In 1957, addressing an international congress of physicians, Pope Pius XII spoke rather presciently on this issue of prolonging life. During this important allocution, the Pope, following St. Thomas Aquinas, stressed that "life, health, and all temporal activities are in fact subordinate to spiritual ends" (Pope Pius XII 1958:396). The Pope went on to say that it is the patient who must decide whether a given medical intervention is obligatory or not and the patient who gives the doctor permission to treat in accord with the patient's wishes. The family's rights and duties depend in general on the wishes of the patient, and generally families are only bound to use what they believe the patient would consider obligatory, that is, ordinary means. Finally, however, in a strange twist of logic, Pius asserted that "if it appears that the attempt at resuscitation constitutes in reality such a burden for the family that one cannot in all conscience impose it upon them, they can lawfully insist that the doctor should discontinue these attempts, and the doctor can lawfully comply" (Pope Pius XII 1958:397). The Pope thus held that not only do we have to consider what the patient wishes; we must also, especially when the patient is unconscious, assess the effects of life-prolonging technologies on the family, and, if these technologies are creating an authentic burden to the family, they may ethically be discontinued. Since these technologies are not physically burdensome to the family, the Pope must have had in mind psychological, economic, or spiritual burdens, among others.

More recently, Kevin O'Rourke, a Dominican priest acknowledged by both critics and admirers alike as a Catholic theologian who does not dissent from official Catholic teaching, has in two different articles (O'Rourke 1986, 1988) shown the evolution of Church teaching with regard to prolonging life. I now want to focus on some of the principles O'Rourke presents.

First, he argues that

in order to pursue the purpose of life, one needs some degree of cognitive-affective function.... Hence, if efforts to restore cognitive-affective function can be judged useless, or if it can be judged that an infant will never develop cognitive-affective function, then if a fatal pathology is present, the adult or infant may be allowed to die.... Physiological function, which can be prolonged long after cognitive-affective function ceases irreparably, is not a sufficient reason for prolonging life. (O'Rourke 1986:322)

In the second article, O'Rourke clarifies what he means by "the purpose of life." For a Christian, the purpose of life is clearly the spiritual goal of loving God: "Hence anything that would make the attainment of the spiritual goal of life less secure or seriously difficult would be a grave burden and would be considered an optional or extraordinary means to prolong life" (O'Rourke 1988:33).

O'Rourke is, in these articles, consolidating the views of most contemporary Catholic theologians on prolonging life by artificial means by stating that these means are optional when they are either (1) useless (for O'Rourke, useless for establishing the potential pursuit of the purpose of life, i.e., loving God); or (2) burdensome (for O'Rourke, any activity that would make the possible pursuit of the purpose of life less secure or seriously difficult).

I would agree with these two criteria and O'Rourke's interpretation of them. I would, however, expand the concept of burden, following Pope Pius XII, by saying that when the family of an unconscious person finds the pursuit of its responsibility of loving God (directly and through other family members) hindered because of its attempts to prolong the person's life, it may lawfully assess this as a disproportionate burden and thus cease the attempt. In sum, while in the Catholic tradition we are never allowed directly to take the life of the innocent, we are allowed to let a fatal pathology run its course without medical intervention in many circumstances, as I hope is now clear from this brief historical review.

THE JEWISH TRADITION

I began my treatment of the Catholic tradition by examining whether or not there is a right to die or its moral equivalent within that community of faith. I will now consider the same issue within Judaism since I believe that a response to this question will help us understand the Jewish attitude toward prolongation of life by artificial means. Jews, like Catholics, believe that God is the author of life and that it is God, and only God, who gives life and who can legitimately take it away. Jews also believe that we are stewards, not masters, of our lives and therefore that we must preserve and protect our lives as the gifts of God that they are. However, the Jewish faith is a this-worldly religion and, in general, does not have a well-developed theology of death and afterlife, although it would be inaccurate to say that religious Jews have no belief in life after death at all. Nevertheless, Jewish faith is certain of this life and also certain that any length of human life, however short, is infinitely precious before God. Thus Jewish teaching holds that there is an obligation to prolong life as long as possible until a person is clearly in the throes of death, at which time it is acceptable to stand back and allow the person to die. Hence, in Judaism, there is clearly no right to die, but on the contrary, a responsibility to live. Right until the end, the devout Jew is called to use whatever means, no matter how burdensome, will be useful in prolonging life. While this stance is subject to much interpretation, even within the more strict Orthodox tradition, and while it is made even more flexible within Conservative and Reform Judaism, it is my experience that most Jews whom I know have this tendency toward vitalism, which is stronger the more seriously they practice their religion. As the Code of Jewish Law expresses it, "All laws of the Torah are suspended on the possibility that life is in danger, however remote the likelihood" (Feldman 1986:25).

Yet even this command to promote health and prolong life is not absolute. Rabbi Shapiro relates the following Talmudic story:

On the day that Rabbi Judah was dying the rabbis announced a public fast and prayed that Rabbi Judah not die. Rabbi Judah's maid climbed to the roof of his home and prayed: *The angels want Rabbi to join them, and the mortals want Rabbi to remain with them; may it be God's will that the mortals overpower the angels.* But just then she thought of Rabbi Judah and how he suffered. She stopped and re-worded her prayer: *May it be the will of God that the angels overpower the mortals.* Then, while the rabbis continued to hold death at bay with their prayers, the maid picked up a clay pitcher and flung it from the roof onto the ground in their midst. For a moment the stunned rabbis ceased their prayers, and the soul of Rabbi Judah departed his body. (Ketubbot, 104a [Shapiro 1986:25])

There are several interpretations of this story. T. Jakobovits points out that "Rabbi Isserles permits the removal of anything causing a hindrance to the departure of the soul . . . since such action involves no active hastening of death but only the removal of the impediment" (Jakobovits 1959:123). Thus, "removing a hindrance to natural death is permitted" (Feldman 1986:94–95). But is this hindrance to be understood as extraneous to the patient (such as the rabbis' prayers for Rabbi Judah) or intrinsic, as in the case of a respirator or feeding tubes? F. Rosner holds that Jewish law "sanctions the withdrawal of any factor, whether extraneous to the patient or not—which may artifically delay his demise in the final moments of life" (Rosner 1983:235). Jakobovits agrees with this interpretation but emphasizes that it may only be employed when death is imminent, that is, when the person has truly become *Goses,* that is, moribund or in the process of dying (Jakobovits 1959:121–25). Rabbi Shapiro says that "while Judaism certainly comes out in favor of prolonging one's life, it is not in favor of prolonging one's dying" (Shapiro 1986:25). D. M. Feldman sees this as a dilemma but resolves it in favor of not treating:

The dialectic between the two moral thrusts, that of the preciousness of life and the imperative to extend mercy to our fellow-man, even to the convicted criminal, allows the application of the practical principle of *shev v'al ta' aseh,* "sit back and take no action," that is, let nature take its course. In such cases, "do not resuscitate" would be the proper procedure. (Feldman 1986:96)

Rosner, however, maintains that "human life is not regarded as a goal to be preserved for the sake of other values, but as an absolute basic good. Neither technological complexity nor financial expense should be spared where prolongation of life or potential cure is deemed possible" (Rosner 1983:235).

Feldman suggests that physicians should first initiate life-prolonging procedures to give the patient every chance for life but that they may discontinue them if they subsequently determine that their function is not the prolongation of living but rather the prolongation of dying (Feldman 1986:95). I am in genuine sympathy with this approach but I know of several rabbis who hold that once a medical procedure such as a respirator is initiated, fidelity to the patient demands that the respirator be continued and that, in fact, the removal of the respirator in these cases would be the moral equivalent of killing the patient. Thus they would hold that the Jewish tradition allows the withholding of treatment from patients whose death is imminent but not their withdrawal once begun (personal correspondence with Rabbis Kasztl and Schiff). In fact, a suggestion has been made that Jewish patients in this situation be put on a respirator run on batteries so that when the batteries run down a new decision can be made as to whether the respirator should be provided or withheld. I have often heard this interpretation of Jewish teaching suggested. However, I am not able to find any authors writing in English who suggest it. Thus it seems to me, on the bases of scholarly writings in English by Jewish sources, that the Jewish tradition will allow both the withholding and the withdrawal of any medical interventions that only prolong dying when death itself is imminent.

I would like to end this section with a quotation from the late Rabbi Seymour Siegel which is a fitting summary of all that has been said thus far about both the Jewish and Christian traditions.

Therefore, in conclusion, we are guided by the principle that life is precious; that we are bidden to preserve and guard our health; that we are bidden to intervene in nature to raise the human estate; and that our lives are not our own, but are part of the legacy bequeathed to us by the Creator. In our community there are differences of approach and interpretation. Let us discuss these issues with reason and prayerful dialogue, hoping that God will guide us in our decision-making so that we can better serve Him and our fellowman. (Siegel 1980:33)

FLORIDA LAW, THE RIGHT TO DIE, AND RELIGIOUS VALUES

In this concluding section, I would like to examine certain sections of Florida's Life-Prolonging Procedures Act (*Florida Statutes* 765) and Florida case law in the light of the religious values of the Catholic and Jewish tradition previously discussed. This will be done first to examine whether Florida law is consonant with these religious values and also to show that, while there is basic agreement on religious principles, in the application of these principles to public policy there are various convictions as to how the law should be written and interpreted.

Florida's Life-Prolonging Procedures Act went into effect on October 1, 1984. This statute established as a legal document what it refers to as a "declaration" and what many refer to as a "living will." This declaration or living will is simply an instructional directive made in advance of terminal illness (hence it is often called an "advance directive") so that physicians or significant others will know the patient's wishes should the patient not be able to communicate them because of lack of consciousness or incompetence. The Florida statute also allows persons to assign a proxy (i.e., a proxy directive) to make their health care decisions when they are unable to do so in the context of terminal illness. It also provides for surrogate decision makers when the patients have not chosen one. And while the Life-Prolonging Procedures Act deals, strictly speaking, only with terminal illness, a case decided by Florida's highest court (*John F. Kennedy Memorial Hospital, Inc. v. Bludworth*) applies almost the same approach to persons irreversibly comatose or in a persistent vegetative state. Thus advance directives can apply both to persons terminally ill (by statute) as well as those who are permanently unconscious (by case law). (In fact, the Florida Supreme Court in *John F. Kennedy* in its dicta implies that it believes that those permanently unconscious are by definition terminally ill. I have argued elsewhere that I very much agree with this position. Be that as it may, it is clear that the holding in *John F. Kennedy* is directed toward the permanently unconscious.)

I will now consider some of the language of the statute, which has caused some debate and disagreement within both the Catholic and Jewish communities of faith. First, the statute defines "terminal condition" as "a condition caused by injury, disease, or illness from which, to a reasonable degree of medical certainty, there can be no recovery and which makes death imminent" (*Florida Statutes* 765.03). The first part of this definition is not difficult conceptually and often not that hard for physicians to determine. It is the second part of this definition, "which makes death imminent," that causes difficulty. Is this phrase to be interpreted as "which makes death imminent without the use of life-prolonging procedures" or as "which makes death imminent even with the use of life-prolonging procedures"?

I believe that religious Jews and "crypto-vitalist" Catholics would be much more comfortable with the latter interpretation since they believe that biological life is of such immeasurable value that it should be preserved up until the point of death. Thus they would justify almost any life-prolonging intervention up until the time when it is clear that the person is dying, intervention or not. Catholics who follow the evolving tradition, however, would be comfortable with the former interpretation. We would believe that in the context of a fatal pathology which might be somewhat offset or slowed down by life-prolonging procedures, the precise ethical question that should be asked is not whether we can prolong this person's life, but whether we should. Answering this question demands an analysis of how useful the procedure will be in helping the person attain his or her spiritual end or how much of a burden it will be. The statute, while providing flexibility in interpretation, also invites disagreement and conflicting points of view.

Second, the word "imminent" is laden with ambiguity. Does it mean that death will occur within a few minutes, hours, days, or years? Again, the statute itself gives no indication of what it understands "imminent" to mean. I have argued that the statute must mean "imminent" to be longer than minutes or hours; otherwise the statute would be superfluous, since its provisions would not go into effect until right before the person expired. Here again, however, Orthodox Jews and vitalist-oriented Catholics would want to interpret "imminent" narrowly so that people with terminal conditions are not allowed to die "prematurely." Relying on the recently enacted New York "Orders Not to Resuscitate" Law and statutes in other states, St. Francis Hospital in Miami Beach, Florida (a Catholic hospital sponsored by the Allegany Franciscan Sisters) has interpreted "imminent" to mean that death will occur within one year for purposes of implementing *Florida Statute* 765 in accordance with hospital policy. Since the legislature has given no guidance as to what it means by "imminent," I believe that this interpretation is as valid as any other. In closing this particular section, I should point out that Kevin O'Rourke argues (rightly, in my estimation) that "if a fatal pathology is present, the significant ethical question is not whether death is imminent, *but rather whether there is a moral obligation to seek to remove the fatal pathology or at least to circumvent its effects*" (O'Rourke 1986:322).

One of the sections of the statute that has caused the most controversy since its enactment states that "the term 'life-prolonging procedure' does not include the provision of sustenance or the administration of medication or performance of any medical procedure deemed necessary to provide comfort care or to alleviate pain" (*Florida Statute* 765.03).

First, this statement is ambiguous. Does it imply that the provision of sustenance is not a life-prolonging procedure at any time or only "the provision of sustenance . . . deemed necessary to provide comfort care or to alleviate pain"? The answer depends on the interpretation of the first "or" in the clause. If it is a strong "or," provision of sustenance is not one of the life-prolonging procedures that may be withheld or withdrawn under the act. If it is a weak "or," only the provision of sustenance used for pain relief or comfort care may not be withdrawn.

On this issue, the Florida Catholic Conference, supported by many right-to-life groups, has advocated a clear vitalist position that holds that artificial sustenance should rarely be withdrawn or withheld. Its justification for this stance was articulated by William E. May and several authors in a recent edition of *Issues in Law and Medicine* (May et al. 1987). The presuppositions and principles presented in this article include the belief that human life "is inherently good, not merely instrumental to other goods," and the belief that "remaining alive is never rightly regarded as a burden" (May et al. 1987:204–5). This belief leads the authors to "conclude that, in the ordinary circumstances of life in our society today, it is not morally right, nor ought it be legally permissable [sic], to withhold or withdraw nutrition and hydration provided by artificial means to the permanently unconscious or other categories of seriously debilitated but nonterminal persons" (May et al. 1987:211).

Since the authors seem to interpret "imminent death" very narrowly, it is clear that they are referring to almost all persons now kept alive through the artificial delivery of food and fluids.

I am convinced that these authors are not faithful to traditional Catholic teaching regarding the prolongation of life both because they see human life as an inherent rather than temporal good that must always be understood as instrumental in helping us achieve our spiritual goal (union with God), and because they believe that remaining alive is never rightly regarded as a burden. Clearly this latter position was not shared by Pius XII, nor would it be shared by anyone who believes that the prolongation of living with great suffering could lead to despair and thus be a burden to one's Christian vocation. Having rejected these claims, I would nevertheless hold with them that we are never allowed directly to kill the innocent, not because human bodily life is inherently good or because continued living is never rightly regarded as a burden, but because only God is the author of life and may legitimately take it away. This is an argument based on revealed religious truth and not on the natural law.

Thus I believe that the position taken by the Florida Catholic Conference with regard to the sustenance issue is mistaken and will lead to great confusion among the faithful, especially when other bishops (in Chicago and Providence, for example) have taken an official position that much more accurately reflects the tradition outlined in Part 1. Finally, it should be mentioned that the Jewish tradition would see the provision of food and fluids as a necessary means of prolonging life until the person is on the brink of death, at which time the feeding tubes could be withdrawn.

In a case decided recently (*Corbett v. D'Alessandro*), a Florida Court of Appeals interpreted the Florida statute in the strong sense and held that the provision of sustenance is not to be considered a life-prolonging procedure, but that there is a constitutional right of privacy and a common-law right of self-determination that would allow patients to refuse sustenance, the restrictions of the statute notwithstanding. Thus it is now Florida law that patients may refuse artificial sustenance even though it may not be provided for in the statute. The legislature recently worked to amend the statute to conform with *Corbett* but was unsuccessful in that session. It will, however, probably be done in years to come.

Thus we can say that Florida law clearly recognizes the rights of patients or their proxies to refuse artificial life-prolonging procedures, including artificially delivered food and fluids. If this is construed as a right to die, so be it; I would prefer to construe it as a "right to refuse medical treatment" based on a more fundamental "right of self-determination and personal privacy." However it is described, the law itself does not believe that it is legitimizing suicide, mercy killing, or euthanasia or that it is permitting "any affirmative or deliberate act or omission to end life other than to permit the natural process of dying" (*Florida Statutes* 765.11). And even though concrete applications of these principles may be controversial, it is clear to me that both the Catholic and Jewish traditions, because of the arguments we have previously discussed, can and should be comfortable with the state of current Florida law with regard to the right of the terminally ill to refuse life-prolonging treatment while at the same time expecting competent and compassionate care.

REFERENCES

Atkinson, G. M. 1981. "Theological History of Catholic Teaching on Prolonging Life." In *Moral Responsibility in Prolonging Life Decisions*. St. Louis: Pope John Center.

Corbett v. D'Alessandro. 487 So.2d 368 (Florida 1986).

Feldman, D. M. 1986. *Health and Medicine in the Jewish Tradition*. New York: Crossroad.

Génicot, E. 1902. *Theologiae Moralis Institutiones I*. Louvain, Belgium: Polleunis et Ceuterick.

Jakobovits, I. 1959. *Jewish Medical Ethics*. New York: Bloch Publishing Co.

John F. Kennedy Memorial Hospital v. Bludworth. 452 So.2d. 921 (Florida 1984).

Life-Prolonging Procedure Act of Florida. *Florida Statutes*, Chapter 765.

May, W. E. et al. 1987. "Feeding and Hydrating the Permanently Unconscious and Other Vulnerable Persons." *Issues in Law and Medicine* 3(3): 203–17.

McCartney, J. J. 1986. "Catholic Positions on Withholding Sustenance for the Terminally Ill." *Health Progress* (October): 38–40.

———. 1980. "The Development of the Doctrine of Ordinary and Extraordinary Means of Preserving Life in Catholic Moral Theology before the Karen Quinlan Case." *Linacre Quarterly* 47(3): 215–24.

O'Rourke, K. 1988. "Evolution of Church Teaching on Prolonging Life." *Health Progress* (January-February): 28–35.

———. 1986. "The A.M.A. Statement on Tube Feeding: An Ethical Analysis." *America* (November 22): 321–24.

Pius XII, Pope. 1958. "The Prolongation of Life." *The Pope Speaks* 4: 393–98.

Rosner, F. 1983. "The Traditionalist Jewish Physician and Modern Biomedical Ethical Problems." *Journal of Medicine and Philosophy* 8(3): 225–41.

Shapiro, Rabbi R. M. 1986. *Open Hands: A Jewish Guide on Dying, Death and Bereavement*. Miami Beach: Riverside Memorial Chapel.

Siegel, Rabbi S. 1980. "Healing and the Definition of Death." In I. Franck, ed., *Biomedical Ethics in Perspective of Jewish Teaching and Tradition*. Washington, DC: College of Jewish Studies of Greater Washington.

3 Ethical Perspectives on the Right to Die: A Case Study

Helene A. Lutz

Euthanasia or, more precisely, active killing for mercy, the right to die, and death with dignity have been subjects of numerous studies and debates. I do not wish to review here the concerns of these debates, important as they are, since I would only be repeating arguments that have been raised time and again.[1] Neither do I wish to argue for or against the right either to die or to be killed. Indeed, I fear that discussion of this matter is already becoming a politically charged, polarized debate similar to that concerning abortion—that is, a situation wherein genuine moral inquiry and discourse has instead become a moral impasse that is both socially fragmenting and self-deceptive.

My fear of such an impasse leads me to hesitate even to speak of death as a right. This is not because I am opposed to the notion of a right to die under certain circumstances; I am not. My concern is rather about moral discourse, specifically that discussion and debate about the right to die will become a battle of rights versus rights. The danger of such an approach is that moral discussion and decision-making are often subsumed under conflicts of unresolvable oppositions. Both sides of a rights debate can have legitimate positions. Of course every human being has a right to life, as well as a right to a "good death"—the literal meaning of euthanasia. Of course a fetus has a right to life, but a woman also has a right to control her own body. What does such a focus on rights tell us about responsibility, however? Not much, and because of that it provides little moral illumination, except to point to a need for a broader basis of discussion than simply the matter of rights.

Contemporary ethical discussion attempts this broadening by using ethical principles or rules as a foundation for making impartial judgments about right or wrong. Although important tools for guiding ethical discernment and decision making, principles nevertheless do have the disadvantage of being abstract, and consequently can lead to an overlooking of relevant subjective values and experiences.

In contrast to an ethical method based primarily on principles or rights, I would advocate an approach that arises from experience. Such a method has its roots in a traditional Aristotelian ethic of virtue. It places its emphasis not on philosophical concepts that can be known a priori, but on the moral agents who are making ethical judgments and decisions. Its starting point is: What is going on here, in this concrete situation? What are the experiences of the persons involved? What are their values, questions, understandings, emotions, motivations, hopes, desires? How reasonable and responsible are their judgments and decisions, as well as the method or process by which they judge and decide? In other words, persons making ethical judgments should pay attention to what is happening, what values are at stake, what is being understood, and what is being overlooked, within both the situation and themselves. In addition, it is important that moral agents allow themselves to be affected and even transformed by the situation; otherwise abstract reflection, lack of interest (masking as objectivity), and self-deception are likely to replace compassionate and honest reflection and behavior.

THE CASE OF REBECCA MULLER

A recent medical-become-legal case illustrates well the ability of experience to transform those who would make ethical and legal judgments. It also illustrates the potential for abstract reasoning and judgments, based on ethical and legal precedents and principles, to minimize or overlook concrete, subjective realities and issues that have ethical implications.

It was personal involvement by visitation to the bedside that enabled Judge Vernon Evans of Tampa, Florida, to grant Barbara and Alan Muller's desire to have their terminally ill daughter, Rebecca, taken off a respirator.

Rebecca Muller was born in November 1987 with severe brain, lung, kidney, spinal, and intestinal damage. She was also deaf and blind, and her eyes, when opened, rolled back until only the whites showed. The moment after she was born, her heart was shocked into beating by cardiac paddles, a treatment that was to be repeated many more times over the course of her short life. Her first and all subsequent breaths were forced by a respirator. Food was poured into her stomach by a feeding tube, but since her stomach was incapable of digesting anything, she was subsequently fed predigested foods intravenously.

When touched, Rebecca would become rigid, stop breathing, and turn reddish-purple. She was completely unaware of her surroundings. The only thing to which she appeared to respond was pain.

For two months after her birth, Rebecca was given numerous tests in an attempt to discover the cause of her medical problems. None provided a clear answer. Her physician then proposed surgery (tracheotomy and gastrostomy) to insert tubes into her throat and stomach in order to make nursing care easier. Rebecca's parents refused permission for the surgery, claiming that Rebecca had suffered enough. They requested that Rebecca be taken off the respirator and allowed to die.

Because Rebecca had minimal brainstem activity, hospital authorities would not allow the removal of life-sustaining technology without a court order. Florida law permits the withdrawal of life-sustaining measures from infants who are brain dead, but is unclear about cases such as Rebecca's—even though, in Rebecca's case, everyone involved, including physicians, nurses, lawyers, clergy, and parents, agreed that Rebecca had no chance of surviving for more than another few months, even with the technological support.

Legal proceedings were a nightmare for the Mullers. The court appointed an attorney to represent Rebecca's interests. He, not the child's parents, had complete legal control over the infant. Various people who had never seen Rebecca accused the Mullers of such things as child abuse and abandonment. Fortunately, all those who were personally involved with Rebecca's case, including health care providers and attorneys, supported the Mullers' desire to stop life-prolonging measures, stating that Rebecca had no chance to survive. After visiting the infant's bedside twice, Judge Evans authorized the withdrawal of the respirator. Rebecca died less than two minutes after the respirator was removed.

On the first day of the court hearing, the Mullers issued the following statement:

Our decision to stop artificial life support was reached after two months of hour by hour, minute by minute prayer. If the medical tests had shown even a small ray of hope, we would have kept our vigil, forever if necessary, to give her a chance at life. To us, there can be no personal price too great to bear if there were at least the slightest hope, and if there were no pain for Rebecca. Her condition has progressed to the point where even routine care is very painful to her. We have watched her suffer great pain for so long that it is now clear to us that by using the hospital's life support systems where there is no hope, that we are actually interfering with God's will.

COMMENTARY

The case of Rebecca Muller is a tragic one, not only because an infant and her parents suffered so greatly, but because there is no ethical, medical, or legal justification for such futile treatment.

Rebecca Muller was born terminally ill. She was shocked into life and shocked into staying alive. From all the evidence I have seen and heard, the baby was struggling to die: She had numerous cardiac arrests, multiple organ failure, and permanent incapacity to breathe on her own, or to eat and digest foods. She had minimal brainstem activity and would never have emerged into a cognitive state. Nevertheless, technology and misinformed and misguided decision making prevented her body from following its natural course toward death.

It appears instead that every effort was made to keep Rebecca alive, regardless of the cost to her or to her family. When it was finally acknowledged that these efforts were futile, and that the infant should be allowed to die, recourse was made to the courts rather than to the medical-ethical tradition for guidance. It is profoundly disturbing that the current climate of litigation and fear of litigation has turned what are essentially ethical matters into legal problems.

Once medicine had done all that it could to diagnose and treat Rebecca's condition, the question of her future ceased to be a purely medical issue. It had become an ethical issue as well. Whether a terminally ill patient should live or be allowed to die; under what conditions a person should live or die; what burdens individuals should be made to bear, and for what hoped-for benefit; at what point we draw the line between treating and not treating severely handicapped or terminally ill patients; who decides whether treatment should be stopped; and who speaks for those who are unable to speak for themselves—all are ethical questions, not scientific judgments. They concern values and assumptions about the meaning of human life and death. As value judgments, they are moral choices and should be treated as such. Judicial scrutiny should be the last resort when deciding ethical matters, and not the first resort, as it became in the Muller case.

Withholding and Withdrawing Life-Sustaining Treatment

It is likely that part of the problem in Rebecca Muller's case, and in those like it, was a confusion about the morality and legality of withholding and withdrawing life-sustaining treatments. It is fairly common for health care professionals to think that once certain life-sustaining treatments have been initiated, they cannot ethically and legally be stopped, even if they prove to be a futile means of improving a patient's medical condition. Unfortunately, however, this mistaken notion frequently leads to undesirable consequences:

1. overtreatment of some patients, even to the point at which it causes positive harm without compensating benefits;[2]

2. failure to initiate treatments that might be beneficial for fear that once begun, the treatments cannot be stopped.

According to the President's Commission for the Study of Ethical Problems in Medicine and Biomedical and Behavioral Research (1983:76), there should, in fact, be greater justification for withdrawing treatment than for withholding it:

Whether a particular treatment will have positive effects is often highly uncertain before the therapy has been tried. If a trial of therapy makes clear that it is not helpful to the patient, this is actual evidence (rather than surmise) to support stopping because the therapeutic benefit that earlier was a possibility has been found to be clearly unobtainable.

An additional obstacle to withdrawing therapy that has already begun is a fear of legal liability. Many worry that stopping treatment, even when ethically justifiable, will constitute wrongful killing. This supposition is based on two fallacies. The first is that the terminally ill or permanently incapacitated patient's death is caused by the act of withdrawing treatment. This is simply not true. Such a patient dies from a particular illness or other medical problem, not from the act of withdrawing futile treatment. The withdrawal of such treatment merely allows death to occur from whatever necessitated the treatment in the first place. If Rebecca Muller had never been hooked up to sophisticated machinery after birth, we would say she died of multiple organ failure. That she was hooked up to machinery that was powerless to improve her medical condition or to save her life did not change the cause of her death. The machinery only kept her mechanically alive and prolonged and exaggerated her dying process (for example, the ventilator was scarring her lung tissues, thereby slowly killing her). The act of withdrawing Rebecca from mechanical ventilation was not an act of killing; it was a ceasing to provide futile and excessively burdensome treatment.

A second fallacy is that withdrawing life-prolonging treatment will result in legal prosecution. On the contrary, says the President's Commission (1983:77):

Little if any legal significance attaches to the distinction between withholding and withdrawing. Nothing in law—certainly not in the context of the doctor–patient relationship—makes stopping treatment a more serious legal issue than not starting treatment. In fact, not starting treatment that *might* be in a patient's best interests is more likely to be held a civil or criminal wrong than stopping the same treatment when it has proved unavailing.

Although it may be psychologically more difficult for many to withdraw life-sustaining treatment than it would be to refrain from starting such treatment in the first place, it is important to recognize that there is simply no moral significance to the distinction between withholding and withdrawing. If a treatment is medically and ethically warranted, it is wrong to withhold or withdraw it. If, however, there is no good reason for employing a particular treatment, then there is no moral objection to either withholding or withdrawing such treatment. The criterion, then, of moral judgment in this matter is whether or not the treatment is morally indicated in a given situation, not whether stopping a treatment is a greater evil than not starting it.

Unfortunately, in our current litigious environment, many health care professionals fear unjustified lawsuits or prosecution. More unfortunate, however, is that the patient frequently pays the price of this fear. It is a fear that does not constitute "a compelling moral reason for physicians or others to deny infants [and by extension any patient] the care that is most likely to be in their best interests," say the authors of a Hastings Center report on the ethics of neonatal care (Caplan et al. 1987:23). Until the public comes to understand that withdrawing a treatment is not ethically different from withholding it, "the remote possibility of legal entanglement simply may be one of the risks of providing competent and ethical care. The specter of public confusion reinforces the need to educate the public and the professions on this matter" (ibid.).

Extraordinary and Ordinary Means

So confused has the meaning of "ordinary" and "extraordinary" care become that most ethicists recommend dropping the terms altogether and substituting more precise terms such as benefits or burdens, mandatory or optional, proportionate or disproportionate. Although I agree with the intent of this recommendation, I think it would be a mistake to abandon the "ordinary–extraordinary" distinction altogether, simply because the terms are still used so frequently in medicine. Instead of complete abandonment, I suggest an effort to clarify their traditional meaning and to correct inappropriate usage.

The distinction "extraordinary means" arose in sixteenth-century Roman Catholic moral theology, and referred primarily not to the technique or means employed in medical care, but to the condition of the patient (Beauchamp and Childress 1983:126–36; Kelly 1958:129; President's Commission 1983:82–90). Historically, in both the moral and Hippocratic tradition (Amundsen 1978), even the most basic remedy, if offering no hope of benefit to the patient, was deemed "extraordinary" and hence morally optional. In this tradition, the patient's condition is the decisive factor. If a treatment is extraordinary, it is because the patient's condition is extraordinary, not because the treatment is technological, expensive, or complex. The emphasis of treatment decisions is therefore not on technique, but on the effect of such treatments on the patient. The implication of this is that no remedy is obligatory unless it offers a reasonable hope of checking or curing an illness.

The crucial issue is to discover some substantive standard that allows us to say that for some patients a certain treatment would be considered ordinary (i.e., morally obligatory) medical care, whereas for others the same treatment would be extraordinary (i.e., morally optional). A criterion generally proposed by ethicists is that of proportional benefit or burden. Will a proposed treatment or procedure offer a patient a reasonable hope of benefit, that is, will it provide the possibility of improved medical status or quality of life? Or will the treatment simply prolong a dying process already in motion? Will the treatment help alleviate pain or suffering? Are the burdens associated with the treatment excessive, or are they sufficiently bearable in light of the hoped-for benefit?

These types of questions should be asked when determining whether a treatment is ordinary or extraordinary, and hence mandatory or optional. Failure to make proper distinctions in this regard has, like the confusion between withdrawing and withholding, led to the imposition of unnecessary and burdensome treatments on many dying patients. Public and professional education is needed about this matter every bit as much as about withholding and withdrawing treatments.

PATIENT AND FAMILY AUTONOMY

Parents should be the surrogates for a seriously ill newborn unless they are disqualified by decisionmaking incapacity, an unresolvable disagreement between them, or their choice of a course of action that is clearly against the infant's best interests....

Decisions should be referred to public agencies (including courts) for review when necessary to determine whether parents should be disqualified as decisionmakers and, if so, who should decide the course of treatment that would be in the best interests of their child. (President's Commission 1983:6–8)

The ethical basis for parents' authority to make decisions on behalf of their children is the presumption that parental love will lead to choices that are in their children's best interests. This presumption cannot always be guaranteed, however, and so the law makes provision for appointing guardians for those children whose parents are unable or unwilling to act for the child's welfare. A decision to appoint a nonparental guardian for a child should be based on clear evidence of parental incapacity or negligence.

The Mullers' dedicated, compassionate, and generous love for their child was never in doubt; neither does there appear to have been any evidence of their interests being in conflict with those of Rebecca. In addition, when Rebecca's case went to court, everyone involved in it, including parents, physicians, nurses, clergy, hospital administrators, lawyers, concurred that life-prolonging treatment was futile and burdensome. There was, consequently, no basis for disqualifying Rebecca Muller's parents as her surrogate decision makers. Nevertheless, from the moment Rebecca's case was brought to court, her parents were legally disqualified as decision makers on her behalf, and an attorney was appointed in their place. This action (although not unusual in such circumstances) not only represents a gross interference in the fundamental relationship between parents and child and a lack of respect for them as persons; it also violates the recommendation of the President's Commission that disqualification of parents as primary decision makers should be based on evidence of incapacity, unresolvable disagreements, negligence, or abuse.

It is regrettable that this case ever went to court, for it not only robbed a family in very tragic circumstances of their privacy and autonomy, but it also transformed what was basically a medical-ethical matter into a legal problem. A reason given by hospital authorities for seeking a legal ruling on terminating treatment in a case such as Rebecca Muller's was that Florida law does not specifically cover the circumstances of Rebecca's medical condition. Florida law permits the removal of life-sustaining equipment from infants who are brain dead, that is, whose entire brain has ceased to function. Rebecca did not meet this criterion because she had minimal brainstem activity, shed tears, and appeared to experience pain. It was precisely the testimony about Rebecca's shedding tears that led the presiding judge in the case to hesitate in granting the request to terminate treatment. Judge Evans stated, "In this case, there is in my opinion cognitive brain function [because of the tears], and no doubt about it" (*St. Petersburg Times*, January 30, 1988:1-B). He noted that past cases in which courts have allowed infants' respirators to be removed involved babies who were comatose and apparently lacked the ability to think or feel.

The data of the case point to another conclusion than that reached by Judge Evans. Evans was mistaken in his opinion that Rebecca was capable of cognitive experiences, since the infant's neurological capacity was limited to brainstem activity. According to the American Academy of Neurology (1986):

No conscious experience of pain and suffering is possible without the integrated functioning of the brainstem and cerebral cortex.... Noxious stimuli may activate peripherally located nerves, but only a brain with the capacity for consciousness can translate that neural activity into an experience.

Since Rebecca Muller had only minimal brainstem function, she had no cognitive ability. Consequently, her tears and seemingly pained reactions to physical stimuli did not represent cognitive brain function, but reflex reactions. If Judge Evans had made his final decision on the presumption of cognitive ability, it would have been based on a mistaken interpretation of medical evidence. Fortunately, he did not.[3]

The second problem with Judge Evans's standard for withdrawing treatment from infants is that it restricts removal of life-support systems to comatose infants and makes no additional provision for the cessation of treatments that are futile or excessively burdensome. Attention to comatose infants is itself legally complicated by the "medical oxymoron" (Cranford 1988:29), "chronically and irreversibly comatose," employed in the Amendments to the Child Abuse Prevention and Treatment Act of 1984 and the implementing Health and Human Services regulations of 1985 (Federal Register 1985). Says Cranford (1988:32), "the class of patients called 'chronically and irreversibly comatose' simply does not exist in any meaningful sense," since the lifespan of a truly comatose patient is limited to weeks or months—hardly a chronic state. In addition, the term "irreversibly comatose" is variously used by different physicians to indicate very different conditions: whole brain death, persistent vegetative state, and all types of permanently unconscious patients. This imprecise and inaccurate use of language leads to clinically and ethically confusing consequences, maintains Cranford (1988:28). It is a confusion that was evident in the terminology used to report Rebecca's medical condition and in the decision making concerning withdrawal of her treatment.

Federal regulations (Federal Register 1985) define medically indicated treatment for infants as that which will most likely be effective in ameliorating or correcting life-threatening conditions. There are three exceptions to the requirements to provide such treatment: (1) infants who are irreversibly comatose; (2) infants for whom such treatment would merely prolong dying, not correct all the life-threatening conditions, or be useless in ensuring survival; and (3) infants for whom such treatment would be "virtually futile" and its provision inhumane. In all cases nutrition, hydration, and appropriate medication is to be provided (Cohen 1987:9).[4]

Rebecca Muller clearly met exceptions (2) and (3). (Exception 1 is problematic in its wording and intention, as Cranford has indicated; see above.) Consequently, I see no legal or ethical reason why hospital officials hesitated to allow the removal of her respirator. Hospital officials were concerned about violating a Florida law regulating withdrawal of treatments from infants and about the possibility of litigation and loss of federal funding. Liability fears were unfounded, in my judgment, since federal laws would not have been violated by terminating Rebecca's treatment. The Florida law is itself a problem since it is based on a fallacious notion that ceasing to treat a brain-dead infant is terminating the child's life. If someone is brain dead, there is no life to terminate, and no life to sustain by the treatment—other than purely physical life for the purpose of organ transplantation, for instance. By limiting the removal of life supports to brain-dead infants, the law makes no provision for stopping futile and burdensome treatment for the terminally ill, a problem that is not unique to Florida. It is for this category of patient that guidelines concerning the withdrawal of life-sustaining treatments are needed, and not for patients who are already legally dead.[5]

The lack of an adequate standard in Florida law for terminating treatment (such as futility or burden–benefit) apparently led to Judge Evans's initial reluctance to permit removal of the respirator from Rebecca. The appearance of minimal cognitive awareness (e.g., the ability to experience pain) by Rebecca was another. This latter point needs comment. The fact that a terminally ill child has even minimal cognitive ability, such as the ability to experience pain (debatable in the Muller case), is an insufficient criterion, on ethical grounds, for refusing to cease treatment that is both futile and burdensome. In fact, the ability to suffer on account of such treatment is itself an ethically sufficient criterion for stopping life-prolonging treatment if such treatment is futile and if the burdens of the treatment outweigh any hoped-for benefit. Laws should be changed to reflect more appropriate ethical and medical judgments concerning removal of life-sustaining treatments from infants and children, including the cessation of futile and inappropriate administrations of artificial fluids and hydration (admittedly a more volatile issue than termination of respiratory support, but one that nonetheless needs careful study and reassessment; see Paris and Fletcher 1985).

CONCLUSION

I began this chapter by claiming that principle- and rights-based ethics are insufficient for dealing with the complexities of experiences on which ethical judgments are made. Principles and rights are not starting points; they are conclusions that are based on experience and understanding. They are abstractions that reflect only part of the whole. They can never be the whole. Experience must be a factor in making ethical judgments and decisions.

Every person involved in Rebecca Muller's case was trying to do the right thing. There is no indication of bad intent on anyone's part. Nevertheless, the tendency when seeking the right thing is to find clear answers to a problem: lawyers and judges through the law and in rights, philosophers through principles. Neither laws, rights, nor principles, however, can fully account for the experiences of living beings in concrete situations. Abstractions can be useful, and often necessary, guides when making decisions, but they cannot replace intelligence in the decision-making process, and intelligent decision making must be based on the experience of all data pertinent to a case. Judge Evans was unable to make a decision about removing Rebecca Muller's respirator simply on the basis of legal precedent. He had to experience for himself the condition of the child.

The ethic I am proposing is not based on a rejection of principles or rights as valuable guides. I am claiming, however, that neither principles, rights, nor the law are sufficient when making ethical decisions. None of the major decisions of life is based on principles. People do not marry because of principles; people do not have children because of principles; people do not choose a career because of principles. A vast array of experience leads people to make the choices they make, and this array must receive our attention if we are to make intelligent, reasonable, and responsible judgments and decisions.

The primary focus of an ethics of virtue is on moral agents, that is, on the attitudes and dispositions that inform and affect people's actions and judgments. It is concerned with such factors as one's intentions, values, and motives, and one's biases, blind spots, and oversights. To use more philosophical language, virtue is concerned with moral character, with one's conscious intentionality and interiority—with what one is doing when one is experiencing, understanding, judging, and deciding. It begins not with principles and rights from which one tries to deduce correct action but with the foundations of rights and principles: How do I know? What am I to do? Why?

What difference might such an approach have made in Rebecca Muller's case? First, it would have broadened the basis of concern from what tasks needed to be done to keep Rebecca alive or to protect health care providers or institutions from legal liability, or even from whether ethical principles were being upheld or violated, to a consideration of the moral experiences, perceptions, and sentiments of those involved in her care. It also would have considered such things as the values, feelings, emotions, understandings, and responsibilities of Rebecca's parents to be data morally relevant to the decision-making process.[6]

Also relevant are the experiences, motives, and goals of the health care professionals. What were they trying to accomplish by their various testing and treatments? For what benefit? When the benefits of treatments ceased, what were their responsibilities toward the patient? Why? What should have been the course of action when nothing more could be done to save the life or improve the health of the patient? Attention to goals is important here. Is the goal of medicine to maintain life at any cost? That has certainly never been the Hippocratic tradition (Amundsen 1978). What were the motives for the actions and decisions of health care providers and hospital officials? Compassion for the baby and her parents? Hope for a remedy or a diagnosis? Desire for self-protection, medical experimentation, or a need to be doing something? (Alan Muller reported to me that he once overheard one of the physicians order further tests—after everyone had already admitted nothing more could be done for Rebecca—because, said the physician, "We have to be doing something. We can't just let her lie there.") Questions such as these focus on the intentions of moral agents (and we are all moral agents).

The criteria for the rightness or goodness of ethical acts lie in the presence or absence of the honesty, integrity, intelligence, and responsibility—that is, the authenticity—of those who make ethical judgments and decisions. By authenticity I mean that the moral agent is attentive to all the data relevant to a particular question for judgment, that the agent seeks to understand these data, is open to questions and to other viewpoints, and is reasonable and responsible when judging and deciding. The agent should be attentive not only to data "out there," but to his or her inner processes of experiencing, raising questions, seeking to understand, to judge, or to decide. Principles, rules, or laws can be useful as well, for they are transcendental values that can help sort out and clarify the significance and merit of the data of experience and act as a check against mere subjectivism, situationism, bias, or fear. They cannot, however, substitute for the data of experience and for the issues and questions that arise from experience. Once again, legal precedent did not enable Judge Evans to decide about the ethical and legal probity of disconnecting Rebecca Muller from the respirator and allowing her to die. Direct involvement with and experience of the infant was necessary to him to make a judgment and decision about what was in the best interests of the child.[7]

There is a presumption on the part of many individuals that curative, restorative, or stabilizing treatment always serves an infant's best interests. Such a presumption does not always hold up against facts, however. According to J. Glaser (1985:85), in some situations providing merely comforting care can be in an infant's (and, in my opinion, in any patient's) best interests if the following conditions are met:

1. Treatment would be useless and only prolong the dying process.
2. There is no hope of the patient's achieving even a minimal capacity for an experience of relationships.
3. The patient's life would be dominated by intractable pain and/or the struggle to survive.

Rebecca Muller's case met all of these conditions.

In conclusion, it is evident to me that if the law and the fear of lawsuits continue to form the basis of decisions that impose burdensome and futile medical treatments on patients and their loved ones, neither society nor individuals are being well served. In addition, sound ethical and medical values and traditions are being compromised and marginalized in a legalized decision-making process. Says G. J. Annas (1988:30):

A major problem in medical practice over the past decade has been the trend for physicians to abdicate their responsibility for medical decisions to hospital administrators, lawyers, and courts, resulting in an increasing bureaucratization of medicine to the detriment of both physicians and patients. . . . [The courts] should not routinely permit themselves to be used by doctors, hospital administrators, and their lawyers to avoid taking professional responsibility for their decisions. . . . Hospital administrators and lawyers often forge "solutions" to medical practice "problems" that are disconnected from biological reality and compassionate medical practice.[8]

There is an urgent need for the general public, and especially for health care and legal professionals, to become educated about the ethical aspects of terminating life-sustaining treatment. There is an equally urgent need for laws concerning the termination of life-sustaining treatment that will be informed by and based on established ethical and medical insights, values, traditions, and principles. These laws will allow patients and their loved ones to accept or refuse treatments according to their own values and understanding of their own best interests. Ultimately, this will be in society's and in medicine's best interest as well.

NOTES

1. My decision not to discuss euthanasia in this chapter does not imply that I think discussion of the matter is not needed. On the contrary, there is considerable evidence that such debate is urgently needed, lest policies, practices, or proscriptions become standard without careful ethical, legal, medical, or social reflection. Recently the need for such reflection and debate was glaringly demonstrated by the publication of an anonymous letter in the *Journal of the American Medical Association* about a medical resident's injecting a fatal dose of morphine into a cancer patient ("It's Over, Debbie," 1988) and in the ensuing responses to this letter (Gaylin et al. 1988; "Letters" 1988; Lundberg 1988; Vaux 1988). For an example of some recent discussions of euthanasia, see Campbell and Crigger (1989).

2. Overtreatment can itself result in a lawsuit (*Leach v. Shapiro* 1982 and *Leach v. Akron General Medical Center* 1982).

3. Rebecca Muller's parents understandably disagree with the contention that the infant did not experience pain. I make my judgment on the basis of testimony of neurologists (American Academy of Neurology 1986; Cranford 1988:31). Whether or not the Mullers' understanding of Rebecca's reactions to physical stimuli is correct, her body contortions and turning purple each time she was touched should not be minimized. In my opinion, these reactions themselves

indicate that violence was being inflicted on the child's body even if she could not feel it.

4. See Paris and Fletcher (1985) for a challenge to this stipulation on medical and ethical grounds.

5. Even brain-dead patients are not always immune from the imposition of continued "life-sustaining" treatments, however. According to Annas (1988:30), "Great discomfort and uncertainty about brain death persists. Surveys consistently show that [hospital] administrators are uncertain about brain death, and this translates into inappropriate actions."

6. Though not irrelevant within a system based on ethical or legal abstractions (except in an extreme deontological system such as Kant's), such issues as personal values, feelings, emotions, and burdens are considered subjective and therefore secondary at best to principles and laws.

7. It is unrealistic to expect judges to visit the bedside (or, by extension, any living quarters) of every case that comes before the court. The point here is not that Judge Evans had to visit Rebecca in the hospital (although the visit was decisive in his determination in this case) but that he broadened his criteria for judgment beyond case law to the data of experience.

8. Annas's remarks are included in a study of a New Jersey case in which physicians, hospital administrators, and lawyers refused for three days to discontinue mechanical bodily support systems from a 20-year-old man pronounced brain dead. Although Rebecca Muller's case differs from this one since she was not brain dead when her parents requested termination of life-support systems, it does indicate that the problem of not honoring parents' requests to terminate futile treatments for their children is not peculiar to Florida.

REFERENCES

American Academy of Neurology. 1986. *Brophy v. New England Sinai Hospital, Inc.* Amicus Curiae Brief.

Amundsen, D. 1978. "The Physician's Obligation to Prolong Life: A Medical Duty Without Classical Roots." *Hastings Center Report* 8(4): 23–30.

Annas, G. J. 1988. "At Law: Brain Death and Organ Donation: You *Can* Have One Without the Other." *Hastings Center Report* 18(3): 28–30.

Beauchamp, T. L., and Childress, J. F., 1983. *Principles of Biomedical Ethics*, 2nd ed. New York: Oxford University Press.

Campbell, C. S., and B. J. Crigger, eds. 1989. "Mercy, Murder, and Morality: Perspectives on Euthanasia." Special Supplement to the *Hastings Center Report* 19(1).

Caplan, A., Capron, A. M., Murray, T., and Penticuff, J. 1987. "Deciding Not to Employ Aggressive Measures." *Hastings Center Report* 17(6): 22–25.

Cohen, C., Levin, B. and Powderly, K. 1987. "A History of Neonatal Intensive Care and Decisionmaking." *Hastings Center Report* 17(6): 7–9.

Cranford, R. E. 1988. "The Persistent Vegetative State: The Medical Reality (Getting the Facts Straight)." *Hastings Center Report* 18(1): 27–32.

Federal Register. April 15, 1985. *Child Abuse and Neglect: Prevention and Treatment.* 45CFR 1340, DHHS Part IV.

Gaylin, W., Kass, L. R., Pellegrino, E. D., and Siegler, M. 1988. "Doctors Must

Not Kill." Commentary. *Journal of the American Medical Association* 259(14): 2139–40.

Glaser, J. 1985. "Caring for Newborns With Disabilities." In J. Glaser, ed. *Caring for the Special Child*. Kansas City, MO: Leaven Press, pp. 89–90.

"It's Over, Debbie." 1988. *Journal of the American Medical Association* 259(2): 272.

Kelly, G. 1958. *Medico-Moral Problems*. St. Louis: Catholic Health Association.

Leach v. Shapiro. 1982. Civ. Action C–81–2559A, Summit County, Ohio; *Leach v. Akron General Medical Center*. 1982. 426 N.E. 2d 809. Ohio Com. Pl. Cited in President's Commission. 1983, p.75, n.96.

Letters to the Editor. 1988. *Journal of the American Medical Association* 259(14): 2094–98.

Lundberg, G. 1988. " 'It's Over, Debbie' and the Euthanasia Debate." Editorial. *Journal of the American Medical Association* 259(14): 2142–43.

Paris, J., and Fletcher, A. 1985. "Infant Doe and the Absolute Requirement to Use Nourishment and Fluids for the Dying Infant." In J. Glaser, ed. *Caring for the Special Child*, op. cit., pp. 72–75.

President's Commission for the Study of Ethical Problems in Medicine and Biomedical and Behavioral Research. 1983. *Deciding to Forgo Life-Sustaining Treatment*. U.S. Government Printing Office.

St. Petersburg Times. January 30, 1988. "Tears May Tell Fate of Terminally Ill Baby." 1-B.

Vaux, K. 1988. "Debbie's Dying: Mercy Killing and the Good Death." Commentary. *Journal of American Medical Association* 259(14): 2140–41.

II Cross-Cultural Views

4 On the Question of the Right to Die: An African View

Kwasi Wiredu

Let me start with an abstract. To be or not to be is an agonizing question. Is it to be left to individuals to answer for themselves as they may see fit? Even the most individualistic societies set very definite limits to the individual's rights over his or her life in the prohibition of suicide. The question that is becoming increasingly urgent in societies with scientific and technological facilities for prolonging life—even when it has ebbed to an irreversibly vegetative level—is whether the community has an absolute right over the individual in this matter.

It is well known that African societies are deeply communalistic. An individual is regarded as amounting to nothing except in the context of the community. Consequently, it might be expected that the right to make the ultimate decision of life and death will be vested in the community rather than the individual. In fact, the contrary is the case. Although individuals are regarded as nothing without the community, once situated in society, they are regarded as having a value that is, in principle, overriding; for, by explicit doctrine, each individual is a child of God and none is a child of the earth. Every individual is unique not just in a logical sense but also in a special sense defined by his or her destiny. Life itself is a gift of God, and destiny is strictly a matter between God and the given prenatal hopeful. Death normally fixes the outer limit of the destiny prescribed by God, but malevolent forces may interfere with that destiny. Moreover, human knowledge is uncertain, and it is always an open question whether a threatening death is the decree of destiny or of some countervailing force. Accordingly, African societies have an abundance of both ordinary and special procedures for warding off premature death. But when all effort fails, the inference is that perhaps destiny is taking its course, and it is considered a person's last right or privilege—the distinction does not matter at this stage—to be able to die in dignity and to receive a fitting burial and a well-attended funeral. Life, in this way of thinking, is meaningless except in terms of social interactions aimed at the well-being of all concerned. Thus, when the will to live has been drained away in circumstances of total incapacitation, not to obstruct a death wish may be the proper way to pay last respects.

At every point in the above abstract there are issues of doctrine calling for elucidation. I propose to supply the needed elaboration with particular reference to the traditional thought of the Akans of Ghana, the ethnic group in Africa of which the present writer has an understanding from the inside.

It is necessary at the outset to have some understanding of the great value that is placed on human life in Akan society. No sacrifice is thought to be too great for the preservation of human life. In circumstances requiring sacrifices to this purpose an Akan would be apt to quote the popular Akan maxim *Onipa na ohia*, which is literally translated as "It is a human being that there is need for" or, more idiomatically, "It is a human being that is important." A slightly more expansive Akan maxim points out that when you call on any worldly possession there is no reply, but when you call on a human being there is a response. This sense of the importance of human life is incapsulated in the very conception of a person that is held by the Akans. That conception has two aspects: descriptive and normative.

Descriptively, a human person is held to consist of three basic elements: the body (*nipadua*, literally, the person-tree), the life-principle (*okra*, not to be confused with Western concepts of the soul), and *sunsum*, which is regarded as the basis of the unique personal presence that every individual has. Quite subtle problems arise in the characterization of the ontological nature of these elements and their relations which must be left unexplored here. Suffice it to say that while the second and the third elements, unlike the body, are not material, neither are they fully immaterial, being conceived on a partially material model.[1] The important thing to note here, however, is that the *okra* (the life-principle) is supposed to be a portion of God himself which he contributes as a *direct* gift in the making of a person.[2] The traditional account of the initial stages of person-making takes a somewhat dramatic form. It is not a bedroom drama but rather a theological one. When God has formed the *okra* (out of himself) he is believed to conduct a ceremony with it at which he announces its destiny to it. The *okra* thereupon takes leave of God and heads downward to incarnation on earth. A well-known Akan lyric says, "I saw God and took leave of him before coming" (*Mihuu Nyame na mekraa no ansa na mereba*). The destiny, of course, comprehends absolutely the entire life-process, but the announcement of destiny naturally mentions only the principal outlines of a person's earthly career. Again, all sorts of questions arise here which we cannot pursue, but there are two points of particular relevance for our discussion. First, the idea that the *okra* is a speck of God in man gives a person, any person, an aspect of divinity, however diminutive in degree. Second, destiny is an exhaustive principle of individuation; no two destinies are exactly alike. Each individual comes endowed with unique potentialities and responsibilities, tendencies and contingencies, and this uniqueness is much prized by the Akans in spite of their deeply communalistic orientation. Thus a common maxim says, "When I was taking leave of my God there was nobody there" (*Merekra me nyame na obiara nni ho*), exulting in the one-to-one character of the destiny ceremony. The implication is that ultimately one is solely responsible for one's own life and conduct.

We are brought to another aspect of the Akan concept of a person very relevant to our discussion when we come, still on the descriptive plane, to the next phase of the making of a person after the destiny-investiture of the *okra*. One way or another, the *okra* has to be born of a woman, and this is a biological process in which both parents have obvious roles. In recognition of this the Akans hold that a person's father contributes a factor (*ntoro*) which is responsible for the emergence of the *sunsum*, the unique impression that one communicates to others by one's sheer presence. To the mother is attributed a person's blood (*mogya*). These two factors, the *ntoro* and the *mogya*, have a direct social significance. The Akans are a matrilineal people and therefore ascribe a greater social significance to the *mogya* (blood) than to the *ntoro*, the paternal input into the biological make-up of a person. The "blood" is taken as the basis of family, or more strictly, clan identity. Membership in a clan situates a person in a quite extensive network of kinship relations to which are attached various degrees of rights and obligations. Similarly, the paternal factor automatically makes one a member of a patrilineal grouping, which also means a definite set of rights and obligations, although of a rather less intensive and pervasive sort. The point here is that, on this showing, a person is by definition a social being. Aristotle said that man is by nature a social being. One Akan way of articulating the same idea is picturesque: "When a person descends onto this earth he lands in a town." But the remarks just made about the social significance of the *mogya* and the *ntoro* show that the Akans went further than Aristotle. People are not social just be virtue of circumstances having to do with their lives in the world. They are already social at conception— by virtue of their internal constitution as biological combinations of *mogya*, *ntoro*, and *okra*.

This thought has an even more fundamental implication, namely, that the essence of human existence is social. The meaning of human life, as conceived by the Akans, consists of the fulfillment of social functions and the enjoyment of the consequent reciprocities. The social functions are defined, first, by kinship relations; second, by membership in the political set-up of a town, division, and nation; and, third, by membership in the family of humankind, all human beings being emphatically children of God as far as the Akans are concerned.[3] The kinship level of relations, as mentioned above, is founded on the individual's *mogya* and *ntoro*. The wider range of solidarity extending to the whole of humankind is founded on the idea that we all have within us little apportionments of the divine substance.[4]

But what are all these concentric circles of human relations for? The Akan answer is simple: human well-being. This is the most fundamental concept of Akan ethics. The goodness or badness of anything, be it an object, situation, or conduct, is judged by its subservience to the goal of human well-being. This is true of all appraisals that are, broadly speaking, ethical. But there is also a narrower concept of the ethical in which ethics (at least for the Akans) deals with nothing but the principles of the harmonious adaptation of the interests of the individual to the interests of the community. Here it is evident that ethics is concerned with human well-being at two levels, the individual and the social. This conception of ethics may be called humanistic in a strict sense. I shall return to it in due course. The following point, however, cannot be further delayed. If the criterion of goodness or badness (and, derivatively, of rightness or wrongness) is conduciveness to human well-being either in general or from the point of view of the harmonization of the interests of individuals with those of society, then it becomes possible to formulate the question of the right to die in a quite manageable way. The question is simply whether recognizing individuals' right to terminate their lives in certain circumstances is, in itself, prejudicial to human interests in either of the two perspectives just mentioned. To this question too I shall return later.

But it is important at this stage to probe a little further the bearing of the Akan conception of a person on the issue at stake. Although Akan conceptions of life and death evolved in the absence of those technological facilities for prolonging life, the use of which under certain conditions has played a great part in stimulating the controversy regarding the right to die in recent times, those conceptions nonetheless have definite relevant implications. As the reader must have begun to see by now, that conception of a person is very crucial in this connection. It is apparent that the descriptive aspect of that concept is intrinsically oriented in a social direction. This is even more explicit in its normative aspect. The natural translation of the English word "person" in Akan in *onipa*. The latter, however, shrouds a subtle ambiguity. In many important contexts, to call someone *onipa* is to commend that person; conversely, to say that someone is not an *onipa* is to condemn him or her

quite decidedly. Moreover, to risk a verbal hybrid, *onipa*hood is suscep-
tible of degrees in either direction. In this sense *onipa* does not mean
just a human being; it means a human being who has attained a certain
status. The problem is that in certain circumstances the word means a
person in the sense simply of a human being. Even the humblest nitwit
is still an *onipa* and is entitled to all the sympathy, consideration, and
basic respect due to all the children of God.

Thus personhood is, in one sense, something we are born with, but
in another sense it is something we strive for. This second sense is the
important one from a social point of view. In this sense, a person in
Akan thought is a human being who has attained adulthood, married,
established a household, and shown an ability through hard work and
judicious thinking to shoulder responsibilities to himself, his household,
his wider clan, and his community. Those raised in Akan society come
to understand and to appreciate through their own reflection that this
is what is expected of everybody. Consequently, those Akan-born, repeatedly faced with the failure to measure up to this expectation, will
almost certainly be constrained to ask themselves whether they are ever
going to become persons (*Se mere beye onipa ni?*) unless their basic good
sense has been eclipsed by some infirmity of mind. Among the Akans
such moments of self-questioning are accompanied by the deepest sense
of personal tragedy. If in this moment of deepest despair, overcome by
pessimism, one should take one's own life, the event would be viewed
with the greatest grief and dismay by the individual's relations and community, but not without understanding. Life is not thought to be worth
living at any and every cost. From an Akan standpoint, a meaningless
life is not worth living.

Notice that the criterion of meaningfulness is the ability to function
socially in a manner that takes due account of one's own interests along
with those of the community. This is evident from the Akan concept of
a person in both its descriptive and normative aspects. We see that in
Akan society the struggle to become a person *is* the struggle for meaning
in life. The necessity to harmonize one's interests with those of the
community, which is involved in this concept of meaning, is nothing
other than what might be called the moral imperative. It is an imperative
that the Akan mind imposes on itself. In Kantian idiom it is an autonomous rather than a heteronomous imperative, although, since the mind
itself evolves in a cultural matrix, it is also a social product. Beyond this
moral imperative there is also the social imperative of communal use-
fulness which the Akan individual comes to internalize in the process of
socialization. Thus both strictly moral and broadly social considerations
lie behind the thinking of those who, perceiving themselves to be faced
with the prospect of lives without meaning, decide to take their own life.
The remarkable thing is that this thinking reflects values embedded in

the very concept of a person that is held by the Akans. This is why the individual's extreme action, although regretted, is met with understanding.

Nevertheless, most Akans would feel that Akan values are misapplied in the self-destroyer's reasoning. Such pessimism would invariably be of a metaphysical sort. From a presumably unbroken succession of failures one concludes that destiny holds nothing better in store for one. Now, notions of personal destiny play quite a large part in Akan thinking about human life. As previously noted, these notions are an integral part of the Akan concept of a person, providing, indeed, the definition of an individual's identity. Interestingly, the same notion motivates both pessimism and optimism. Pessimists infer that present reverses infallibly portend a uniformly unhappy future. Nonpessimists rejoin that there is a non sequitur in the inference: The future is not always like the past. In this the latter have an Akan maxim on their side: "If bad days befall you, do not give up life; better days may come" (*Ehia wo a enwu; da pa be ba*).[5] This is not to suggest that an Akan optimist is necessarily steeled against the fallacy, for present fortune will sometimes encourage an optimist, with a similar lack of logic, to infer a rosy future.

But although logic is not on the side of pessimists, their right not to continue to live a meaningless life is not in question. What is illogical is the inference that leads them to the conclusion that they will never achieve meaning, not the belief that a meaningless life is not worth living. In fact, the Akans recognized an additional ground for suicide: the avoidance of a major disgrace not involving willful misconduct. Two relevant Akan maxims may be cited here. One of the most characteristic expressions of the Akan code of honor translates approximately as "Disgrace does not befit an Akan-born" (*Animguase mfata okanniba*). Perhaps the English translation does not capture the depth of feeling behind this saying, which renders it intelligible to the Akan understanding as a possible explanation of suicide. In any case, the Akans also say, quite bluntly, "Death is preferable to disgrace" (*Animguase de efanyinam owuo*). In precolonial times, when the Ashantis, a branch of the Akan ethnic group, were often at war, it was standard behavior for a general suffering an ignominious defeat in the field to commit suicide rather than come home in disgrace. This was regarded as the right thing to do. This right to die, however, was not restricted to discomfited generals.

But it would be a mistake to suppose from the foregoing that the traditional Akans generally took suicide lightly. On the contrary, their attitude to suicide was, as a rule, rather harsh. People who committed suicide were usually "punished" by means of extremely drastic symbolism. As K. A. Busia (1968:64) puts it, " 'Suicide' applied to one who had killed himself in order to avoid the consequence of some wrongful deed or from unknown motives, which the Ashanti therefore presumed to be evil. The suicide was tried, found guilty and *decapitated*" (my emphasis). When suicide was committed for known motives of an honorable kind, however, the reaction was different. Thus the Akans recognized a right to suicide under very restricted circumstances.

However, the right of a person of a sound mind in a sound body to commit suicide is not the kind of right to die that is currently most intensely discussed. That issue has increasingly been precipitated by the use of advanced technology to prolong life in circumstances of radical and irremediable impairment of body and (sometimes) mind. There are a number of issues to be sorted out of this connection. The first is the question of whether we are ever in a position to determine that a given state of impairment is irreversible. In order to avoid an epistemological digresson we might restrict the issue so that the question of the right to die is raised on the explicit hypothesis of irreversibility. This hypothesis would have the advantage of highlighting the fact that at this stage we are dealing with a matter of principle rather than of practicality. But we ought not to leave the question of irreversibility without noting that in the traditional Akan context the question often took the form of whether the apparent imminence of death was the decree of destiny or the machination of some evil force. Needless to say, this is not the question that pressed itself on the Akan consciousness at the first sign of ill health or mental impairment. Everything was done to overcome any incidence of ill health by ordinary means. The traditional Akans, like other African peoples, had an impressive repertory of effective herbal cures for all manner of health problems. This resource, incidentally, has generally not been tapped by contemporary African authorities as a complement to the Western health delivery systems that have become established in our urban centers.

Most ordinary afflictions of the body were satisfactorily cured purely by herbal methods. But more intractable illnesses were approached on three planes: physiological, psychological, and spiritual.[6] In such cases herbal medicine was supplemented with psychological analysis and treatment and, if necessary, with the invocation of (alleged) extra-human forces. The object of psychological investigation was to find out possible dislocations in the patients' social relations, for it was thought that such situations could cause or aggravate illness. Thus if a married woman had a health problem that seemed to withstand all the best medicines, the traditional healer would inquire, for example, whether her chastity had been questionable. If the answer should turn out to be in the negative, she would be encouraged to confess it to the appropriate people in a program designed to reestablish satisfactory relations with all concerned. Perhaps, the patient was a successful man who had fallen seriously ill and had been getting worse in spite of the most expert herbal treatment. Then the question might be whether he had harbored evil thoughts against others or perhaps taken undue advantage of some rivals. If all such lines of investigation proved negative, the suspicion would begin to fall on evil forces, such as witchcraft. The healer would then resort to various procedures for (supposedly) invoking the assistance of better inclined and more powerful extra-human forces. It was when all these methods failed that the hypothesis of destiny came into the picture. The thought then was that perhaps the person's destined end was at hand. The Akan doctrine of destiny, however, is quite tangled logically, for sometimes attempts were made through spiritual means to improve a gloomy destiny, ascertained to be gloomy by an equally spiritual methodology. However, if by one mode of inference or another an approaching death is thought to be in accordance with the inevitable schedule of destiny, it would strike the traditional Akans as irrational to try to prolong life by such means as artificial respiration and as positively wicked to do so in opposition to the death wishes of the patient concerned.

This brings us to the second set of issues to be considered. It is clear from the above that in Akan thought one has the right to terminate one's own life in certain circumstances. But do others have a duty to help the patient die? This raises some of the problems of euthanasia. The difficult question here is not whether it is ever right to help a person to die when the continuation of life is seen by all parties to be painfully pointless, but rather whether, when an individual in such circumstances asks to be helped to die, others have an obligation to oblige. When the help sought is merely the passive one of dicontinuing the operation of special systems of life support, the question can be answered in the affirmative on the basis of the Akan considerations already discussed. But when help involves quite active life-termination measures, the issue is more difficult. To make the problem more concrete, suppose your own brother, inextricably caught in a conflagration, is certain to die slowly in unspeakable pain. He cannot be saved, but his dying pains can be shortened. For example, if he is shot in the head or hit hard with a heavy object, he will die quickly with much less pain. He implores you to favor him with the quicker dispatch. Ought you to do it? Can you do it? If "ought" implies "can," perhaps the question can be reduced to whether it is psychologically possible for you to do it. To be sure, the question is not whether if you did it, you would be right, but rather if you did not do it, you would be wrong. Perhaps it is not urgent to pursue this question here as it concerns not just the right to die but the right to be helped to die. But I might observe that the Akans are generally cautious about people with the equanimity and emotional strength that would enable one to shoot one's own brother even though for reasons of mercy or compassion. Indeed, the same attitude is adopted toward a person who is able to endure extraordinary pain with perfect composure.

The fear is that such stoicism might easily turn into wickedness in other situations. Thus the same expression which, when used in certain contexts, means wickedness may be used in another context to refer to this kind of willpower. In both contexts we say *Ne tirimu ye den*, which literally means "The inside of his head is hard." Most likely, this shows more about Akan psychology than about Akan ethics.

As far as ethics is concerned, the Akan position regarding the right to die is clearcut. If human well-being is the sole basis of moral evaluation, it is difficult to imagine any valid grounds for denying the right to die to the terminally ill. Their interests are not served, for they have no prospect of any sort of personal well-being to look forward to; and if they wish to die, they have no living interests. Neither can the legitimate interests of others be infringed on by their wishes to put an end to their pointless suffering. The anguish of relatives at the approach of the demise of a loved one is, of course, understandable, but solicitude degenerates into involuntary sadism if it causes nothing but the prolongation of suffering for its object. Such an attitude would be absolutely un-Akan.

But suppose the prolonged suffering of a universally loved, terminally ill patient would result in a greater overall balance of happiness over pain, owing to the great misery that a premature death would bring to many earnest well-wishers. Would not considerations of human well-being override accommodating the patient's will to die? This question provides an opportunity to distinguish the Akan moral outlook from utilitarianism as frequently understood. Insofar as the Akans appeal to nothing beyond the empirical conditions of human well-being in their moral evaluations, their ethics may be characterized as humanistic. The word "humanistic" is used here in just this sense. Humanism, as thus strictly construed, is not to be confused with humanitarianism. There is also a humanitarian strain in the Akan ethic, but an ethic can be humanitarian without being humanistic. The fundamental reason why Akan ethics must uphold the right to die, in the sort of circumstances under discussion, is to be found not just in any humanitarian feelings, but in the humanistic basis of their outlook.

Now, utilitarianism is a humanistic theory of ethics, but not all humanistic ethical systems are utilitarian. Commonly, utilitarianism is understood to be the philosophy of morals which holds an action to be morally right (in the strict sense) in proportion as it promotes the greatest happiness of the greatest number of people, happiness being defined in terms of pleasure. Two points need to be made immediately. The first is that the idea of promoting happiness is not in itself a moral or ethical topic in the narrow meaning of these concepts (in which we will hereafter use them unless otherwise specified). In the broad sense, anything having to do with human conduct is moral or ethical. But in the narrow sense morality concerns the adjustment of the interests of an individual to the interests of others. In this sense ethics deals not with the promotion of happiness as such but rather with the manner of promoting it. By any except perhaps the most masochistic reckoning, happiness is a value, a good; however, moral problems arise precisely because in the pursuit of this good people are apt to be oblivious to the interests of others. Thus, given only that an action does promote the greatest happiness of the greatest number of people, we are still in the dark as to its moral status. Suppose, for example, that we are told that the action involved the enslavement of a considerable number of persons. At this point moral evaluation can begin. If one's moral feelings are jarred by the idea of the happiness of some being promoted through the enslavement of others, the reason surely is that such a situation is inequitable; it fails to accord to all concerned the basic respect, dignity and sympathy due to all human beings. In particular, it fails to treat all parties concerned with the kind of impartiality that comes from the imaginative identification of oneself with others. A genuinely moral action must satisfy all these requirements. However, it is not easy to define with precision what these requirements actually consist of. Within Akan moral thought they are articulated informally in a number of sayings:

- *Wo yonko da ne wo da* (your fellow's plight is your plight).
- *Etua wo yonko ho a etua dua mu* (sticking into your fellow's flesh it might just as well be sticking into a piece of wood). This is said in remonstrance with a person who has acted without due consideration for others.
- *Yede ye wo a ebeye wo de?* (would you like it if it were done to you?). Again, this a common form of moral expostulation.
- *Kwasia na ose wode me yonko* (it is a fool who says it is aimed at somebody other than I).
- *Obi de aba, obi de nam kwan so* (somebody's turn has come; another's is on the way).
- The same stick that was used to beat Gyasi will be used to beat Birago. (Gyasi and Birago are twins; humankind is here viewed as pairs of twins.)

The ethical thought and the general philosophy of the traditional Akans is to be found in an oral tradition rich in proverbs, epigrams, conundrums, and so on. Presumably, sentiments similar to those quoted above can be found in the folk thinking of all other people. However, when technical philosophers come to give precise, rigorous, and systematic formulations of these sentiments, unanimity seems to elude their efforts. It seems clear, however, that the above sayings converge in the direction of those principles of universability, sympathy, impartiality, and respect which raise the interest in the happiness of the greatest number into an ethical interest. Thus, although human well-being is the fundamental value of Akan ethics, the Akan conception of ethical life is not the pursuit of this aim per se but as subject to the requirements of those principles.

The second of the two points that need to be made is that the idea of defining happiness in terms of pleasure would sound very strange in Akan ears. The concept (*Ahoto*) that, in the Akan notion of conduct, corresponds to happiness is a broad concept within which what approximates to the concept of pleasure (which cannot be rendered by any one term in Akan) can only count as one element. Without elaborating here on this it should still be quite clear from the few remarks above that Akan ethics is not utilitarian in the understanding so far specified.

In Judeo-Christian thought one encounters an attempt at a unified formulation of the principles discussed above, which for lack of a better name I will call the principles of sympathetic impartiality, in the Golden Rule. But perhaps the most philosophically interesting formulation is to be found in the Categorical Imperative of Kant as propounded, for example, in *The Fundamental Principles of the Metaphysic of Morals*: "Act only on that maxim whereby thou canst at the same time will that it should become a universal law" (Abbott 1898:39). Kant's philosophy of morals is often contrasted with that of John Stuart Mill and the utilitarians, and in some ways there are good reasons for that. In respect of the requirement of sympathetic impartiality, however, there is no fundamental difference between them. Mill (1897:25) is explicit, even passionate in advancing that requirement:

The happiness which forms the utilitarian standard of what is right in conduct, is not the agent's own happiness, but that of all concerned. As between his own happiness and that of others, utilitarianism requires him to be as strictly impartial as a disinterested and benevolent spectator. In the golden rule of Jesus of Nazareth, we read the complete spirit of the ethics of utility. To do as one would be done by, and to love one's neighbour as oneself, constitute the ideal perfection of utilitarian morality.

The problem with Mill is that in his concise formulations of the principle of utility he makes it seem as if the promotion of happiness in itself were the criterion of moral rightness.

If the principle of utility is understood to include the principle of sympathetic impartiality as an absolutely essential part, the difference between utilitarian and Akan ethics is reduced, although it does not vanish; for in regard to the conception of happiness, quite deep disparities of conceptualization remain. Nevertheless, if we return to the terminally ill, we find that utilitarianism and Akan ethics are united in conceding their right to die. And it should now be obvious that the reason why the pain of well-wishers cannot nullify this right is that to suppose so would be to forget the requirements of sympathetic impartiality.

Another feature that Akan ethics has in common with utilitarianism is its nonsupernaturalistic character. This is a tautological consequence of its being humanistic. This feature of Akan ethics has an important impact on arguments concerning the right to die. As is well known, some denials of this right are based on religious dogma. If it is held, for example, that terminating human life in the circumstances of terminal illness is contrary to the law of God, then any considerations of sympathetic impartiality relative to human well-being are of no avail. From an Akan point of view, however, this would constitute a *reductio ad absurdum* of any such dogma. The Akans do, indeed, believe in the existence of a Supreme Being (*Onyame*), and they believe also that this being hates evil. But in their humanistic ethics, evil is what is contrary to human well-being, conceived within the framework of the principles of universality, sympathy, impartiality, and so on. Hence the suggestion is ruled out of court that terminating human suffering through death by choice in the sort of circumstances that we have been discussing is contrary to any law of God. Only if good and evil are defined in terms of the will of God or in terms of some extra-human factors is it logically possible to discount human well-being and considerations related thereto in any context of moral evaluation. But that would be supernaturalism in ethics, which is altogether foreign to Akan thinking.

Finally, in thinking about the right to die we are normally thinking of, or indeed *from*, the point of view of the individual concerned, be it of a person contemplating suicide in dire circumstances or of a terminally ill patient seeking an end to a pointless and humiliating distress. But it might happen that the individual is in no position to make a judgment either because of total incapacitation of body and mind or because of extreme youth. In such a case, if no previous indications of wishes are available, the question naturally arises: What individual or group has the right to decide the question of life or death for the unfortunate one? In Akan society there can be no question that this right lies with the "family," taken as including both parents and the close clan relatives of the patient. They would not necessarily be the ones to decide whether the patient's condition is irremediable; but if the best-instructed opinion should foresee nothing but irreversible deterioration, the last words would belong to the family. Let these be our own last words here.

NOTES

1. See note 6 below.
2. Christians believe that human beings were made in the image of God. Akan philosophy goes further. Human beings are made of the very stuff of God.
3. The late J. B. Danquah, jurist, politician, philosopher, and the most famous

exponent of Akan philosophy, quotes, among other Akan maxims, the one alluded to here. This he translates as "All men are the offspring of God; no one is the offspring of the Earth." In explaining the Akan notion of family he states that

> it would appear [that] bounds cannot be set to the meaning of "family" until every trace of the quality which is other than beastly is exhausted; to embrace, that is, not only the Akan, but the entire race of that quality, the manlike family of humanity. (Danquah 1968: xxix)

Of course when the meaning of "family" has been extended to cover all humankind, literal sense has merged with metaphor. Nevertheless, the underlying thought motivates definite modes of behavior, as exemplified in note 4.

4. Strangers to Ghana have often been struck by Ghanaian hospitality. This attitude flows from this folk philosophy of universal brotherhood reinforced by an acute sense of the general vulnerability of human beings when they find themselves in unfamiliar surroundings far from home. One line of a lyric sums up this feeling: "[Think of all] the contingencies of travel [and realize that] the plight of a traveller is pitiable" (*Akwantu mu nsem! Okwantuni ye mmobo*). By the way, although my direct references are to the Akans, who constitute over half of Ghana's population of fourteen million, most of the points made in this discussion apply with equal force to all the ethnic groups of Ghana. I restrict my direct references to the Akans only because Akan is my native language.

5. Literally, this means, "If bad days befall you, do not give up life; better days *will* come." But this also would commit a non sequitur. To keep within the dictates of logic one would have to say, *na na pa betumi aba*, or "Better days *may* come." But that wording in Akan would ruin the poetry.

6. I use the word "spiritual" here for lack of a better word, but it should not be taken, in a Cartesian sense, to mean that which is not extended. In Akan ontology, as I understand it, there are no such things as nonextended objects. All objects are in space, but some are supposed to be less constrained than others by the commonsense causal laws of the familiar world such as that you cannot move an object without making contact with it, that you cannot be at another place than a previous one without traversing the intervening space, that you cannot pass through a solid wall without boring a hole through it, or that the presence or motion of an object should be detectable directly or indirectly by means of at least one of the five senses. In the English language too one can designate by the word "spirits" objects that allegedly contravene some or all of these commonsense laws, although the adjective "spiritual" is often reserved for definitively Cartesian uses. Sometimes, however, the word "spiritual" is applied to alleged beings that are not nonphysical in absolutely all respects. Angels, for example, are described, by those who talk of such things, as spiritual beings. But these are supposed to be beings that have wings, and some of them can apparently sing. Therefore, they are conceived of on at least a partially material model. Of course, angels are not supposed to be visible to the naked eyes of living mortals; but, to speak with fundamentalist Christians for the moment, we have full assurance that when we die and our bodies are resurrected on the Day of Judgment with vastly improved eyes and ears, we shall be able to see them and hear their singing. It seems to me that such beings cannot rightly be called

spiritual in the Cartesian sense, that is, in the sense of completely nonmaterial (or nonphysical) beings, for they are described in unmistakably material imagery, although they are not held to be subject to all the laws of the physical world. Accordingly, I suggest calling such objects quasi-material (or quasi-physical). Such terminology should help us avoid confusing the ontological status of beings like angels with that of, say, the mind, conceived as an immaterial substance after the manner of Descartes. Surely if angels, or at least some of them, can sing and can be spoken of in terms of being well-behaved or (in the exceptional case) refractory, then they must have minds, and their minds and thoughts can hardly have the same ontological status as, for example, their wings, at least if we have a Cartesian conception of mind. It has to be recognized, then, that angels, witches (in witchcraft), poltergeists, African ancestor "spirits," and a host of alleged beings of like character are of the quasi-material category. The point is that in Akan thought only quasi-material objects are postulated besides material objects, whereas in Western thought there are influential philosophies in which there are thought to exist, besides all these, purely spiritual objects in the sense of totally immaterial, totally nonphysical objects. In Akan thought, perhaps the word "spiritual" should not be used at all, but it is not easy to find economical replacements in contexts such as the above. The reader will note that the *okra* and the *sunsum*, the two constituents of a person besides the body postulated by the Akans, belong to the quasi-material category of being. The fact that only the material and quasi-material categories of being have a place in Akan ontology is a reflection of the general empirical orientation of Akan thought, which, at the ethical level, takes the form of an ethic based exclusively on considerations of human well-being.

REFERENCES

Primary Sources

Abbott, T. K. trans. 1898. *Kant's Critique of Practical Reason and Other Works on the Theory of Ethics*. London: Longmans, Green.

Busia, K. A. 1968. *The Position of the Chief in the Modern Political System of Ashanti*. London: Frank Cass & Co.

Danquah, J. B. 1968. *The Akan Doctrine of God*, 2nd ed. London: Frank Cass & Co.

Mill, John Stuart. 1897. *Utilitarianism*. London: Longmans, Green.

Secondary Sources

Abraham, W. E. 1962. *The Mind of Africa*. Chicago: University of Chicago Press.

Gyekye, Kwame. 1987. *An Essay on African Philosophical Thought*. New York: Cambridge University Press.

Idowu, E. B. 1962. *Olodumare, God in Yoruba Belief*. London: Longmans, Green.

Menkiti, Ifeanyi A. 1984. "Person and Community in African Traditional Thought." In Richard A. Wright, ed., *African Philosophy: An Introduction*. New York: University Press of America.

Oguah, B. E. 1984. "African and Western Philosophy: A Comparative Study." In Richard A. Wright, ed., *African Philosophy: An Introduction*. New York: University Press of America.

Opoku, K. A. *West African Traditional Religion*. London: F.E.P. International Publishers.

Wiredu, Kwasi. 1983a. "The Akan Concept of Mind." *Ibadan Journal of Humanistic Studies*. Also in Guttorm Floistad, ed., *Contemporary Philosophy*, Vol. 5, *African Philosophy*. Netherlands: Martinus Nijhoff, 1987.

———. 1983b. "Morality and Religion in Akan Thought." In H. Odera Oruka and D. A. Masolo, eds., *Philosophy and Culture*. Nairobi, Kenya: Bookwise Ltd.

———. 1980. *Philosophy and African Culture*. New York: Cambridge University Press.

5 An Islamic Perspective on Terminating Life-Sustaining Measures

M. Adil Al Aseer

Advances in medical science over the past half-century have given society the ability to prolong human life to a hitherto unimagined extent. Use of "extraordinary" means to sustain the life of a terminally ill patient with little or no chance of recovery is now commonplace in most hospitals. Patients whose major organs no longer function are kept alive with sophisticated machinery; in cases of severe brain damage, the body and its organs can be sustained for indefinite periods.

The prohibitive financial burden placed on a patient's family and society is another dimension of this issue. Medical equipment used in sustaining terminally ill patients is among the most sophisticated and expensive equipment found in hospitals. In addition, the cost of long-term hospital patient care is well beyond the means of most families. Such costs can be borne only by insurance companies or the government. It is estimated that ten billion dollars per year is expended for the care of the terminally ill. Although human life is to be valued above any financial concerns, the burden placed on society is an issue that cannot be ignored.

Medical advances in sustaining life have outpaced society's ability to deal with the profound legal, ethical, and moral aspects of this issue. Until recently, the medical profession and the patient's family were allowed to determine the courses of action. The right to die invoked by terminally ill patients and their families has raised society's awareness and forced it to recognize the ethical and moral implications. We are currently grappling with the many questions raised by this issue.

Do we have a choice in this case or not? How can we die? What if we cannot make a choice? What if we are too sick? What if we are mentally confused or mentally incompetent? Who makes the choice for us—the spouse, the physician, the court, the next of kin? And what if these people disagree with each other? Who takes over then? Should this issue remain a private matter between the doctor and the family or should laws and regulations be established by the government? What is the role of religion in defining and resolving the moral aspects of this issue?

This chapter presents the Islamic perspective on this issue and attempts to answer the above questions in that context.

THE ISLAMIC VIEW OF LIFE AND DEATH

Islam views death merely as a stage in human existence. When life as we understand it ceases, human existence does not also cease; rather, it moves to another level which precedes Judgment Day and eternal life (according to Chapter 2, verse 28; Chapter 53, verses 44–47; and Chapter 67, verse 2 of the Qur'an).[1] This is made very clear in the case of martyrs dying in the cause of God, who live eternally in Paradise (Chapter 3, verses 169–71).

Death is not an evil to be feared by a believer. Only those who have led a life of sin and ignored God's command need fear it (Chapter 23, verses 99–101). Spiritual death is the form of death that human beings should truly fear (Chapter 6, verse 123).

What is life from the Islamic perspective? The Holy Qur'an shows that this word was used in many forms: The word *Hayat* is derived from *Hayya*; *Hayya* or *Ahya* means "to give life." The Qur'an used this term in the context of "to give life to a dead country" (50.11); "He gives to give life to the land" (35:9); "He gives life to the bones" (36:78); and "gives life to the dead." God says, "He brings death and grants life" (53:44). In fact the Holy Qur'an speaks about two types of lives. God says, "How do you disbelieve in God seeing you were dead and He gave you life and then He shall cause you to die, then He shall give you life, then unto Him you shall be returned" (2:28). This Qur'anic verse presents the religious ethics concerning the Day of Judgment, or Day of Accounting.

Another verse of the Qur'an (39:32) presents death and life as if they were a form of sleep. God says, "It is God that takes care of the soul in case of death, and in case of those on whom He has passed the decree of death He keeps back, but the rest he sends to their bodies for a term appointed."

The mystery of life and death is a fascinating riddle. God sets forth death before life, saying, "He who created death and life to try which of you is best in deed" (67:2). This wisdom introduces death as an irresistible and overpowering issue in the sense that the human being will never be able to defeat death, no matter how much progress is made in science and technology.

The Qur'an also acknowledges that the soul or the spirit will continue living after death in the *Barzakh* state until the Day of Hereafter. God says, "And before them is Barzakh until the Day of Resurrection" (23:100). Therefore it is the nature of the body to die and that of the soul to live.

I am not, however, as pessimistic as the great Arab poet Al Ma'arri who said, "All life is a place of fatigue and restlessness and I wonder for those who like to prolong their life." It is, however, very hard to accept the definition of life by Anatole France, who maintained that human life is summed up by three words: "born; suffers; dies."

Speaking about life, the Holy Qur'an reads, "What is the life of this world but amusement and play?" (6:32). To summarize the Qur'anic attitude toward life, we see that amusement and play have no lasting significance except to prepare us for the serious work of life. Thus life is but an interlude and preparation for the real life in the hereafter. The varieties of this world are therefore to be taken for what they are, but they are not to be allowed to deflect our minds from requirements of the inner life that really matter.

The second point that the Islamic scriptures emphasize is the prohibition against committing suicide. Life is a gift from God and it is He who takes life. This is a guideline in Islam. God speaks about this gift as part of the honor that God bestowed on the human being. The Qur'anic verse states, "Indeed We have honored the human beings" (17:70). To be sure, life is a trust in one's hands and one has no right to destroy it. This is why it is prohibited to commit suicide. The prophet Muhammad let peace be upon him, says,

Whoso hurls himself down from a mountain and thus kills himself will be in Hell hurling himself down therein, abiding therein and being accommodated therein forever; whoso takes poison and thus kills himself, his poison will be in his hand; he will be tasting it in Hell, always abiding therein, and being accommodated therein forever; and whoso kills himself with a gun, his gun will be in his hand; he will be shooting himself therewith against his belly in Hell, abiding therein and being accommodated therein forever.

The Qur'anic view therefore is that the patient has neither the right to choose death nor the right to die. The same answers concern the family: None of the patient's family members has the right to decide to kill the patient.

Moreover, the Qur'an does not allow the taking of anybody's life, except in the case of self-defense, or if the court gives a decision for capital punishment. These cases are exempted. God says, "The one who kills one person, as if he kills the whole mankind; and the one who gives life to one person as if he gives life to whole mankind" (5:35).

THE ROLE OF THE ISLAMIC PATIENT AND FAMILY

No matter how much pain and suffering is experienced, the patient and his or her family are prohibited from praying for death as a release. The prophet Muhammad said, "O God, keep me alive if life is better and let me die if death is better for me."[2] The loss of a loved one should never be regarded as a punishment for the family; neither should the family question God's wisdom in these matters.

The patient's suffering is not a sufficient reason for terminating life-sustaining measures. Similarly, the pain and burden borne by the family and society is also not an acceptable justification for this action.

With this understanding of the issue of life and death, the question of whether there is a right to die will now be discussed.

THE RESOLUTION GIVEN BY ISLAMIC LAW

As we are speaking from an Islamic point of view, it is important to mention that reasoning is a source of this religion and individual reasoning is open for any qualified Muslim. Joseph Schacht (1966), in his work on Islamic law, states, "Reasoning was inherent in the Islamic law from its very beginning." Islam sets forth the rule that in case a question comes up for which the answer was not given in the divine text (*Al Shari'ah*), that is, in the Qur'an or the teaching and practice of the prophet Muhammad (*Sunnah*), reasoning plays its role.

There are, however, subordinate sources. If the question was answered in the divine text, then there is no possibility for other answers to be given. If the question is not mentioned, or was not answered in the divine text, or if it is a new question, then, in order to bridge the gap between the unchangeable text and day-to-day needs, the Muslim expert is supposed to refer to subordinate sources. These sources also help enforce the public interest and stop what causes damage in society (Al Ghazzali [n.d.]:287).

One of these sources is *Saddu al Dhara'a*, which means preventing the means from becoming an end (Abu Zahrah [n.d.]:275–81). Take the example of using artificial means to enable a patient to recover and to live a healthy life. This is a sound and ethical objective. But for a case such as brain death, this objective cannot be attained. Rather than prolonging the life of this patient for recovery, it turns out that the means have become the objective. Because of advanced medical technology or because of the request of a family who left grandma in a nursing home for years but now feel guilty, her life is prolonged despite the impossibility of recovery. This act is immoral and contradicts the principle of *Saddu al Dhara'a* (Al Qarafi 1928: vol. 2, 32). The court, following systematic reasoning, can enforce this rule and decide to take such a patient off artificial life support (Al Shatibi 1969: vol. 2, 249–59).

The other subordinate source of Islamic law (*Al Shari'ah*) is the *Maslahah*, or public interest (Abu Zahrah [n.d.]:267–68). In the event that the divine text did not deal with the question, this source allows the Muslim scholar (*Al Mujtahid*) the right to pursue "the public interest" (Al Shatibi [n.d.]:vol. 3, 307). If an action is good for society the scholar may adopt it, but if it hurts society the scholar does not do so. If artificial methods are used for severely brain-damaged patients and similar cases, the patient and family suffer continuously. Moreover, such cases require much time from doctors, nurses, and other experts and cost billions of dollars. Needless to say, the treatment of brain-death cases is not in the public interest. Medical treatment can be stopped.

The systematic reasoning expressed in both above-mentioned sources of the Islamic law (*Al Shari'ah*) can be utilized to answer the question concerning terminating, in certain cases, extraordinary life-sustaining measures.

SIGNS OF DEATH

Before further discussion, however, it is important to determine when the human being is considered dead. Medical expression defines life as the potential for survival. For example, in this age of greater knowledge of a baby's metabolism and nutrition, physicians are able to save the lives of smaller infants.

I am not a medical doctor. I will therefore quote Dr. Wasim Ali, professor of obstetrics and gynecology, who gave a lecture at "The Symposium on Life and Death" in Houston, Texas, in July 1987:

Well, time has changed, we have seen the presence or the absence of pulse. This does not necessarily mean that the person is dead. In a similar way, the presence or absence of heartbeat does not mean a person is alive or a person is dead. What is important is that [we have] a criteria [sic], which is called a brain death. Now brain death is being described by many scientists in different categories and different criteria.... In the past, people used to have the idea of loss of consciousness, lack of pulse, lack of heartbeat; and [people] were pronounced dead. But nowadays we have seen the picture completely different. Now these people can be put on a respirator and their heart and blood pressure can be monitored by medication, or [in] other ways it can be manipulated by the physicians.

Therefore the criterion of death is not the absence of pulse or the absence of heartbeat, as it was recognized for a long time, but is now brain death. This fact was not known until recently.

The Islamic scriptures did not define criteria for physical death. Acknowledging the two sources of Islamic law mentioned above, and acknowledging the fact that the criterion of death is now brain death, opens the way for the court to decide in many cases to discontinue artificial life support.

THE ROLE OF THE ISLAMIC COURT

The body of law that guides the Islamic community is the *Shari'ah*. The *Shari'ah* is composed of the Qur'an and the *Sunnah* (prophet Muhammad's teaching and practice). The Islamic court uses this body of law to adjudicate all cases within the guidelines of Islam. As such, the Islamic court is empowered by the community and *Shari'ah* to decide whether terminating life-sustaining measures for a terminally ill patient, such as a case of severe brain damage, is appropriate. In so doing, it must weigh several factors. First, the medical professionals concerned should clarify the condition of the patient and his or her chances for recovery. The court throughout its history has utilized the opinions of scientific experts and professionals in many cases. Two or more recognized experts would present medical evidence and give expert testimony. On the basis of this testimony the court can determine the chances, if any, for the patient's recovery.

The court also takes into account the suffering and welfare of the family. The financial and emotional burdens faced by the family are key factors since the family's support is essential in treating these patients. The court, however, must not be influenced by emotional appeals of family members to end a human life because of the family's and the patient's suffering.

The court must also weigh financial and related demands imposed on the state. Since extending the life of a patient requires a substantial portion of the state's resources, the court must balance this need against the use of those resources to provide medical care to needier patients who have a better chance of recovery. The primary duty of the Islamic court is to ensure the safety and welfare of the entire Islamic state rather than that of the individual. This approach is referred to as *Al Haq Al 'Am*, or public rights.

THE NEED FOR SPECIAL COURTS

In the United States, courts expend much money and time in trying such cases. Consider the well-publicized case of a Missouri woman who suffered severe brain damage in an automobile accident. The court took three years to determine whether artificial support sustaining her life could be withdrawn. This delay exacerbated the case by adding to the emotional trauma of the family and patient. It also put an additional financial burden on the family and the state. The involvement of the media in such cases only clouds the issue and heightens the emotional atmosphere.

To avoid such costly and drawn-out cases, the Islamic court system would empower a special court to handle these cases. Such a court would gain expertise in these matters that would allow it to review cases rapidly and efficiently. Its rulings in these cases would be final.

NOTES

1. The Holy Qur'an is the scripture of Islam. It was revealed to the prophet Muhammad from God through the Angel Gabriel over a period of twenty-three years (571–633). The Qur'an has been translated from Arabic into many languages, but the translations are human work.

2. This saying of the Prophet was reported by Anas b. Malik and is narrated in the collections of Al Bukhari and Muslim. (See Fazlul Karim, *Al-Hadis of Mishkat al Masabih*, vol. 3, p. 9, no. 3.)

REFERENCES

Abu Zahrah, M. *Usul Al Figh*. Cairo: Arab Thought House Press, n.d., pp. 275–81.

Al Ghazzali, *Al Musta'fa fi 'Ilm al Usul*, 2 vols. Cairo: Halabi Press, n.d., vol. 1, p. 287.

Al Qarafi, S. *Al Furuq*, 4 vols. Cairo: Ihia' Al Kutub Al 'Arabiy yah Press, 1928, vol. 2, p. 32.

Al Shatibi, I. *Al Muafaqat fi Usul Al Ahkam*, 4 vols. Cairo: Madani Press, 1969, vol. 2, pp. 249–59.

———. *Al I'tisam*, 4 vols. Cairo: Madani Press, n.d., vol. 3, p. 307.

Schacht, J. *An Introduction to Islamic Law*. Oxford: Clarendon Press, 1966.

6 Japanese Perspectives on Euthanasia

Shigeru Kato

Tenrei Ōta, a famous physician and important proponent of euthanasia in Japan, has published an article entitled "Conception of Euthanasia" (1974) in which he distinguishes both a broad and a narrow sense of the word "euthanasia." Following his example, I will begin by classifying its meaning.

Euthanasia interpreted in a broad sense connotes the natural death all of us would like to experience, that is, painless in body and peaceful in mind. Indeed, the prefix "eu-" in Greek means "good," "easy," or "natural." Such is the death everyone yearns for since nobody can escape the final termination of life.

We usually translate euthanasia into *Anraku-shi* (death) in Japanese. *Anraku*, which is synonymous with paradise or the land of bliss in Buddhism, means the ideal of happiness without pain and agony. A Chinese Buddhist writing (*Fa-hua-wên-chü* 8) defined it, saying, "*An* means without danger in Body, and *Raku*, without anxiety in mind" (*Encyclopedia of Buddhism* 1935). Thus it may be said that euthanasia in a broad sense has the pre-Baconian meaning of dying well or having an easy death "by leading a temperate life or by cultivating an acceptance of mortality" (Gruman et al. 1978).

Euthanasia in its narrow sense means "specifically measures taken by the physician, including the possibility of hastening death" (Gruman et al. 1978). This definition has increasingly called forth arguments, from Francis Bacon's "Advancement of Learning," written in 1605 (Bacon 1908–9), to the present day. T. Ōta (1974) further divided this narrowly defined euthanasia into three cases. Euthanasia implies:

1. Putting to death patients who have no useful and effective life, such as infants afflicted with an incurable hereditary disease or with idiocy, or, recently, and with increasing frequency, comatose patients.
2. The legal killing of or causing death to persons such as criminals.
3. Letting sufferers die voluntarily from a disease known to be incurable and to cause unbearable pain or to destroy human dignity.

Some people say that it is not appropriate to count case (1) among cases of euthanasia lest it cause gratuitous prejudice in euthanasia arguments by reminding us of Nazi genocide (Gruman et al. 1978:267), which slaughtered "living beings with no value to live."

Should one try to legalize euthanasia, including case (1), one would inevitably encounter opposing views, such as the time-honored religious belief that a human being to whom life is given has no right whatever to control birth and death, or the humane ethical creed that human life is too sacred and valuable to be taken except under a few very restricted conditions. However, is it not natural to allow severely handicapped infants the right to die on humane grounds, even if the Nazis' case is out of the question? I think generally it is desirable to deal flexibly, on a case-by-case basis, with a few very definite cases while still respecting strictly holistic (religious or humanistic) principles as such.

Of course, case (3) is the main subject of argument today: euthanasia as specialized care to ease the distress—bodily pain, mental unease, and spiritual worry—of the dying. This problem is peculiar to the age of artificial prolongation of life by biomedical science. We do not want, painfully and inhumanely, to postpone dying with extraordinary daily measures. Case (3), however, is not necessarily the antithesis of the prolongation of a quality of life that all living beings yearn for. Such prolongation is an illegitimate child of the present-day biomedical revolution in which longevity and easy, natural death cannot, unhappily, always be reconciled, contrary to the optimistic expectation of thinkers such as microbiologist Ilya Mechnikov who believed it possible to ameliorate senescence and achieve longer life—up to 120 years (Gruman et al. 1978:265). The result is that euthanasia is opposed not to increasing longevity but to unnatural (inhuman) "life support" (Gruman et al. 1978:262). The question therefore is: Is euthanasia an inherent right to die with freedom, dignity, and well-being, or the "unnatural" and arrogant intervention by the mortal into the sphere of life and death?

In Japan, in recent decades, euthanasia has come to be argued in various interdisciplinary spheres—medicine, law, religion, philosophy, public opinion, and so on. In such discussions today, we tend to prefer the word *songen-shi* (death with dignity) to *anraku-shi*, which is a literal translation of "euthanasia." Why? The reason, I guess, is that while the latter is apt to sound like something hedonistic, emphasizing solely an escape from bodily pain, the former, more grave and serious, warns us of the urgent crisis that is the loss of human reason which may follow the bodily pain. In sum, to assert one's right to die painlessly and with freedom and dignity, but without extraordinary measures, we ordinarily speak of as *songen-shi*.

The Japanese Society of Anraku-shi—later renamed Songen-shi—was founded on January 20, 1976, by T. Ōta, Tadashi Uematsu, and others. Since then its members and those who succeeded in legalizing the Living Will—the written rejection of unnatural life support—have increased in number year after year (Miyano 1982).

Before examining the euthanasia arguments of our contemporaries, I will summarize the history of views on suicide and euthanasia.

SUICIDE AND EUTHANASIA

Voluntary euthanasia is a sort of suicide, a means by which an individual hastens death in order to end unbearable distress. It is feared that suicide would become more common if voluntary euthanasia were made legal. Nevertheless, present-day euthanasia differs from suicide proper[1] (Kato 1981) in the following points:

First, euthanasia releases the patient from unbearable pain or long-term senility, in short, primarily from physical maladies. In this sense it has nothing to do with purely mental or spiritual distress as in suicide in general.

Second, euthanasia is always social suicide. The one who wishes to die is in communication with others, such as physician and family, and has public opinion as a background. For this reason it raises the problem of criminal suicide by the person in question who is not able to die without help and at the same time raises the question of the implication of the assistant in a "crime" of homicide.

Third, since euthanasia is social suicide that implicates an accomplice, it raises not only ethical and religious but also legal controversies.

In order to carry out voluntary euthanasia, it is necessary that the patient's will to die be complemented by the assistance of an accomplice. According to the degree of such assistance, or the consent of the assistant, we may classify euthanasia as (1) murder by assent; (2) aiding or abetting suicide; and (3) murder by contract. Incidentally, these three cases are all punished equally by a sentence of from six months to seven years at hard labor or imprisonment under Article 202 of the Japanese Criminal Law (Uematsu 1974).

BUDDHISM AND SUICIDE

We will first survey Buddhist views of suicide in order to explain the Japanese perspectives on suicide and euthanasia. Japan has been under the influence of Buddhism for more than 1,500 years. I will focus my description on the subject of suicide (Nishimoto 1962) but will not go deeply into Buddhist philosophy as such.[2]

Sakyamuni Buddha taught that not only life but also death are equally delusion and suffering, that is, spiritual darkness (*avidya*) from which we must emancipate ourselves by means of the insight and practice of the Fourfold Noble Truths (suffering, cause of suffering, extinction of suffering, path to Nirvāṇa) and the Eightfold Holy Path (right view, right thought, right speech, right act, right living, right effort, right mindfulness, right meditation).[3] To pass beyond both life and death, to keep away from the two extremes of permanence and nonexistence, and to persevere in moderation—these are the main points of Buddhism.[4] It is therefore natural that suicide—usually a mere act of escape from reality or insanity—is not thought to be a fundamental resolution of human troubles according to the essential teaching of the Buddha. In fact, the Buddha rejected suicide as a form of clinging to nonexistence as well as a killing of a living being (Poussin 1922). For example, he admonished his disciples, "Life is precious and dear for every living being. Judging from your own life's valuableness don't kill and don't let kill" (Nakamura 1983). And yet Buddhists as a whole do not condemn the dead, but accept with motherly love and the spirit of tolerance those who have committed suicide no matter what their reasons. For instance, Buddha's disciple Vakkali, in unbearable distress, asked for euthanasia and committed suicide in spite of the prohibition against taking life. This prohibition is the most important Buddhist precept and therefore its breach deserves *Harai* (*pārājika*, or the expulsion from the *samgha*). Yet the Buddha was compassionate to the dead, saying, "Vakkali entered Nirvāṇa, accomplishing the Fourfold Noble Truth."[5] Buddhist tolerance is sharply opposed to the rigor with which Christianity has condemned suicides. Yet during the age of Hīnayāna Buddhism, the original teaching of the Buddha (the spiritual emancipation from the endless cycle of births and deaths in the world of transmigration) was disregarded. People misinterpreted death as itself being Nirvāṇa, as suggested by the word *nirupadhiśesanirvāṇa* (Nirvāṇa without rest) (Poussin 1922:25). This Hīnayāna conception that death is itself Nirvāṇa does not necessarily result in an affirmative view of suicide. One may, however, easily imagine that from this concept originated the idea that whoever passes away can become a Buddha. Moreover, the original precept of prohibiting suicide was gradually relaxed.

While on the one hand Hīnayāna was conservative and self-contained, on the other hand Mahāyāna, which tried to convey all sentient beings to the other shore of the Buddha land, was progressive and open-hearted. It is characteristic of Mahāyāna that is emphasizes transforming sentient beings below as well as seeking enlightenment above. It also idealizes the *Bodhisattva*'s self-sacrifice for all sentient beings and the *darma*, that is, compassion and wisdom.[6] But later the religious idealism of Mahāyāna became misunderstood by the common people—especially by some fanatical believers in Pure Land Buddhism—to mean that Buddhism recommended suicide. From about the fifth century in China, and the tenth century in Japan, *shashin-ōjō* began to prevail (Nishimoto 1962). In this form of suicide or self-sacrifice by setting oneself on fire, fasting, drowning oneself, and so on, believers expressed their worship of Amida-Buddha and their yearning for birth in the Pure Land. For instance, *Ichigonhōdan*, the analects of followers of the Pure Land Gate in the Kamakura period in Japan, quite clearly recommended religious suicide in their sayings "Delight in dying" and "Hasten your death" (Morishita 1983:28). The so-called *nen-shi* (Morishita 1983:25) meant that the ideal of "disliking and leaving this world," or "aspiring to birth in the Pure Land" (Genshin 1970:10; Ippen 1985:32), Pure Land Buddhism's motto, was understood literally and translated into action. It was from such misapprehensions as this that the *sashin-ōjō* was hastily performed by some followers in the Middle Ages of Japan.

THE JAPANESE CONCEPTS OF LIFE AND DEATH

Can we say that Buddhism has influenced Japanese views of suicide at all? If we can, then in what way?

Japan has the reputation of being "a kingdom of suicide," perhaps owing to the circulation of words like *harakiri* and *kamikaze*. In fact, Japan has produced the greatest number of suicides among the Asian Buddhist countries although a recent investigation by the World Health Organization shows that Japan is not always among the countries with the highest percentage of suicides in the world. It may not be appropriate to say that Buddhism alone has made Japan "a kingdom of suicide," but we cannot deny that it has strengthened the Japanese tendency to beautify suicide or absolve suicide of a sense of sin.

Long before Buddhism was brought into Japan from the continent in about the sixth century (in other words, since the age of ancient Shintoism), the Japanese as a whole are said to have tended to:

- be indifferent to and without tenacity for life, especially the life that Westerners have differentiated sharply from death.
- have a feeling of intimacy with death instinctively and beyond reason, believing that there is no clear borderline between life and death such as Christianity has recognized. Indeed, this feeling or belief is too immediate for us to transmit through "media" (Yanagida 1982:342; Savata 1968:124–25, 129).
- devote themselves to or take refuge in the holistic being or something great that transcends them, such as Buddha, God (Kami), nature, Tao, heaven, and

so on. Stated conversely, the Japanese lack, or at least have no clear consciousness of, personal identity.

If this is the case, it may be said that Japanese suicide as a whole is not motivated by the clear consciousness of the right to die for the individual, which has characterized Western cases, but is instead the result of a lack of tenacity for life, a yearning for death, and a religious holism swallowing individual consciousness. We cannot therefore deny that Japanese views of euthanasia have something to do with the traditional conception of life and death in Japan.

It seems that this native conception of life and death, beginning with the ancient Shintoism indigenous to Japan, which did not explicitly exclude suicide, has been fueled by the newly adopted religion. For Buddhism taught that everything in this world is transient and egoless, in a word, śūnyatā, and that we should emanicipate ourselves from any attachment to it. At the same time, Buddhism made us believe in *saṃsāra* as the repeated cycle of suffering, life, and death. It was first received as if it were a religion of "the next world," wherein the believer could escape from life in this world. In short, Buddhism strengthened the Japanese belief in the continuation of life and death and the feeling of intimacy with death (Nishimoto 1968:90–92; Savata 1968:135).

JAPANESE SUICIDE

I shall now turn to the history of the relation between Buddhism and suicide. The old Buddhism from India and China, consisting of both the Hīnayāna belief that death is itself Buddha-land and the *Bodhisattva*'s *tao* of self-sacrifice in Mahāyāna, was, so to speak, dissolved to form a better organization of Japanese Buddhism. Since the Middle Ages, the influence of Pure Land Gate teaching to "dislike and leave this defiled world" and the Zen Gate recommendation to "throw away one's own body-mind," and exist "without all attachments" (Dōgen 1972:185–93) have been extended over common believers.[7] This Japanese Buddhism mixed with the old Shintoism, both equally tolerant of suicide (unlike Christianity), thereafter played a role in aiding and abetting suicide and created an unsuspected trend to affirm or even idealize suicide.

While Pure Land Gate spread to people of the lower classes, Zen Gate was, from the Kamakura period, solidly supported by the samurai warrior classes. The lower classes caused the above-mentioned *shashin-ōjō* during the Middle Ages and began the fashion of *shinjū* or *aitai-shi* (dying between two parties). This, for the townspeople, was a death pact between unhappy lovers who hoped to enter into a happier life in the next world. Monzaemon Chikamatsu described this vividly during the Tokugawa period.[8] On the other hand, Zen Gate became a sort of guiding principle of the samurai classes, idealizing active resignation or renunciation of one's life and cultivating the spirit of preparing for death. It ultimately created the custom of *harakiri* or *seppuku* (belly-cutting) through the Middle and modern (pre-Meiji) ages (Harada 1922:33–35).

Thus *harakiri* was a samurai's means of expressing his devotion to his lord or master; *junshi* was a form of *harakiri* with the idea of following one's lord into the next world; and *shinjū* was a dedication to love. These suicides are said to be secular and popular expressions of Buddhist holism or transpersonalism, which has influenced Japanese life and death views since the sixth century.

It seems that the religious resignation found in Dōgen (1238), the high priest representative of Zen Gate, and the Pure Land teachings of "hastening death" in *Ichigonhōdan* (1294) then merged in the *Hagakure* (1716) of "Bushidō means a way of dying"[9] (Naramoto 1969:58). The Kamikaze corps in World War II in its turn found the latter a spiritual support. Although the religion has weakened gradually, the trend affirming suicide continues today.

Does Buddhism then have nothing at all to do with the present-day Japanese views of suicide? In understanding Buddhism as a modern sect, we may say so. Not only has present-day Japanese life relinquished its traditions through increasing Westernization, but Buddhism has also lost the authority it had in ancient times by divorcing itself from real life. If, however, we understand Buddhism as a combination of vague yet deep-rooted conceptions of life and death, value and nature, customs and habits, that have developed in the Japanese mind as a sort of collective unconscious, then we can say with certainty that it has influenced the views of suicide and euthanasia.

THE HISTORY OF EUTHANASIA

There have been more than a few recorded cases of voluntary euthanasia in Japan. An example is *rinjū-gyōgi* (the ceremony at the moment of death), which took place in Mujō-dō (a temple where priests with fatal illness spent their last days) during the Heian period (Genshin 1970:206–7). This temple was a sort of terminal care hospice wherein the dying sought a "good" and "beautiful" death by taking refuge in Amida Buddha. *Ichigonhōdan*, insofar as it taught hastening a good death (*shashin-ōjō*), is a book recommending religious voluntary euthanasia in Pure Land Gate.

According to *Hagakure*, the samurai warriors' best accomplishment was to die beautifully or with dignity. It recommended that they be firmly prepared for death in battle for one's lord's sake and that they keep themselves always clean and tidy in everyday life lest they be shamelessly killed (*Hagakure*:40–41). Even during the Meiji period this *bushido* (Japanese chivalry) or samurai spirit of "sacrificing oneself willingly" was encouraged as the best model of national life. Indeed, this same esthetic holism governed Japanese military life in the World Wars during this century. We remember the sorrowful esthetics of "falling down like cherry blossoms" which prevailed among the Kamikaze corps (the suicide pilots who served in a special air attack corps of the Japanese Imperial Army and Navy).

Since *harakiri* was a way to avoid the humiliation of public condemnation and punishment or the supposed disgrace of capture by the enemy's forces in war, the ceremony might be said to be a form of euthanasia for the condemned who wanted to escape, while keeping their dignity, from a mental distress more painful than *harakiri* itself. The act of assisting *harakiri* is known as *kaishaku*. A second at the commission of *harakiri* was a kinsman or special friend of the condemned. The ceremony having been performed, the duty of the assistant was to behead the sufferer so that his last agony might be as short as possible (Harada 1922:37). In this sense, the assistant is like a doctor who administers poison at the wish of the patient.

This solemn "ceremony of the moment," compassionately tended by the golden Buddhist images in the *mujō-dō*, these samurais who fell on the field of battle with a smile, the Kamikaze corps who departed, crying, "Long live the Emperor!"—this *harakiri* and *kaishaku* share one characteristic in common: the time-honored esthetics of "downfall" or "falling blossom" expressed by the Japanese who say, "I would like to die beautifully or with a smile," or "I wish to accomplish the virtue of making the end well." This is why, I think, many of us Japanese prefer *songen-shi* to *anraku-shi*, as mentioned above. As evidence, the former has taken root and displaced the latter in recent decades.

I will cite another instance that does not belong to voluntary euthanasia. Long ago, people used to abandon "useless" old women in distant mountains because of the poor economic conditions in those days. The legend of "throwing-old-women" told in *Narayama-bushi-ko* by Shichiro Hukasawa (1965:249–84) shows that there were cases of "thrift euthanasia" based on the principle of "scarcity economics" (Gruman et al. 1978:20) in some now deserted villages of old Japan.

It was Ōgai Mori, a writer and doctor, who first foresaw and called attention to present-day euthanasia (case (3) above). He told the story impressively in his famous novel *Takase-bune* (1979) about a younger brother who was seriously ill. Despair drove him to attempt suicide, but he was not able to kill himself. The elder brother, no longer able to stand by, let his younger brother die mercifully but was accused of murder. Hearing this sad story, a boatman who was transporting the criminal under guard said, "How can that be, I wonder?" He thought that although such a case might be murder, it was not a crime because its compassionate motive was to release the patient from his dying struggle. Thus Ōgai Mori hinted at our fear of unnatural life support of the dying by present-day biomedicine.

More than twenty years ago a patricidal son, indicted for a murder by contract, was let off with a light sentence. This adjudication in Nagoya High Court on December 23, 1962, marked an epoch in the history of euthanasia arguments in Japan (Hasegawa 1974:19). It was the first case to prescribe the following six requisites, the fulfillment of which would legally be recognized as euthanasia:

1. The incurability of the patient's disease and the imminence of death as judged by present-day biomedicine must be established.
2. The patient must be judged to be suffering unbearable pain.
3. The main purpose of the measures that cause death must be to ease or soften the pain.
4. The measures must be taken in accordance with the patient's consent, if the individual can indicate his or her intention.
5. In principle, it must be done at the hands of a physician.
6. The ethical appropriateness of the measures that the physician takes must be established.

This Nagoya adjudication has since caused heated arguments even in public opinion in Japan.

THE HOSPICE MOVEMENT

As mentioned above, the Japanese (historically speaking) seem to be so esthetic and religious that euthanasia for them signifies "death with dignity" rather than *anraku-shi*. They indeed have tended to value the heroic way to kill themselves and the *katachi* (form) of the dying hour. Now it is the role of the hospice that brings such death with dignity into institutional operation.

The present-day hospice takes care of the dying in order to enable them to complete their remaining days with dignity and beauty by easing not only bodily but also mental or spiritual distress by means of dialogue and religious or artistic care. In this sense, for the past ten years in Japan, the euthanasia problem may be said to have been resolved by formation of a better hospice organization.

It is a Buddhist tenet that has characterized the Japanese-style hospice. It is worth notice that lately the Buddhist hospices named *Bihāra* (meaning in Sanskrit a temple for the terminal patient to rest and fulfill his or her life in, not merely to die in) have begun to be organized by twos and threes. The *Bihāra* seems to me to reorganize the previous *Mujō-dō* or *Ōjō-in* of the Heian period wherein Pure Land Gate Buddhists provided a variety of terminal care for incurable patients. Similarly, in the modern *Mujō-dō* that present Pure Land Gate Buddhists (as *Jōdo-shū* or *Jōdo-shin-shū*) have organized, doctors, nurses, counselors and Buddhist monks cooperate to carry out naturally and openly a sort of passive and voluntary euthanasia (not taking useless and extraordinary measures, yet not exercising active euthanasia). There the patients are able to enjoy conversations with others, hear religious discourses, appreciate arts or films, and so on, as they wish.

PRESENT-DAY EUTHANASIA ARGUMENTS

What social changes have we experienced today? Westernization with its emphasis on individuality, rationalism, and the biomedical revolution has brought euthanasia from the past to become a "problem" in Japan today. Present-day euthanasia arguments have sprung up from several sources.

First, there is a sense of growing crisis about the advent of the "compulsion of prolongation of life" (unnatural life-sustaining measures) by the medical skill of resuscitation.

Second, society has aged as a byproduct of this biomedical revolution.

Third, the modern person yearns to prolong or maintain as long as possible human life with dignity and well-being—in short, yearns for "quality of life."

At first sight there appears to be no feature that is especially "Japanese" in present-day euthanasia arguments. Some emphasize the right and freedom of the individual to die; some respect above all the overriding will of something holistic; and some are obliged to maintain a neutrality that neither affirms nor denies euthanasia.

Arguments of Jurists

According to Tadashi Uematsu, a jurist of great influence who advocates both voluntary and passive euthanasia, no one has the right to punish those who, with mercy and good intentions, aid suicide or murder the sufferer by contract (Uematsu 1974:27–28). He thinks that we must respect "above all" (Uematsu 1974:29) the free will of the patient who begs earnestly for such mercy killing in a situation that requires artificial maintenance of his or her life. Why do some people obstinately refuse to recognize this right to die? The answer is found in the religious premise that "we must sustain his life even without regard for his own will to die" (Uematsu 1974:27). It is a sin against God's will for mortals artificially to control their lives, which are a godsend. This old-fashioned dogma of religion has prevented us from meeting the needs of the new age by an epoch-making control of death as well as of life. Thus it appears that euthanasia is opposed by religion, as in Christianity, instead of by a reckless, driving biomedical science. For Uematsu, religion is nothing but a "superstition in the twentieth century" (p. 28) to compel us—that is, modern people apart from all religions—to prolong "unnatural" living, and thereby violates our right to die well.

It seems to me that Uematsu goes too far in saying that religion is but a superstition compelling the undue prolongation of life in this century. I am sure that true religion, which makes our lives better and meaningful, does not repudiate euthanasia but instinctively seeks to eliminate it gradually somehow. Nevertheless, we should consider Uematsu's juridical point of view: For the patient suffering from an incurable and unbearable disease, the continuation of existence is a violation of the fundamental right of the individual.

Generally speaking, to go to an extreme and affirm or deny something is a danger at best for us and much more so in such a complicated and subtle problem as euthanasia. Thus I will introduce opposing views in order to counter the unqualified optimism about it.

Kōichi Bai, another famous jurist, disapproves of euthanasia (active or passive) from his moderate standpoint of a humanism that respects unconditionally the value of all human life. He regards euthanasia as making the absolute into the relative and says, first, that "euthanasia may involve a risk of causing the ranking of lives of men, from the valuable (useful) ones to unvaluable ones, from 'above' to 'below.' " Second, it may lead us to the argument of relating life having absolute value in itself with other things—that is, the financial burden to the patient's family, the management situation of the hospital, insurance problems, and so on (Hasegawa 1974:21).

The view that human life, without (or with few) exceptions, should always have an absolute value in itself we may call a humanistic holism. There is another, religious holism, however. A time-honored religious belief states that human beings have no right to manipulate arbitrarily and selfishly their "own" lives, which are transiently borrowed and must be returned soon to the holistic Being. (After all, such manipulation may come down to a sort of "clinging" or "attachment" to life and death, according to Buddhism.)[10] We can never dismiss this religious holism as an outdated superstition; we must keep it as a brake against the drive toward euthanasia. In this sense, the religious philosopher Hidehiko Hori (1975:18–19) says that there is a serious and unique meaning proper to the human being in that last distress—bodily, mental, or spiritual. If the patient can endure it, then perhaps we have no right to bring about an easy and painless death. This is, I think, the fundamental attitude of Buddhism to euthanasia as mentioned above.

Arguments of Physicians

The opponents of euthanasia usually point to two additional difficulties. First, should the supreme principle of unconditional respect of life be destroyed and euthanasia be made a legal concept, the result would be the corruption of medical treatments and the abuse of euthanasia or suicide. The second problem involves the unresolved ambiguity and inexactitude of the key words used in the prescription of euthanasia, such as "incurable," "the imminence of death," "the degree of the patient's pain," and so on.

To be sure, considering the rapid advance of biomedical science and the subjectivity of the "pain" experience, we may find difficulty in clarifying the essential vagueness of these words.

We have never seen so consistent and open an advocate of voluntary and passive euthanasia as Tenrei Ōta, who has appealed for its legalization. There is, indeed, a persuasion in his arguments because he anticipated the above objections.

First, as to holism, religious or humanistic, like his friend Uematsu, Ōta opposes imported modern individualism and rationalism. He insists that it is true humanism for us to eliminate a patient's pain as much as possible and not to torture the sufferer by compelling the useless sustaining of life (Ōta 1972:185). Both Uematsu and Ōta earnestly advocate euthanasia, but the former does so from the standpoint of the legal protection of the rights of the individual, while the latter does so for the purpose of releasing patients from unbearable pain. In fact, according to Ōta, it is as important a duty for the physician to ease a patient's pain, even though the consequence is a hastening of death, as to aid the patient in recovering health; a doctor must not only cure but also care (Ōta 1972:191). Ōta is confident that a good physician, if requested earnestly, can let a terminal patient die well and beautifully. In thinking so, Ōta may be said to one of those Japanese who have tended traditionally to value a beautiful death with dignity. As to "pain," Ōta means not only bodily pain but also the indefinable ensemble of mental unease and spiritual worries of a human being facing the end of life (Ōta 1972:189).

With regard to the fear of the abuse of euthanasia, Ōta proposed obtaining the assent of the family as well as that of the patient (if the latter can express his or her will) in the presence of a lawyer (Ōta 1972:19).

Finally, concerning ambiguity and inexactitude in medical diagnoses,

Ōta proposed that medical care be decided through the prudent mutual consent of more than two physicians (p. 187).

It was on the basis of the above principles that he, together with Uematsu, founded in 1976 the Japanese Society of Songen-shi, which aimed at a legalization of voluntary and involuntary euthanasia without precedent in the world (Ōta 1972:193).

It seems to me that Mitchio Matsuda, a prolific writer and physician, is more prudent and therefore more persuasive than Ōta in taking into account the truth of the above objections. And while Ōta's arguments were somewhat idealistic, Matsuda's appear real and pessimistic. On the one hand, he, too, appeals for the protection of the right of the weak, that is, for the right of individuals to die by their own will. His criticisms of hospitals are bitter and sharp: "To maintain the moribund's life artificially, this is to the profit of the hospital" (Matsuda and Hashimoto 1972:307). The ethics of medicine to sustain a patient's life as long as possible coincides with the commercialism of the hospital. The patient's will to cling to life and the last satisfaction which the family may find even in the vanishing remainder of that life (such as the breathing and warmth of the patient's body) also cooperate to support sustaining life by medical machines and contribute to the profits of the hospital. This is why many physicians have tended to support euthanasia, for their consciences' sake, as a private affair. Partly for this reason, Matsuda doesn't hesitate to agree to euthanasia, for he is well aware of the deceptive hope for life that physicians may give patients. He well knows that the sufferer, if injected with a unit of narcotic, can pass away painlessly (Matsuda 1975:156–57). The problem, however, remains a difficult one.

Matsuda argues, however, that on the whole it is more dangerous and unsound for the hospital to stop medical treatments too soon and accept euthanasia too easily than to persist in the attempt to prolong life as long as possible. If euthanasia is legalized, he warns, then the physician will lose the main ethic to reject murder in any form and the hospital will be robbed of its proper function to prolong life; both would be overwhelmed with terror (Matsuda 1972:153, 158). This is why in this context he denies euthanasia. It is worth noting his warnings as he has seen much of the real state of affairs in hospitals. Although he defends the right of the weak to self-determination, Matsuda also recommends that doctors adhere to the time-honored principle of medicine, which coincides with humanistic holism. For this reason he calls his own standpoint "the negative theory of partial affirmation" (Matsuda 1975:129).

CONCLUSION

The Japanese as a whole (at least at the level of the common people influenced by Buddhism) have tended traditionally to idealize suicide, and the fact that they prefer *songen-shi* (beautiful death with dignity) to *anraku-shi* may signify a distant echo of such a traditional attitude toward suicide. In this sense, for instance, Tenrei Ōta, who has striven for the idealization of *songen-shi*, belongs to a samurai-like way of thinking. As for the right to die, the Japanese have never become acquainted with this Western conception in spite of today's modernization. It seems that Japanese views of suicide and euthanasia, negative or affirmative, have not taken root in the notion of individual consciousness and rationalism but in the traditional holistic and Buddhist concept of life and death.

In my own view, we should respect holism, humanistic or religious, which emphasizes the unconditional value of life, as a major premise or at least as a brake against euthanasia arguments, as the opponents of euthanasia have admonished. At the same time, the right to die well and with dignity should never be neglected as an actual condition, as the advocates of euthanasia stressed. It follows, then, that the best way to choose is to consider prudently and flexibly each particular case, making allowances for the circumstances of each case and yet harmoniously carrying through the other principle. This may be a laborious and difficult task, but is not this solemn control over life and death worth taking trouble for?

"Don't hold your own life dear, and yet, hold your own life dear" (Dōgen 1972:34). This remark of Dogen's is indeed full of implications. It seems to me that there is a truth in the "middle"—between holism and individualism; between duty and right; in sum, between negation and affirmation. Thus, after long deliberation we come to Buddha's wisdom: "Being perfect, keep away from extremes of prejudice and preserve a moderation that is beyond all words to describe" (*Avatamsaka-sutra* 32).

NOTES

1. I will not go deeply into the philosophical and religious problems of suicide proper, about which I have written a book, *Why Does the Human Being Suicide?* (in Japanese). Tokyo: Keisoshobō, 1981.

2. As to the essence of Buddha's teaching, "suffering, impermanence, egolessness, enlightenment," see *Aṅguttara Nikāya* 4–185, *samaṇa-sūtra*. The sutras (or suttas) belong to Buddhist canonical literature and are quoted, as is the Bible, without reference to any particular collection or edition.

3. "Everything is changeable, everything appears and disappears; there is no blissful peace until one passes beyond the agony of life and death" (*Mahā-parinirvāṇa-sūtra*).

4. As to this point, for instance, see *Laṅkāvatāra-sūtra* and *Avataṃsaka-sūtra* 32, *Sutta-nipāta* 634, 636, and 642.

5. See *Saṃyuktāgama* 47 and *Ekottarāgama* 19.

6. For instance, see Prince Sattva's self-surrendering in *Suvarṇaprabhāsa-sūtra* 26.

7. "Go up, furthermore, on the top of a high pole"; "Obey Buddhism without ego and all its precepts, for even a day, or for only an instant, even if you are dying from starvation or cold, and you will achieve eternal enlightenment." Dōgen (1200–53). *Shōbōgenzō-zuimonki* (in Japanese). Tokyo: Kōdansha, 1972, pp. 185–93.

8. See "double suicide pieces" such as *Shinjū-tennoamijima* or *Sonesaki-shinjū* in Kabuki and Bunraku plays made popular in the seventeenth century by Chikamatsu (1653–1724), a distinguished playwright.

9. Compare this saying with *Ichigonhōdan*'s sayings: "The acme of the entire world means only one thing: death and nothing but" (p. 26); "All teachings of the Buddha teach only one word: death, and nothing but" (p. 27). You will understand that the Tao of Buddhism was merely replaced by the Tao of Bushi.

10. "One should always remember that nothing in the world can strictly be called 'mine.' What comes to a person comes to him because of a combination of causes and conditions: it can be kept by him only temporarily and, therefore, he must not use it selfishly or for unworthy purposes" (*Dhammmapada Aṭṭhakathā* 1). Also see *Laṅkāvatāra-sūtra* and *Śrīmālādevīsimhanāda-sūtra*.

REFERENCES

Bacon, F., "Advancement of Learning." In J. E. Spingarn, ed. *Critical Essays of the Seventeenth Century*, vol. 1. Oxford: Clarendon Press, 1908–9, pp. 1–9.

Dōgen (1200–53). *Shōbōgenzō-zuimonki* (in Japanese). Tokyo: Kōdansha, 1972, pp. 185–93.

Encyclopaedia of Buddhism (University of Ryūkoku, ed.) Tokyo: Fuzanbō, 1935, p. 106.

Genshin (942–1017). *Ōjō-yōshū* (The Essential Collection Concerning Birth) (in Japanese). Tokyo: Iwanamishoten, 1970, p. 10.

Gruman, G., Bok, J. S., and Veatch, R. M. "Death and Dying: Euthanasia and Sustaining Life." In W. T. Reich, ed. *Encyclopedia of Bioethics*, vol. 1. New York: The Free Press, 1978, p. 261.

Harada, T. "Suicide (Japanese)." In J. Hastings, ed. *Encyclopaedia of Religion and Ethics*. New York: Charles Scribner's Sons, 1922, pp. 35–37.

Hasegawa, S. "Euthanasia." In *L'esprit d'Aujourd'hui*, No. 83, *Euthanasia* (in Japanese). Tokyo: Shibundō, 1974, p. 19.

Hori, H. 1975. "Euthanasia. The Problem of Life–Death and Today." In S. Gorai, K. Sasaki, S. Katsumata, and H. Hori, eds. *Life and Requiem* (in Japanese). Tokyo: Kawadeshobōshinsha, 1975, pp. 198–99.

Hukasawa, S. "Narayama-bushi-kō." In *A Collection of Shichiro Hukasawa. Modern Literature*, vol. 31 (in Japanese). Tokyo: Kawadeshobōshinsha, 1965, pp. 249–84.

Ippen (1239–89). *The Analects of Ippen-shōnin* (in Japanese). Tokyo: Iwanamishoten, 1985, p. 32.

Kato, S. *Why Does the Human Being Suicide?* (in Japanese). Tokyo: Keīsoshobō, 1981.

Matsuda, M. *On the Dignity of the Human Being* (in Japanese). Tokyo: Tchiku-
    mashobō, 1975, pp. 156–57.
Matsuda, M., and Hashimoto, M. "A Conversation: On Death." In *On Death* (pt.
    6 of Series *Life*) (in Japenese). Tokyo: Tchikumashobō, 1972, p. 307.
Miyano, A. *Euthanasia. Does Man Have the Right to Die?* (in Japanese). Tokyo:
    Nipponkeizai-shinbunsha, 1982, pp. 70, 156.
Mori, O. "Takase-bune." In *A Collection of Ogai Mori*, vol. 2. *A Whole System of
    Japanese Modern Literature 12* (in Japanese). Tokyo: Kadokawashoten,
    1979, pp. 440–41.
Morishita, J., ed. *Ichgon-hōdan-sho* (in Japanese). Tokyo: Iwanamishoten, 1983,
    p. 25.
Nakamura, H. "Dhammapada, No. 130." In his *Dhammapada and Udānavarga.*
    Tokyo: Iwanamishoten, 1983, p. 28.
Naramoto, T., ed. *Hagakure. Japanese Classics 17* (in Japanese). Tokyo: Chūō-
    kōronsha, 1969, p. 58.
Nishimoto, S. "Ōjō of the Pure Land Buddhism." In K. Sato, ed. *L'Esprit d'au-
    jourd'hui*, No. 34. *Dialogue with Death* (in Japanese). Tokyo: Shibundō,
    1968, pp. 90–92.
———. 1962. "Buddhism and Suicide." *The Scientific Report of Kyoto Prefectural
    University. Humanistic Science* 14:59–67.
Ōta, T. "A New Interpretation of Euthanasia and its Legalization." In M. Mat-
    suda, ed. *My Anthology*, vol. 7. *Death.* Tokyo: Tchikumashobō, 1972, p. 185.
———. "Conception of Euthanasia." In S. Hasegawa, ed. *L'Esprit d'aujourd'hui*,
    No. 83. *Euthanasia* (in Japanese). Tokyo: Shibundō, 1974, pp. 22–25.
Poussin, L. de la V. "Suicide (Buddhist)." In J. Hastings, ed. *Encyclopaedia of
    Religion and Ethics*, vol. 12. New York: Charles Scribner's Sons, 1922, p. 25.
Savata, T. "The Opposite Views of Life and Death." In K. Sato, ed. *L'Esprit
    d'Aujourd'hui*, No. 34. *Dialogue with Death* (in Japanese). Tokyo: Shibundō,
    1968, pp. 124–25, 129.
Uematsu, T. "Freedom to Choose Euthanasia. Superstition in the 20th Century—
    The Compulsion of Prolongation of Life." In S. Hasegawa, ed. *L'Esprit
    d'Aujourd'hui*, No. 83. *Euthanasia* (in Japanese). Tokyo: Shibundō, 1974,
    p. 27.
Yanagida, K. *A Discourse of our Ancestors* (in Japanese). Tokyo: Tikuma-Shobō,
    1982, p. 342.

III Cross-Legal Views

7 Euthanasia: An English Perspective

Mary Rose Barrington

More than one innovative idea for improving the lot of the disadvantaged has been formulated in England, although the initial lead is not always maintained. It seems to have been widely accepted for most of this century (at least) that doctors occasionally give their patients euthanasia—far too often, according to opponents, but not nearly often enough according to the rest of us. I say "rest of us" bearing in mind that opinion polls taken over the last twenty years, putting questions in reasonably neutral terms, show that the public favors empowering doctors to give euthanasia to patients in suitable cases.[1] The idea has been stoutly resisted by the spokesmen of the medical establishment although the current position appears to be that around two medical practitioners in five would be prepared to give euthanasia in suitable cases if the law were to be changed.[2] (They would presumably be equally prepared to take part in other acts of deliverance, for example, giving drugs to patients to enable an act of self-deliverance to be undertaken by the patient.)

The law in its existing state takes no cognizance of euthanasia; whether the motive is merciful and altruistic or merciless and greedy, the deliberate taking of life is classed as murder. This has been recognized as embarrassingly crude, and suggestions have been made from time to time (Criminal Law Revision Committee 1976) that it would be appropriate to create a separate offense of mercy killing punishable by a relatively short sentence. Even the most doctrinaire judge can hardly relish having to impose a life sentence on a mercy killer, this being the mandatory sentence for murder.

The rigor of the law is mitigated in the case of a person who is prepared to plead before the court that he committed his "offence" while "suffering" from such abnormality of mind ... as substantially to impair his mental responsibility for his acts" (S.2(1) Homicide Act 1957). A finding of diminished responsibility will result in a conviction for manslaughter (not carrying a mandatory life sentence) rather than murder, and the same reduction will be made if a defendant is found to be the survivor of a genuine suicide pact who failed to die after killing the other party (S.4(1) Homicide Act 1957).

The other highly relevant item of legislation affecting the position is the Suicide Act 1961. Before the enactment of this legislation the law of the Middle Ages prevailed, and persons attempting suicide, but not succeeding in the attempt, could be arrested and put on trial for a criminal act. It was obviously an offense to assist a suicide or attempted suicide, since both were classed as crimes, but when suicide was decriminalized one might have expected the assistance of suicide to have gone the same way. It was not to be, and the position is governed by S2(1) of the Act: "A person who aids, abets, counsels or procures the suicide of another, or an attempt by another to commit suicide, shall be liable on conviction on indictment to imprisonment for a term not exceeding 14 years." In this area the law of Scotland differs significantly because under Scots law suicide was never a criminal offense so that the Suicide Act 1961 does not apply to Scotland. While Scots may rejoice in the freedom to assist suicide, they may in some cases be at greater risk of finding themselves charged with murder in circumstances where the 1961 Act might have been used in England.

There is one area of law entirely free from legislation and from judicial authority since it has never been in doubt. Persons who are mentally competent (and others, too, subject to some qualification) may refuse medical treatment (Dimond 1984:694)[3] so that imposing treatment on them against their express wishes would be an assault in both criminal and civil law. Nor can they be forced to take nourishment against their will. From the viewpoint of the deliverist these are valuable rights, provided the patient is in a position to claim and enforce these rights. There are of course situations in which a person's consent to treatment is reasonably assumed. Mangled victims of road accidents who are brought into the hospital casualty department cannot usually be asked whether they want all steps taken to save their lives, and it is hardly to be imagined that an action in court could be sustained against a doctor who, for instance, removed an irrecoverably damaged limb, only to find the patient complaining of assault and battery. One can, however, imagine a situation in which the patient's life could be saved only by massive mutilation and the doctor's attention is drawn to the patient's written statement saying that in such circumstances the patient would not consent to extremes of suffering and impairment.

This position has not been tested in court. The clarity of the position is reinforced by the absence in English law of any general duty to assist, save, or rescue a stranger. There is a duty imposed on people who have helpless persons in their care to protect their helpless state by, for example, fetching a doctor or getting them to a hospital. But if one elects to extricate oneself from the care of the doctor, the doctor does not have to assert a contrary duty to give the sort of care the patient does not want. In theory, the wishes of the patient have supreme authority as long as the patient is undeniably *compos mentis* (Dimond 1984:694). Provided one is not in the hands of a doctor who intends to override one's wishes regardless, the right not to be handled in any way against one's will can (at any rate in theory) bring about one's death, although it may be a more stressful procedure than would be the case if one could effectively request positive steps to be taken to secure this end. I shall return to these aspects of refusal of treatment after dealing with various attempts made over the years to promote the cause of voluntary euthanasia and self-deliverance.

Doctors who discreetly practice euthanasia usually carry their discretion to the point of not consulting the patient. This implies no malice on their part, but a benevolent paternalism under which they make the decision they believe (on reasonable grounds) that the patient would make if the patient had the right to do so. This veterinarian sort of initiative is mercy killing rather than voluntary euthanasia, but it may well be that many people would prefer to be humanely dispatched by a kindly doctor without prior consultation rather than face up to participation in the event. I deduce this from public opinion polls indicating greater public enthusiasm for euthanasia than for self-deliverance,[4] although empowering a third person to take a patient's life is a more revolutionary concept than merely empowering someone to give assistance to patients who are strong-minded enough to take their own lives.

In the 1930s doctors were reputedly administering humane overdoses in suitable cases, and it has recently come to light that Lord Dawson of Penn, physician of King George V, having ascertained that Queen Mary saw no virtue in allowing the King's suffering to continue, took whatever steps were needed to cut it short.

Later in that same year (1936) the newly formed Voluntary Euthanasia Society initiated a bill in the House of Lords. The Voluntary Euthanasia (Legalisation) Bill was intended "to legalise under certain conditions the administration of euthanasia to persons desiring it and who are suffering from illness of a fatal and incurable character involving severe pain." It will be seen that this bill had extremely limited objectives and by its definitions excluded many cases in which euthanasia might be appropriate—for example, cases of severe stroke, catastrophic accident, nonfatal degenerative disease, and so on. The requirements of the bill were entirely rational but not very appealing. A deathbed form had to be signed, witnessed, and forwarded with medical certificates to "a euthanasia referee" appointed by the Minister of Health. The deed was to be carried out by a medical practitioner licensed for the purpose (somewhat reminiscent, one must say, of the slaughterhouse) in the presence of an official witness.

Whatever proposals are put forward in Parliament, the opponents of euthanasia will castigate them either as hedged about with repulsive formalities or as intolerably lax, affording opportunities for unscrupulous doctors, grasping relations, and other evildoers to make away with unwilling victims. The 1936 bill could (with some reason) be attacked on both grounds. No one, however, seriously expected the bill to survive its second reading and the debate was not wholly unsympathetic. Thirty-three years were to pass before another attempt was made to secure legislation.

Between 1936 and 1969 two developments took place, one that must rank as a major event in world history and the other local to England, both of which set back the cause of voluntary euthanasia. The larger development was the so-called "euthanasia" imposed by the Nazis on mentally ill and sub-normal patients; some opponents of euthanasia, in their determination to equate euthanasia with mass murder, will even use "euthanasia" to describe the attempted extermination of the Jews. However grotesque such reasoning may be, it has to be conceded that the practices of Nazi Germany, and in particular the willingness of respectable citizens to kill those considered to be useless, unproductive, or otherwise substandard, opened a frightening window on the capacity of apparently civilized people to commit undreamed-of atrocities. The shock waves continue.

The immeasurably smaller event sent a cold shudder through the medical profession, although the general public has always classed it as black farce. This was the trial of Dr. John Bodkin Adams in 1957 (Devlin 1985). With a name and appearance made for comedy, Dr. Adams came within inches of a conviction for murder although, as he put it, all he did was to "ease the passing" of some patients. A prosperous medical practitioner in a seaside resort much frequented by moneyed elderly ladies, Dr. Adams was well liked by his patients, and he had come rather to expect that they would leave him nice little presents in their wills. He was not backward in putting in reminders that he would quite like to have the canteen of silver or the elderly Rolls-Royce. His acquisitiveness was his undoing. Hundreds (or thousands) of doctors at this time might have slipped patients a little extra morphine to ease the passing and later found themselves recipients of minor bounty under wills. It would have been obvious to them and, they would have thought, to everyone else, that the acceleration of those gifts by a few weeks would have been outweighed by the loss of fees they might have collected had the patient lived longer. How aghast they must have been when Dr. Adams was charged with murder, the suggested motivation being these relatively modest bequests. The trial embodied every element doctors might hitherto have considered beyond contemplation. Two nurses gave highly colored accounts of his administration of drugs, and only by various strokes of good fortune was his defending counsel able to show that their evidence was wholly inaccurate. A medical specialist recklessly affirmed that Dr. Adams's treatment had to be interpreted as intent to kill the patient. It was fortunate for Dr. Adams that he had not demonstrably delivered a fatal dose. When the trial started all England expected him to be convicted of murder, but he was acquitted and found guilty only of a very minor offense relating to the misuse of drugs.

The dark question mark that fell over mercy killing at the doctor's discretion has been reinforced over the years by panic reaction of doctors to social drug abuse. In the 1940s and 1950s patients with tiresome coughs could be prescribed a small bottle of linctus containing heroin; anyone wanting a good night's sleep would be allowed to benefit from 100 milligrams of barbiturates. People happily used these medicines for the purposes prescribed, stopped coughing, and went to sleep. It must have been fairly easy in those relaxed days for a doctor or a patient to arrange matters so that a patient who did not want to wake up did not do so. Today doctors who do not hesitate to create diazepam addicts wholesale regard a patient who asks for sodium amytal sleeping capsules as mad, bad, and dangerous to know. Mercy killing is in fact a less comfortable concept than it was a generation or two ago.

By the 1960s the Euthanasia Society had become a small, quiet, inoffensive group not thought likely to cause trouble to anyone, but by the end of the decade things were stirring and the movement suddenly sprang into vigorous activity.[5] The Voluntary Euthanasia Bill moved in the House of Lords in 1969 was a detailed measure fairly summarized in its long title:

An Act to provide in certain circumstances for the administration of euthanasia to persons who request it and who are suffering from an irremediable condition, and to enable persons to request in advance the administration of euthanasia in the event of their suffering from such a condition at a future date.

It will be seen that the revolutionary concept of the living will was proposed to replace the unpleasantness of requiring mortally sick and suffering patients to deal with forms and witnesses while on their sickbeds. This is not to say that the advance declaration was to rank as the patient's last word on the subject. Under clause 4(1) it was proposed that before causing euthanasia to be administered to a mentally responsible patient the physician in charge shall ascertain to his reasonable satisfaction that the declaration and all steps proposed to be taken under it accord with the patient's wishes.

The patient could therefore say "No, not yet." Equally, the patient could ' invite the physician to choose the moment without further reference to the patient. Most important of all, for many people, was the right given to the physician in charge to give euthanasia to a declarant who became demented or suffered catastrophic brain damage. For although the bill entirely excluded suffering due to mental illness, it covered a very much wider field than the bill of 1936, the "irremediable condition" being defined as "a serious physical illness or impairment reasonably thought in the patient's case to be incurable and expected to cause him severe distress or render him incapable of rational existence." The proposers were agreeably surprised when the voting proved to be sixty-one against and forty in favor. The opposition was disagreeably surprised that its victory was not more decisive. The 1969 bill dealt with a wide range of matters and made provision for various contingencies. There was hardly one line that did not give rise to immensely wordy diatribes, often far from the point.

The next attempt by the society to promote legislation consisted of a much shorter bill more limited in scope, the Incurable Patients Bill 1976, which inevitably gave rise to lengthy objections to the words "incurable" and "patients." The long title of the bill was "an act to enlarge and declare the rights of patients to be delivered from incurable suffering." The greater part of the bill was indeed declaratory, that is, its purpose was to spell out rights universally agreed to exist at common law, the most important of these rights being enunciated in clause 1(1):

An incurable patient shall with his consent, and notwithstanding any refusal on his part to receive intensive care or other life-sustaining treatment, be entitled to receive whatever quantity of drugs may be required to give him full relief from pain and physical distress, and to be rendered unconscious if no other treatment is effective to give relief.

No one sought to deny that this truly reflected the existing state of the law, but opponents of the bill considered that it would be highly dangerous to set it down in black and white because unscrupulous people might perhaps enforce their rights to the point of demanding and receiving treatment closely approximating euthanasia. Alerted to the support given to the bill in 1969, the opponents of euthanasia remained in the House while others went away to dinner, and the voting was eighty-five to twenty-three against the bill.

Many public opinion polls taken during the last twenty years have consistently shown that the public greatly favors changes in the law to permit voluntary euthanasia and self-deliverence. Those in favor of such a change in the law usually outnumber opponents by figures varying between 3:1 and 4:1, and even among Roman Catholics a majority declare themselves to be in favor.[6] There appear in fact to be relatively few who are philosophically antipathetic to the right to die. Opposition is nearly always based on practical grounds and the alleged impossibility of shielding helpless people from the wickedness of others who for various unjustifiable reasons want to be rid of them.

By 1979 the frustration of leading members of the Voluntary Euthanasia Society stood at a high level, bearing in mind that three fairly reasonable bills had received increasingly unreasonable treatment in the House of Lords. The time was never considered ripe for the issue to be raised in the House of Commons, where the same performance would perhaps be repeated, though with Members shrieking abuse instead of preserving the dignified hush of the Lords.

The view expressed by one of the influential Dutch organizations was that legislation was best left alone and that attempts should be made to develop a jurisprudential doctrine to the effect that doctors should be regarded as having a special privilege in law to give their patients treatment that would be regarded as homicide if given by anyone other than a medical practitioner. There may be some basis for that view in English law since doctors are clearly excepted from the legal principle that precludes any consent to permit mutilation of one's own person (except accidentally in the course of sport, for example). Surgeons are certainly permitted to mutilate patients with their consent so that the germ of the Dutch idea is firmly sown. The difference, however, between the Netherlands and England is that the Dutch appear to be much more sensible people, their doctors are more courageous, their judges are more humane and (on these matters of life and death) considerably more subtle and sophisticated. The reenactment on English television of the trial of a Dutch woman doctor who gave euthanasia to her senile mother a little earlier than the director of the geriatric home had planned (this appeared to be the major bone of contention) was a masterpiece of civilized debate. In the Netherlands the police have managed to be superbly inactive in restraining the activities of a valiant housewife who has made a practice of broadcasting her willingness to supply a lethal quantity of barbiturates to any sufferer whose doctor refuses to be helpful. One can say with perfect certainty that in England this woman could expect some heavy and unsympathetic attention from police and judges. The Dutch advice has proved very effective in the Netherlands, where there are now medical manuals in circulation advising on euthanasia, but it seemed clear in 1979 (as it does still) that England was not ready for the doctrine of medical privilege.

Such indeed was the noncooperation from the medical profession that the Voluntary Euthanasia Society committee decided to go in the opposite direction. If the professionals were going to refuse to give a service, than the alternative was to mount an exercise in "do-it-yourself." The members of the Society were asked if they would like to be given access to a booklet describing how to end one's life and advising on various methods and pitfalls. The response was overwhelming: The members wanted the booklet and so did thousands of other people who hitherto had not been members but who hastened to join.

The booklet was duly written, entitled *A Guide to Self-Deliverance*, and overprinted "available only to Exit members over 25 years." The renaming of the Voluntary Euthanasia Society as "Exit" was in some ways a symbol of the new militancy abroad in the society. The name was bitterly opposed by some members, and so indeed was the booklet. The legal implications of publication were also fairly alarming, bearing in mind the provisions of the Suicide Act 1961 under which a prison sentence of up to fourteen years awaits anyone who assists the suicide of another person. It was of course a fine legal point whether disseminating information could ever be regarded as assisting any particular act of suicide or as attempting to assist the suicide of anyone who might make use of it. One thing seemed fairly certain: If a juvenile were to be found dead with *A Guide to Self-Deliverance* in his hand, the public would call for someone's head to roll.

In 1980 various cataclysms shook the Society. At a committee meeting attended by relatively few members a decision was rather suddenly taken not to publish the booklet, whereupon the secretary (of whom more later) more or less took command of the Society. This caused some of the committee members who had backed the booklet to withdraw from the committee. Those who lingered were replaced by twelve new members, all declaring that they would go to prison rather than not publish the booklet. Publication was delayed until 1981 as a result of further internal convulsions, and the first booklet was in fact *How to Die with Dignity* (Mair 1980), published by Scottish Exit, a society set up with a view to profiting from the more favorable Scots law. Despite its unruly birth, Exit's *Guide to Self-Deliverance* (Executive Committee of Exit 1981) was a very dignified publication with a preface by Arthur Koestler, and several pages were devoted to "Why you should think again," "Before taking a final decision about seeking self-deliverance," and "Care and distribution of this pamphlet." To discourage impulsive use the pamphlets were in fact numbered and sold only to members of three months' standing. The guts of the booklet, however, were three pages of tables setting out full descriptions of lethal sedatives, nonlethal sedatives, analgesics, antidepressants, and antiemetics, with advice on how many to take. There was also practical advice on what not do to.

These activities did not, of course, go unremarked by the press and by the enemies of euthanasia, who were rumored to be pressing the Attorney General to take some drastic action, such as prosecuting the chairman of the Society for attempting to aid and abet "the suicide of another," to quote the Act.

After some time two thing must have become clear to the department of the Attorney General: first, that dark hints of prosecution were not going to deter the distribution of the booklet, and second, that a prosecution might well fail. If a particular suicide were taken as an example and an attempt were made to show that it resulted directly from advice given in the booklet, this conclusion would have to be strictly proved and that would present considerable difficulties. A far more likely approach would be to prosecute for the offense of attempting to aid or abet the suicide of another. There was already authority for the proposition that the "suicide" did not have to succeed; neither did it even have to be attempted. This had been established in the case of *Regina v. McShane* in 1977, a case as bizarre as any fiction.[7]

Yolanda McShane was in many ways an amiable, hardworking 60-year-old wife and mother, kind to her pets, apparently concerned about her mother, and unfortunately in need of money. The mother lived in a home run by nuns who did not approve of her desire to keep in her possession a supply of lethal barbiturates, which she regarded as her "security" in case she ever wanted to take them. Mrs. McShane promised to bring her mother fourteen capsules of Nembutal (pentobarbitone). Mrs. McShane's sister alerted the nuns, who arranged cover for the police to enable them to videotape the meeting between mother and daughter. This scene was some years later relayed on television by way of entertainment. Mrs. McShane later insisted that she knew her mother had no intention of taking the capsules at that time and that when she told her mother, "Don't make a mess of it this time," this was advice about safeguarding the pills. Despite her age, Mrs. McShane received a two-year prison sentence for attempting to aid and abet. Mrs. McShane's contention that hers was a kindly act was lent some support when her mother, on having the Nembutal taken from her, cried out that her daughter had brought them "because she loves me so much." It was clear, however, that the judge ascribed her actions to hopes of an early inheritance and sentenced her accordingly.

The McShane case gave a clear lead in showing that an attempt to assist a certain person to an act of suicide, even though it resulted in no action whatsoever, could lead to a successful prosecution. But there was still a palpable difference between disseminating information to the multitude and handling out a supply of lethal capsules to an identifiable person. There was also the question of intent. Graphic and detailed descriptions of how to cause the death of others, or oneself, are given in numerous detective stories, presumably with the intent to entertain rather than to instruct. It was obviously a maintainable argument that the purpose of the booklet was to inform, to relieve ignorance, and to give peace of mind, but not necessarily to encourage the reader to put the knowledge to practical use. Three jurors not prepared to interpret publishing information as aiding or abetting an act of suicide would be enough to secure an acquittal, a majority of ten to two being the minimum required for conviction.

The Attorney General decided in the end on a more friendly approach, freely acknowledging that the chairman and committee of Exit were not of criminal disposition in the usual sense of the word, so that the issues would be more properly dealt with in civil litigation. The attorney general moved for a declaration that the supply of the *Guide to Self-Deliverance* amounted to a breach of the law, and the proceedings were conducted without animosity as an intellectual exercise. The outcome was that the Attorney General lost the battle but actually won the war.

Exit's expert witness, Dr. Colin Brewer, drew attention in his affidavit to the existence and availability of other publications containing information of self-deliverance, among them the highly provocative *Suicide: Mode d'Emploi* (Guillon and Le Bonniec 1982). Fairly easily obtained from English booksellers at the time, this book had raised blood pressure in France by summarizing advice given on lethal doses from the *Guide to Self-Deliverance* and other publications that had followed in its wake (Humphrey 1981, 1982).[8] The affidavits sworn on behalf of the Attorney General showed that he had taken more than a passing interest in what he attributed to the effect of the booklet and had apparently been spurred into activity by one rather unusual case.

The suicide of Robert McLeod at Claridge's Hotel at the age of twenty-two had nothing to do with self-deliverance. He was an intelligent and articulate young man who decided on quasi-philosophical grounds that he did not intend to go on living. He was apparently one of the first to utilize the booklet, although his age, if correctly stated, would have disqualified him from obtaining it. After his death, inquiries made of various police forces showed that over a period of eighteen months after the first distribution of the booklet, there were fifteen cases of suicide linked to the booklet and nineteen in which the booklet was thought to have been used but was not found.

One reassuring item of information was that in deciding to seek a declaration from the High Court, the Attorney General had decided that "it would not be right" to bring criminal proceedings in respect to acts done by the defendants in distributing the booklet before the decision of the High Court was made known. It was conceded that in many of the cases linked with the booklet the sufferings of the person committing suicide were pitiable. Using the High Court proceedings to wipe the slate clean was probably as much a relief to the Attorney General as it was to the defendants.

The issues placed before the court were in the form of general propositions unrelated to the actual facts. In its final form the "relief" sought by the Attorney General was a declaration that it would be an offense contrary to Section 2 of the Suicide Act of 1961 for any person intentionally to assist another who later commits or attempts to commit suicide by supplying that person with the booklet known as *A Guide to Self-Deliverance* with the knowledge that either that person wishes to be informed of the methods of suicide or the booklet will increase the likelihood of suicide.

Counsel for Exit committee members argued that, if it was appropriate to grant a declaration, it should be that no offense would be committed if the publisher or supplier of *A Guide to Self-Deliverance* had no knowledge that the recipient presently intended suicide or if the publisher or supplier lacked an intention to persuade a particular recipient to commit suicide or where the publication of the booklet was unlikely to precipitate suicide or suicidal attempts.

Counsel's primary submission was, however, that it was for the criminal courts to interpret and apply the criminal law so that it was not a proper matter to be the subject of a declaration made in a civil court. The judge substantially agreed with this contention, and he therefore refused to make any declaration and awarded costs against the Attorney General. But he added that in the course of his judgment he might be making some useful observations. Although nothing he said could be regarded as absolutely binding on a judge hearing a criminal cause, his views would inevitably be considered the clearest guide to the law available.

It was not for the judge to air his personal views on voluntary euthanasia, and Mr. Justice Woolf remained suitably inscrutable. But he was certainly prepared to give the booklet its due, saying,

Justice requires that I should make it clear that there has been no suggestion made on behalf of the Attorney General that if it is lawful to distribute a booklet of this nature there is anything objectionable about the form or contents of this particular booklet.... If it is appropriate to have distributed a booklet dealing with this subject then this booklet provides as satisfactory a treatment as it would be possible to devise.

The judgment runs to twenty-six pages. The judge considered the words "aiding and abetting" and "counselling or procuring" taken as a whole to indicate a person who is an accessory before the fact (i.e., before the offense is committed). He accepted the view that the conduct of an alleged accessory should indicate "(a) that he knew the particular deed was contemplated and (b) that he approved or assented to it and (c) that his attitude in respect to it in fact encouraged the principal offender to perform (. . . or attempt to perform) the deed."

The judge further said,

The fact that the supply of the booklet could be an offence does not mean that any particular supply is an offence. . . . Is it therefore enough that in any particular case the person responsible for making the supply would appreciate that there is a real likelihood that the booklet is required by one of the substantial number of members of the Society who will be contemplating suicide? It is this aspect of the case in respect of which I find the greatest difficulty."

In the end the judge summarized his conclusion as follows:

Before an offence can be established to have been committed it must at least be proved:
(a) that the alleged offender had the necessary intent, that is he intended the booklet to be used by someone contemplating suicide and intended that person would be assisted by the booklet's contents or otherwise encouraged to attempt to take or to take his own life
(b) that while he still had that intention he distributed the booklet to such a person who read it
(c) in addition, if an offence under Section 2 is to be proved, that such a person was assisted or encouraged by so reading the booklet to attempt to take or to take his own life. Otherwise the alleged offender cannot be guilty of more than an attempt.[9]

The judgment showed that the committee and senior officers of Exit were at considerable risk of prosecution if they continued to distribute the booklet to anyone who requested it. Of course, applicants could have been asked to supply written and signed statements to the effect that they were not contemplating suicide (and the statements might well have been true in the great majority of cases). When the current print run of the booklet ran out, however, there was no reprinting. Exit reverted to its former title, the Voluntary Euthanasia Society, an organization devoted to securing legislation. (However, in October 1989, the society revived "Exit" as an alternative, shorter title to be used concurrently with "Voluntary Euthanasia Society.")

There was another reason for the change of name and renewal of image. During the same eventful years covered by the birth and death of the *Guide of Self-Deliverance*, Exit was also having a share of publicity down at the Central Criminal Court. The general secretary, who had more or less taken command of the Society from October 1980, had embarked on what lawyers called "a frolic of his own," that is, enterprises undertaken while occupied with the business of the Society but outside the scope of his employment. Unwilling to wait for the slow processes of Parliament to bring relief to sufferers who wanted to die, he set about providing a private relief system. When people rang the society begging (as they sometimes do) for someone to help them end their lives, he would send them a helper equipped with capsules and plastic sack. The helper was a more than eccentric elderly member who, incidentally, claimed to be a psychic with a spirit guide called "Dr. Arthur." He was a great talker, and anyone with an average degree of innate caution would not have chosen him as an accomplice. Moreover, some serious misjudgments were made about the sort of people suitable to receive this specialized service. The inevitable result of all this activity was that both were charged with offenses under the Suicide Act 1961 and convicted.

The judge gave the helper a suspended sentence after taking into account the year he had spent in prison awaiting trial. The secretary was sentenced to two and one-half years' imprisonment, reduced on appeal to eighteen months. He served twelve months in an open prison but came out to find that the Society was in effect under new management and that he was considered too dangerous an ingredient to add to a pot that was already having heat applied to it by the attorney general. It is one of the most cautionary tales in the history of the cause.

On the very same day that the *Times* reported the alleged activities of "Dr. Arthur" (the spirit guide) in attempting to bring comfort to those who had asked for his services, and even on the same page of the *Times* (October 15, 1981:3), there was another report of a different trial involving a *real* Dr. Arthur. This Dr. Arthur had come to the conclusion that there was no prospect of a tolerable life for a badly handicapped newborn baby with Down's Syndrome who had been repudiated by the parents, and it was alleged by the prosecution that he had taken steps to ensure that the baby did not continue to live. It was not at all clear how far it was denied that various forms of action or inaction contributed to the baby's death, but the representatives of the medical profession had nothing but praise for a caring doctor and he was acquitted to the general satisfaction of the people.

The coincidence of these two trials might also constitute evidence of a guiding hand engineering human affairs so as to throw up interesting contrasts. Doctors are most unlikely to be charged, convicted, punished, criticized, or disciplined. As long as they do not arrange for a large inheritance, hardly anyone seems to think the worse of them for whatever they may have done. Anyone other than a doctor who assists the deliverance of a stranger (meaning a person to whom one is not bound by emotional ties or family responsibilities) will be treated with rigor, little credit being given to reflect the fact that the crime was undertaken out of altruism, to relieve the suffering of another person, and out of a conviction that the act was morally justified. If anything, this last consideration probably inflames judges into harsher sentencing, for the idea that it would be morally justifiable to flout the law amounts to an affront and an implication that the judge makes a living by upholding unjust and morally offensive laws.

Coming somewhere between the personal and the impersonal was the rather unusual case resulting in the trial of author Charlotte Hough (*Voluntary Euthanasia Society Newsletter* 1984). Out of general kindliness she used to visit an otherwise friendless Miss Harding, now blind and nearly deaf, who earnestly wished to die and persuaded Mrs. Hough to help her. Miss Harding was well able to take the required barbiturates herself, and Mrs. Hough, who hoped and believed that the capsules would take effect fairly soon, promised that she would sit with Miss Harding until she was dead. Time went by, however, hours passed and passed, and Miss Harding continued to live. Rather than go back on her promise, Mrs. Hough felt obliged to finish the job by placing a plastic sack over Miss Harding's head and shoulders, following Miss Harding's detailed instructions given on the assumption that this might prove necessary. And so the promise was fulfilled.

Unfortunately for Mrs. Hough, she told someone about this incident, and he thought it appropriate to pass her confidence on to a London newspaper. Mrs. Hough soon found herself facing a charge of murder. The outcome was one of those compromises that leaves everyone somewhat relieved that something worse did not happen: Mrs. Hough pleaded guilty to attempted murder (a plea underpinned by the precarious logic of the notion that no one could say for sure whether death was caused by the suicidal capsules or by the homicidal plastic sack). Thus she was able to avoid a life sentence and was sentenced to nine months' imprisonment—another cautionary tale.

The sort of prosecution that frequently comes before the court is one in which a family member, sometimes one who has devoted years to caring for an invalid, is driven to desperation by the spectacle of unending suffering and finally resolves the matter by euthanasia or mercy killing. While some may prefer, and be able, to keep silent about their role, so avoiding any confrontation with the law, others immediately confess, admit their guilt, concede their wrongdoing in breaking the law, and plead that they were suffering from diminished responsibility. The result will be a conviction for manslaughter, and in most cases a suspended sentence, or an even more lenient sentence. Defendants of this sort are also treated very sympathetically by the press. The following extract, headed "Man killed his daughter 'out of love,'" is fairly typical:

A man who smothered his severely handicapped daughter because he feared he was too old to look after her was put on probation at the Central Criminal

Court yesterday. Mr. Justice Alliott told...a retired shopkeeper..., "I am satisfied you did what you did out of love and in the sincere belief that what you
did was in her best interests at a time when your mental health had broken down
after years of devoted care." (*Times* March 19, 1988:3)

But if the defendant had claimed to have acted out of a rational belief
that he was doing right in putting an end to his daughter's suffering,
the judge might have thought that a man who pitted his personal moral
philosophy against the statute book needed to be chastised by a term in
prison. To obtain mercy, it is necessary to admit that there is something
irrational and wrong-headed in being moved to an act of deliverance.

A case that should be mentioned as the supreme example of a non-
event is the nonprosecution of Derek Humphrey following publication
of *Jean's Way* (1978), in which he described a loving act of deliverance
given by him to his first wife with her entire cooperation. This is the
sort of case in which public sympathy is so overwhelmingly on the side
of the deliverer that the authorities may feel very little inclination to step
in, even though writing a book on the subject smacks of defying the law.
Several years after the event, however, when there can be no conceivable
shred of objective evidence available, a book that could in theory be pure
fiction does not provide such a solid base for prosecution as to require
action to be taken.

· The conviction and sentence of Mrs. Hough led to considerable public
comment, and the press in general reflected public disquiet at the state
of the law. The Voluntary Euthanasia Society was once again primarily
directing its efforts to securing legislation. One of its members, Lord
Jenkins, introduced in the House of Lords on December 11, 1985, a bill
that was the ultimate in simplicity. It did not even go so far as to propose
the legalization of voluntary euthanasia; it merely sought to ensure that
the bona fide deliverer would not suffer the fate of Mrs. Hough. The
operative clause of the Suicide Act 1961 (Amendment) Bill is concise
enough to quote in full: "It shall be a defence to any charge under this
Act that the accused acted on behalf of the person who committed suicide
and in so acting behaved reasonably and with compassion and in good
faith." This bill was also lost by forty-eight votes to fifteen, the numbers
taking part showing the surprising lack of interest taken in such matters
of life and death.

The fact that the future for legislation is looking ever bleaker in England while euthanasia becomes ever more a normal part of the medical
scene in the Netherlands suggests a change in direction. There have
recently been initiatives to mobilize the substantial minority of doctors
who would be prepared to take part in euthanasia if permitted to do so
by law. It has been reported that a special committee of the British
Medical Association is "trying to forge guidelines, with terms like 'active

termination of life' or 'non-treatment decision' to describe the ending of a patient's life by a doctor" (Vulliamy 1988). The prospect of AIDS patients' lapsing into dementia may encourage the sharpening of hitherto unfocused minds.

A review of the current scene is incomplete without reference to the Enduring Powers of Attorney Act 1985, a statute that has a practical bearing on the enforcement of patients' right not to be treated against their wills. Prior to this enactment it was always possible for an adult *compos mentis*, or with failing but not yet failed mental powers, to appoint another person (called the "attorney," a word that does not in England imply the status of lawyer) to act on that person's behalf generally or in relation to certain transactions. Like most legal matters, a power of attorney is conceived entirely in terms of assets and financial dealings, but there is no doubt that attorneys can also be given power to make more personal arrangements for their appointors, such as putting them into or taking them out of hospitals, engaging nurses to look after them, and so on. Before the passing of the 1985 Act the power of attorney had a serious (and absurd) disadvantage; if the appointor became mentally incompetent the power lapsed, just when it was most needed. This was corrected by the 1985 Act, making the power a more useful tool. A carefully worded special power could ensure that the attorney would be entitled to enforce the terms of any living will made by the appointor so that, if such a person became too helpless to refuse unwanted treatment or nourishment, the attorney could speak authoritatively for that person. These are largely uncharted waters, and one must say that the utility of a power of attorney is effectively limited because the formalities connected with the preparation, execution, and registration of an enduring power cannot easily be dealt with by the layman.

For the patients, or potential patients, who look forward to their last days, weeks, months, or years with anxiety and apprehension, it will of course be a happy day when deliverance ceases to be the business of lawyers and passes into the hands of medical practitioners, where it belongs. A handful of heroic doctors in various European countries have openly written or broadcast about cases in which they have given euthanasia to sufferers. But there is as yet no sign as to which will be the next country to produce a publication equivalent to *Justifiable Euthanasia—A Manual for the Medical Profession* (English language version) prepared by Dr. P. V. Admiraal at the request of the Netherlands Society for Voluntary Euthanasia some ten years ago.[10] It can be said, however, that in the climate of public opinion, which remains solidly in favor of giving doctors the right to accede to requests for euthanasia, English doctors can be reasonably sure that they will not be prosecuted and, if prosecuted, will be acquitted, to the accompaniment of a chorus of approval from their patients.

NOTES

1. *Market & Opinion Research International* (MORI). Their January 1988 poll commissioned by the World Federation of Doctors Who Respect Human Life (British section) and the Human Rights Society, two organizations strongly opposed to voluntary euthanasia. This is the latest poll on the subject, and (inter alia) the finding that 72 percent of the population are in favor, with only 19 percent against, has given rise to public utterances of dismay by representatives of these organizations.

2. *NOP Market Research, Ltd.* Their March 1987 poll commissioned by the Voluntary Euthanasia Society shows that 45 percent of doctors would or might consider giving euthanasia to a patient who suffered from an incurable physical illness that the patient found intolerable, if the patient made a written request for it. (But only one in three actually favored a change in the law.)

3. This article discusses complex issues regarding consent to treatment of the mentally disturbed, and others.

4. *NOP Market Research Ltd.* Their November 1978 poll commissioned by the Voluntary Euthanasia Society shows 62 percent for and 22 percent against doctors' making means of self-deliverance available.

5. *Euthanasia Society* [sic]. At this date "Voluntary" had been omitted from the title of the Society to ensure that its one entry in the telephone book would be found under E.

6. *NOP Market Research Ltd.* Their September 1976 poll commissioned by the Voluntary Euthanasia Society shows Catholics 54 percent in favor and 33 percent against, as compared with Anglicans (72 percent in favor, 13 percent against) and agnostics (87 percent in favor, 6 percent against).

7. *Regina v. McShane* [1978] 66 Criminal Appeal Reports.

8. Derek Humphrey's book is the most notable and comprehensive of these later publications.

9. *H. M. Attorney General v. Able and Others* [1984] 1 All England Reports 277.

10. *Nederlandse Vereniging voor Vrijwillige Euthanasie*, Amsterdam.

REFERENCES

Criminal Law Revision Committee. *Working Paper on Offences against the Person.* London: HMSO, August 1976.

Devlin, P. *Easing the Passing.* London: Bodley Head, 1985.

Dimond, B. "Filling in the Statutory Gaps with the Common Law—An Analysis of the Mental Health Act 1983." *New Law Journal*, August 17, 1984: 693.

Executive Committee of Exit. *A Guide to Self-Deliverance.* London: Exit, 1981.

Guillon, V., and Le Bonniec, Y. *Suicide: Mode d'Emploi—histoire, technique, actualité.* Paris: Editions Alain Moreau, 1982.

Humphrey D. with Wickett, A. *Jean's Way.* London and New York: Quartet Books, 1978.

Humphrey, D. *Let Me Die before I Wake.* Los Angeles: Hemlock Society, 1981 and 1982.

Mair, G. B. *How to Die with Dignity.* Glasgow: Scottish Exit, 1980.

Times (London). March 19, 1988: 3.
————. October 15, 1981: 3.
Voluntary Euthanasia Society Newsletter 23 (December) 1984.
Vulliamy, E. "Life or Death." The *Guardian*, February 17, 1988.

8 Indian Legal Concepts of the Right to Die

Daya Shanker

Of all the creations of God Almighty in this universe the human being is supreme, endowed with knowledge and strength, yet we have been unable to understand the riddle of the wheel of birth and death. We are born free, but throughout life we are chained in bondage and by limitations, restrictions, and restraints. We have an inborn fundamental right to live; have we then the right to die of our own will and desire?

A society, whether primitive or advanced, ancient or modern, cannot flourish or even survive without prescribing moral standards, norms, and rules for the conduct of human beings as individuals or as units of society, for their relationships with other members of society and other human beings in general. Individualism and egoism have given rise to the exploitation of people and natural resources, and to other antisocial methods. They also gave birth to crime, criminal jurisprudence, and the law.

Later on, the great saints, seers, angels, and philosophers of the ancient developed countries evolved the idea of *dharma* (righteousness; social custom and duty) and religion to hold all human beings together, to safeguard the welfare of humanity, and to maintain the social structure and order. The sociological theory of law was ingrained in these principles of *dharma*. The rich and the poor, the weak and the strong were all equal before the philosophy of *dharma* and religion. The great epic writers and poets were also the acknowledged legislators of the world. In India they preached moral standards, norms, rules, rights, duties, and principles of life and religion in the *Vedas, Upanishads, Puranas, Gita, Mahabharata,* and *Ramayana,* and so on, to be followed in life and upon death by the people. The English poet Shelley in *Epipsychidion* rightly sang:

> We—are we not formed, as notes of music are,
> For one another, though dissimilar...?

After industrial, agricultural, and economic developments, the advancement of science and the Renaissance, people began questioning even the existence of God. They turned materialistic in life and irreligious. Legal concepts were developed, customs and usages established, and laws accordingly framed, for the protection of human rights, persons, and property, liberty and freedom, and for the punishment of their breach. The weak could then prevail against the strong through due process of law.

The U.S. Constitution is the oldest written democratic constitution in the world protecting human rights. The Fifth Amendment to the U.S. Constitution provides that "no person...shall be...deprived of life, liberty, or property, without due process of law." Similar limitations were imposed on the state authorities as well by the Fourteenth Amendment to the U.S. Constitution. In the case of *Munn v. Illinois* (reported in (1876) 94 U.S. 113 at page 142), Mr. Justice Field of the U.S. Supreme Court observed,

By the term "life" as here used something more is meant than mere animal existence. The inhibition against its deprivation extends to all these limits and faculties by which life is enjoyed. The provision equally prohibits the mutilation of the body or amputation of an arm or leg or the putting out of an eye or the destruction of any other organ of the body through which the soul communicates with the outer world.... By the term "liberty" as used in the provision something more is meant than mere freedom from physical restraint or the bounds of a prison.

Relying on the English common law maxim that "every man's house is his castle," the presiding lords in the case of Semayne reported in 1604 propounded protection of property and personal liberty.

The Charter of the United Nations Organization affirms the universal declaration that all human beings are born free and equal. It further affirms that they have inherent dignity and inalienable rights. They are endowed with reason and conscience so as to act toward one another with respect for the right to life, liberty, security of person in a spirit of brotherhood without distinction of race, color, sex, language, religion, political or national or social origin, birth or other status in order to lay the foundation of freedom, justice, and peace in the world. In the exercise of one's rights and freedom, however, the charter emphasizes that everyone shall be subject to such limitations as are determined by law, solely for the purpose of securing due recognition and respect for the rights and freedom of others and of meeting the just requirements of morality, public order, and the general welfare in a democratic society.

Part III of the Constitution of India enshrines the fundamental rights of an Indian citizen. Article 21 of the Constitution clarifies the general principles and provides that "no person shall be deprived of his life or personal liberty except according to the procedure established by law." It applies, however, only to the deprivation of life or personal liberty by the state and not by a private individual.

In the case of *Kharak Singh v. State of U.P.*, reported in *All India Reporter* (AIR 1963 S.C. 1295), the Supreme Court of India held that the word "life" in Article 21 of the Indian Constitution "means not merely the right to the continuance of a person's animal existence, but a right to the possession of each of his organs—his arms and legs etc."

In the case of *Maneka Ghandi v. Union of India* (reported in AIR 1978 S.C. 597), the Supreme Court of India considerably widened the scope of the words "personal liberty." Further, in the case of *Francis Coralie v. Union Territory of Delhi* (AIR 1981 S.C. 746), the Supreme Court of India held that the right to life includes the right to live with human dignity. It is thus the duty of the state to protect the life and property of every citizen of India from unjust, unfair, and arbitrary deprivation by the state to enable that person to live with peace and dignity in a decent manner. There is, however, in Article 21 nothing to forbid or restrict individuals from giving up their lives or dying of their own will.

Before we understand life, the right and desire to live, or the right to die, let us recognize what death is and ask whether we can escape from the clutches of death. It is true that it is not easy to understand death. It is subtle in nature. Death is considered by all creatures as painful and full of woes and yet unavoidable. According to the Hindu Vedantic philosophy, death is not the end of life. It is only the *Sthula Sharira*, the physical body, that dies. It is the *Sukshma Sharira*, also called the *Linga Sharira*, the astral body, that does not perish with the death of the body. The *Sukshma Sharira* is very complex, consisting, among other things, of the life breath of vital principle, mind, *buddhi* (intelligence), and, some philosophers believe, of *Ahankaras* (false ego) also. The impressions of past *karmas* (thoughts and deeds) remain in the *Sukshma Sharira* or astral body and are retained even after the death of the physical body. This astral body leaves the *Bhuloka* (earth plane) after death and goes to *Bhuvarloka Antariksha* (the astral plane) and then to *Svargaloka* (heaven, or the mental plane). The astral body then disintegrates and the components are merged in the Ocean of Energy with the Eternal *Parama Brahma*. Thereafter they return by the will of God to another physical body, and the individual is reborn on this earth in accordance with that person's deeds and *karmas*.

The astral body is divided into *Vijyanmaya Kosha, Manomaya Kosha,* and *Pranamaya Kosha*. The *Ahankaras* (false egos) and desires of *Vijyanmaya Kosha* are the root cause of repeated births and deaths. They are the essence of the wheel of birth and death. Death is the separation for a period of time of the astral body from the physical body. Death is thus the beginning of another life; death is not the end of life.

It would not be wrong to say that there is an imperishable ocean of energy which is *Parama Brahma*. It is infinite and self-luminous, free from births and deaths. We all are droplets or lumps or only parts of that great ocean of energy. This droplet of energy enters our bodies which live a life, act, and enjoy. When the body becomes unfit to live, the droplet of energy leaves the body and enters another. This is called "transmigration of the soul." When the soul enters the body we call it birth; when it leaves the body we say it is death. It is a continuous process. In *Bhagwad Gita* (Chapter 2, shloka 22), as translated by Dr. S. Radha-krishnan, the Lord Krishna says, "Just as a person casts off worn-out garments and puts on others that are new, even so does the embodied soul cast off worn out bodies and take on others that are new."

The eternal does not move from place to place, but the embodied soul moves from one abode to another. It takes birth each time and gathers to itself a mind, life, and body formed out of the materials of nature according to its past evolution, *karmas*, and its need for the future. The psychic being is the *vijnyana* which supports the triple manifestation of body (*anna*), life (*prana*), and mind (*manas*). When the gross physical body falls away, the vital and mental sheaths still remain as the vehicle of the soul. When the sould merges with the Almighty, we call it *Moksha* (salvation). Then the person is not born again but is freed from the phenomena of birth, death, and rebirth.

It is universal to all beings, whether plant, animal, or human, that all grow in space and time, age, later decline, leave material possessions, rot, and then perish. One's entire life cannot be full of joy and happiness forever. By old age the limbs and vital organs of the body become slug-gish and inactive and later fail to work. Serious chronic and incurable diseases often engulf the body with great agony and pain. The bonds of attachment and love of family members, neighbors, and friends loosen and later vanish. Life becomes dull and dry; it is no longer worth living. A state of chaos, despair, and utter helplessness may set in with occasional spells of senselessness. The desire to live vanishes. The person prays for death to come and bring relief from all worldly pains, distress, and agony. The person may go through near-death experiences and feelings, but death may not come.

Can one in these circumstances meet death of one's own will and accord? Has one a right to die? Can a medical practitioner, friend, or family member assist one in meeting death? Do custom, ethics, or religion permit it? Is it a part of tort and the human right of citizens to die of their own will? Is it or is it not a crime with legal punishment? Should the law of the land permit it?

The *Bhagwad Gita* is a religious classic and philosophical treatise that sets forth in precise and penetrating words the essential principles of spirituality, *dharma*, truth, righteousness, and reality in life for all who seek to tread the inner way of the heavens. It states that this world is a *dharmakshetre*, the battlefield for a moral struggle of righteousness, which is produced by the Supreme *Brahma* out of his own nature. This world is not only the body of God but is *Isvarasyasesa*, his remainder. The world and God are one, just as body and soul are one. All human beings and creatures are his ramifications and manifestations.

According to Vedantic philosophy as well, the *Parama Brahma* (God) created the human being. God is present in the soul of the human being. Life is offered to us by him in order for us to offer obeisance to God, to obey *dharma*, to perform duties that are assigned to us, and to tread the path of righteousness. God is the material cause and instrumentality of all joys, happiness, woes, sorrows, deeds, and *karmas* of humanity. Just as he gave life to us, he takes it away from us as well. He is the creater as well as the doer and the destroyer of this body.

Paul Deussen's *The Philosophy of the Upanishads* (1908) interprets Mundak Upanishad 2.1.1 in these words "As the tiny sparks leap forth from the fire, so from this *Atman* [universal self, supreme spirit] all vital spirits spring forth, all worlds, all God, all living creatures." It is *Atman* alone who lies outspread before our eyes as the entire universe.

Lord Krishna in *Bhagwad Gita* (Chapter 8, shloka 15), affirms the Vedantic philosophy: Having come to Me, says Lord Krishna, these great souls do not get back to rebirth, the place of sorrow, pain, non-eternal, for they have reached the highest perfection and bliss. Again in Chapter 9, shloka 7, of the *Gita*, the Lord says (in the words of Dr. S. Radhakrishnan), "All living beings, O Son Kunti, return back into nature which is my own, at the end of the cycle, and at the beginning of the next cycle I send them forth. I recreate them." In Chapter 2, shloka 27, of the *Bhagwad Gita*, the Lord declares that for the one that is born, death is certain; and for the one that has died, birth is certain. Since it is inevitable, one should not grieve. Birth and death are the two ends of life.

This takes us to two different philosophies of death. One asks: If life is given and taken away by the will of God alone and we only obey his commands, do we possess the right to do away with our lives at our will whatever may be our circumstances? We are at the mercy of God; we have to obey his commands. We cannot desire death deliberately even if death is inevitable. The other view asks: If the entire universe and all living beings are nothing but the manifestations of God himself and if the world is not only the body of God but his remainder, if we are only a droplet of energy of the great ocean of energy and will finally merge with that ocean of energy, if we arise from him and upon death return to him again, and if God is in us and we are a part of God, then where is the wrong in meeting death of our own free will and desire at any time we like? Since we will then merge with the Almighty, how can it be an act of sin or crime worth punishment?

The great saints, sages, and seers of India from time immemorial have been following the latter law of religious philosophy. They beckoned, welcomed, and met death at will in the later part of their ascetic lives by taking *Samadhi* (complete absorption in God-consciousness) to attain eternal peace and *Moksha*. Many of them were even blessed with the greatest human virtue of *Ichcha Mritya*—commanding death at will. They could not be killed or die otherwise. They were idolized out of reverence and obeisance was made to them. Such saints were worshipped as gods.

In the *Mahabharata* we find that after the victory of good over evil and of *dharma* (righteousness) over *adharma* (sin), and after being freed from obligations and duties to society and the kingdom, both the ancestor and the guru of the *Pandavas* and *Kauravas* beckoned to death and, having *Ichcha Mrityu*, voluntarily died. Many others met death of their own will, including the Lord Rama and his brothers who, after fulfilling their duties and obligations in life, voluntarily gave their lives by taking *samadhi* in the river Saryu in Ayodhya. There were no laws to restrict a saint, seer, or ascetic from taking *samadhi* at will. On the contrary, the practice had religious sanctions. They had the right to die of their own will.

From time immemorial also, the virtuous Aryan women of India had the religious, moral, and social sanction to end their lives on the funeral pyres of their husbands (*sati*). *Sati* was a consequence of the extreme love of the widow for her dead husband or of the desire for the bliss of paradise. It was sometimes committed out of the desire for salvation of the soul or for special social prestige. The spiritual significance of *sati* was stressed in the ancient religious books of the Hindus. *Sati* was said to be a duty and also a right for a Hindu widow to die upon her husband's death. She was idolized and worshipped for committing *sati*. Religious fairs and *yajnas* (sacrifices) were annually or periodically held at such places and *samadhis*. The belief was that if wives died with their husbands the two would never be separated in the heavens or in other lives and rebirths to come.

In Chapter 4 of *Parashar Smriti* and Chapter 10, Mantras 74–76, of *Gautami Mahatma, Brahma Purana,* and *Gurar Purana*, it is prescribed that, if the widow dies on the funeral pyre of her deceased husband, she develops the power to carry her husband away from hell and to live with him in the heavens with all pleasures and happiness for three and a half *crores* (ten million) of years. It is further said that she will be respected and worshipped like Sanyasin Arundhati, the wife of the great saint Rigsi Vashishti. Sanyasin Arundhati met her death by *sati* on the funeral pyre of her deceased husband, and, by her powers and the virtues of *sati*, she can now be seen shining like a star near the Galaxy of the Seven Stars.

In *Maharshi Balniki Ramayana, Ayodhyakand* 66/12, we find that upon the death of the great Dasharatha, Lord Ram's father, his wife wanted to die along with her husband but was not permitted to do so. In *Mahabharata Adiparva* 125/19 we read that King Pandu's wife Madri died on his pyre. The four wives of Lord Krishna's father voluntarily burned themselves upon their husband's death (*Mausal Parva* 7/18), and the wives of Lord Krishna also died with their husband (*Mausal Parva* 7/73 and *Vishnu Puran* 5/38/2). According to *Bhagwad Puran* 1/13/57, King Dhritrashtra's wife Gandhari burned herself along with her husband's dead body.

Only widows who were pregnant at the time of their husband's death or who had infant children were prohibited from committing *sati*. A *Kshatriya* widow invariably committed *sati* upon her husband's death. If a king was defeated in war and there was a chance that the women of the palace would be molested or not respected, the womenfolk were permitted to commit *jauhar* (suicide) by jumping into a fire within the palace in order to save their honor and chastity. *Sati* was a must for *Kshatriya* widows or women during war, but it was not universal for all. It was optional for widows of other communities, such as *Brahmins, Vaish*, and *Shudras*. They could either commit *sati* or *jauhar* or live a very pious and ascetic life with restrictions as prescribed in religious books. In certain states, they could even remarry in special circumstances, but only their husbands' younger brother (called *devar*). This option for widows, however, came into vogue later as a result of the impact of Buddhism on Hindu society in India. Many such women turned Buddhist after the deaths of their husbands, to save themselves from cruelty and torture.

In fact, the ancient Hindu religious scriptures, social order, and customs prescribed very severe and barbarous restrictions on widows. This made their lives so miserable that they lost all hope of leading lives of dignity and self-respect. For them life was made worse then hell. The widow was not allowed to take salt in food for at least one year after her husband's death and could partake of only one austere meal a day throughout the remainder of her life. She was made to sleep on a mattress without bedding on the floor and could not wear ornaments or colorful dress, scent, cosmetic articles, or makeup. She had to live a secluded life as a *sanyasin* (one who has renounced the world). Widows were made to roam like the living dead. They were insulted, tortured, suffered social ostracism, and were left completely at the mercy of their sons and relatives. In poor families they were even forced to lead ignoble lives. This was all done if the widow failed to join her husband on the funeral pyre. For this reason a widow would often burn herself to death rather than live a cruel widowed life. The agony of a few moments in the fire was considered less painful than the misery of physical, mental, and pyschological suffering during her remaining widowed life. Once their husbands and lords were no more, widows had nothing left to live for. They had no alternative but to embrace death, whether under duress or through their own will, for love of their husbands or for the bliss of heaven in accordance with religious tenets.

Another reason for this so-called right of the widow to die was the law of inheritance prevalent in those days among the Hindus. In Bengal, according to the *Dayabhaga* school of inheritance, the widow had rights to her deceased husband's property which barred the claims of his father, mother, brothers, sisters, and daughters. This custom inspired the other members of the family to compel the widow to die by committing *sati* in order to prevent her from being the sole successor. In states where the *Mitakshara* school of law prevailed, however, the surviving widow's rights in her husband's property were circumscribed. It enjoined property distribution among all the successors of the deceased, of whom the widow would be only one. In these states the practice of *sati* or of the widow dying with her husband was a rare phenomenon.

Gradually people began to take offense at the brutal way in which widows were compelled to be burned on the funeral pyres of their deceased husbands. Social reformers protested, Lord Bentinck outlawed *sati* in 1829, but the practice continued, especially in Rajasthan. Recently, in 1987, when a newly married woman named Roop Kanwar committed *sati* in Rajasthan on the pyre of her husband, a great hue and cry was raised by the womenfolk and the people in general. The country was badly shaken. The result was that on January 3, 1988, the Commission of Sati (Prevention) Act of 1987 (Act No. 3 of 1988) was promulgated in India. By this law the widow's right to die either of her own will or under compulsion on the pyre of her husband was prohibited. The attempting, abetting, and glorification of *sati* were all declared punishable by a range of penalties that could include life imprisonment or even the death sentence.

In 1860 the government of India codified the India Penal Code (IPC). Under section 309 of the IPC, the attempt to commit suicide and (under section 306), the abetting of suicide were made punishable by imprisonment. The act of committing suicide, when successful, is not and cannot be regarded as a crime in India, but if unsuccessful it is a crime punishable under the law. In a case reported in AIR 1914 Allahabad 249, a division bench of the Allahabad High Court, held that in a case in which some people gave a widow ghee which she used to pour over her husband's funeral pyre and burn herself, such accused persons were guilty of abetting suicide. In another case reported in 1919 Allahabad

376, the High Court held that, where a woman driven almost frantic by the pains of prolonged labor during childbirth attempted to take her own life and as a result her infant was born dead, she was guilty of attempting to commit suicide. But in another case reported in AIR 1934 Lahore 514, it was held by the erstwhile Punjab High Court that, if a person on account of family discord, destitution, loss of a dear relation, or other cause of a like nature overcomes the instinct of self-preservation and decides to take his or her own life, it is not necessary to inflict a sentence of imprisonment on that person under Section 309 IPC.

The law of homicide is contained in sections 299 and 300 of the IPC. If there is culpable homicide amounting to murder, the punishment is life imprisonment or even the death sentence. In cases of culpable homicide not amounting to murder, there is a reduced punishment. There are, however, several exceptions provided in the Act.

Among Jains also there is a religious festive period called *Sanlekhana*. During this period, according to religious tenets, a Jain is to fast and to perform certain rituals. He may also abstain from drinking water during each day of *sanlekhana* (as in the Hindu *kāyakalpa*). There is a belief that if a Jain dies during *sanlekhana*, he achieves Nirvana. Some Jain saints and men have given up their lives during *sanlekhana*. A religious sanction permits Jains to end their lives by their own will for the bliss of Nirvana or for a better future in the other world or in the next birth to come.

In modern times we know of Acharya Vinobha Bhave, the great disciple of Mahatma Gandhi. Having grown old and being satisfied with his service to humanity, he felt it was time for him to die. In 1983 he voluntarily stopped taking food, medicine, and water. Persuasions by great Indian leaders and personal requests by Indira Gandhi, then prime minister of India, did not dissuade him. He died of his own wish on the auspicious Dipawali day. His act was not regarded as suicide; no criminal action was taken by the state to protect his life.

The other modern case is that of Gopal Shriram Mandlik of Pune, a retired government servant. At 85 years of age, he felt he had enjoyed life well and in old age was facing problems that took away the joy of life. He decided to end his life voluntarily. Considering the criminal laws of the country and perhaps the punishment for the offense of suicide under Section 309 of the Indian Penal Code, he wrote several letters to the state government of Maharastra, the government of India, their ministers, and some members of Parliament in which he asked for permission to die voluntarily. The laws of India being silent on the matter, no one responded to his request. Finally, Mandlik took poison and gave up his life.

The latest case is that of Justice Shashi Kant Varma, retired chief justice of the Allahabad High Court. He was an eminent jurist and a sportsman endowed with vigor and strength even at 70 years of age. He had all the pleasures and blessings in life with health, wealth, fame, and children highly placed in life. He had no unfulfilled ambitions and was fully satisfied and relieved of his responsibilities and obligations. In 1988 he was treated for cancer and recovered. He felt, however, that life no longer held charm for him and was no longer worth living. He decided he had the right to die. One fine evening he retired to his room and fired a shot into his head from his own pistol, thus voluntarily ending his life. It was not a sin or a crime.

During the long war of independence in India against British imperialist rule, many sons, daughters, and nationalist leaders of India offered their lives. They met death, sometimes on the gallows, of their own will for the independence of their motherland. Bhagat Singh, Raj Guru, and Sukhdeo are some of them. There are many others who preferred death rather than to continue to live as slaves. Such martyrs are worshipped by the people and nation of India. They had the right to die for their country. Why then should not others be granted the same right after independence, either for their country or for their own bliss in heaven or for peace?

Since the advancement of science and the development in the world of modern technologies in the medical field, transplantation of vital organs of the human body has become common. The law in advanced countries as well as in India has permitted human beings during their lifetime to donate their kidneys and, after death, their eyes, hearts, and certain other organs for the benefit of others whose organs have failed. The right to donate parts of the human body is an effective and meaningful legal right in the modern world. The process of transplantation of vital organs is hazardous. Donors may lose their lives during the process or afterwards as a result of the donation, yet the government has permitted it. If this can be a legal right, why can we not have the right to do away with our entire body and life? Why do we not have the right to die in other circumstances and for other valid personal reasons?

In India, on August 10, 1971, a statute called the Medical Termination of Pregnancy Act 1971 (Act No. 34 of 1971) received the assent of the president of India. This Act provides for the termination of certain pregnancies by registered medical practitioners in India in certain circumstances upon the will and desire of the pregnant woman or, if she is a minor, upon the consent of her guardian. The Act was apparently a measure to control the enormous population growth in India. Explanation II of Section 3(2)(b) of the Act provides that

Where any pregnancy occurs as a result of failure of any device or method used by any married woman or her husband for the purpose of limiting the number of children, the anguish caused by such unwanted pregnancy may be presumed to constitute a grave injury to the mental health of the pregnant woman.

Does not this Act amount to legalizing the murder of a child in the womb at the will of the mother or her guardian? Similarly, explanation I of Section 3(2)(b) of the Act provides for legalizing abortion for a woman or girl who becomes pregnant as a result of rape. The law permits the removal of such pregnancy if she so desires, partly perhaps because an unmarried pregnant girl or woman, even having been raped, will not be accepted by society. Such a girl or woman may not be allowed to lead a decent life with dignity and honor. On the contrary, she will most likely be an object of hatred. But the law does not permit such a woman to die of her own will even though her life has become a hell. Yet if an unborn child can be consciously allowed to meet death under the law, why should not a living person be allowed the same fate and have the same right to die of his or her own will and desire? The law in India is silent on the matter.

In India the government has prohibited prostitution and punishes a woman involved in it under the provisions of the Suppression of Immoral Traffic in Women and Girls Act. It is well known that normally no person of status and dignity in society is prepared to grant a prostitute a happy and honorable life by marrying her. Since the prohibition of prostitution, these women have no source of livelihood. Prostitutes, generally illiterate, cannot get employment. Further, no family allows a prostitute to do the household work in the family. Thus all doors to earning a livelihood are closed, and the woman is left to lead a life of ignominy, helplessness, and shame. If in these circumstances a prostitute desires to die, the state does not permit her to do so. Is it not a great dilemma for the people and government to solve?

Further, although beggary in India has been prohibited by statute, the government has not provided proper and sufficient rehabilitation centers for beggars. They are disabled and illiterate and are left to lead miserable lives without any source of income. If such a person desires to die to be relieved of great mental agony and humiliation, the law is surely not going to permit it.

There are cases in which men found guilty of murder, dacoity (armed robbery as part of a gang), and other heinous offenses have been sentenced to death, but for one reason or another the infliction of the death penalty has been postponed for years. The condemned are thus made to languish for years in isolated prison cells, segregated from other prisoners and from their family members and friends. These criminals know that life for them is limited; they await death. The fear of death hangs over them for years and causes great mental tension and anguish. Yet the law in India does not permit even such condemned criminals to meet their own deaths as a result of their own will. Because they are criminals they have no right to die, although in similar circumstances of injury to mental and physical health a woman is permitted to end a pregnancy and kill an unborn child.

In every religion of the world sinners have been granted the right to confess sins, to beg pardon, do penance, and bear the punishment awarded for those sins by their guru or God. There are cases in which a person has committed murder but escapes legal punishment. Yet the murderer's conscience is troubled; the mind regrets and repents and the soul is in anguish and feels that it has no right to live. The criminal desires to do penance by ending his or her life for the peace of soul and mind and requests the state for permission to commit suicide. I am sure the state would not permit one to die in the way one desires. People have no liberty to inflict the punishment of death upon themselves in the manner they desire. In India the state has enjoined upon itself the legal obligation to safeguard the life of every human being, whether of a gentleman, sinner, or criminal. The law takes its own course to award punishment to such people by those in authority.

We also have before us the cases of patients who suffer from grave incurable diseases. They suffer unbearable pain and agony; they have no hope of recovery. Life for them is no longer worth living. From the depths of their hearts, they want to end their lives. They request medical practitioners to help them meet their end peacefully, but because of the fear of the law's prohibition, the doctor is helpless and cannot come to the rescue of such persons. Neither the ethics of the medical profession nor the law permits the doctor to help such patients in the act of killing themselves. In a civilized society, it is a crime. Although death at that time would surely grant such persons great relief and peace, the law does not grant them a right to die.

People in the United States and other advanced countries are pleading with their governments to grant the right to die voluntarily under such circumstances. Normally, death under these conditions should not be taken as suicide but as euthanasia. There is much difference between suicide and euthanasia. Religion and *dharma* is many countries permit euthanasia in certain circumstances and at a certain stage of life to attain eternal peace, Nirvana, and *moksha*, but euthanasia was surely not allowed at the costs of moral standards and social order.

We await the day when the law in India and in other advanced countries of the world will come to the rescue of those who live a dreadful life and suffer from mental and physical agony and incurable diseases and have lost all hope of redemption. May the law grant them the liberty and the right to die of their own will, accord, and desire.

REFERENCES

Balmiki, Maharshi. *Ramayana.* Gorakhpur: Geeta Press, 1982.

Besant, A. *The Bhagwad Geeta.* Adyar, Madras: Theosophical Publishing House, 1977.

Deussen, P. (Eng. tr. Rev. A. S. Geden). *The Philosophy of the Upanishads.* Edinburgh: T. & T. Clarks, 1908.

———. (Eng. tr. Rev. A. S. Geden) *The System of Vedanta.* Edinburgh: T. & T. Clarks, 1905.

Radhakrishnan, S. *The Bagwad Geeta.* Bombay: Blackie & Sons (India) Ltd., 1977.

———. *The Indian Philosophy.* Bombay: Blackie & Sons (India) Ltd., 1977.

Shreemad Bagwada Mahapurana (1–13–57), 10th ed. Gorakhpur: Geeta Press, 1982.

9   Active Euthanasia in the Netherlands

Marvin E. Newman

The Netherlands is the only nation in the world that has broadly and legally recognized the right of the individual to choose the manner and time of his or her death. The purpose of this chapter is to discuss how that principle, active voluntary euthanasia, is practiced, how it became legalized in that country, and how the legal and ethical rationale evidenced in Dutch case law justifies the practice. It will also be maintained that the rationale of current case law in the United States bears strong similarities.

Active euthanasia as practiced in the Netherlands must be based on the patient's voluntary decision (Sutorius 1986). Patients may, by means of a written document, unequivocally set forth their personal wish for the procedure to take place. This request is often made during the course of illness. Additionally, it is not unusual for a physician, after due consideration of the patient's hopeless condition, to suggest the option to the patient. Most physicians, however, do not volunteer this suggestion. Those who do often report that the patient almost always acquiesces and frequently expresses gratitude. Physicians report that patients who choose to terminate their lives with medical assistance usually do so as a result of careful deliberation (Admiraal 1986a).

THE PRACTICE OF EUTHANASIA

In 1987 Maria Van Dyke (her name has been changed to protect her privacy) was a patient in a hospital near Delft (Stitler 1987). She was a 27-year-old school teacher. She learned of her cancer when her dentist noticed an unusual sore on her tongue and urged her to get it checked.

Six months and several surgeries later she had no tongue and parts of her jaw had been cut away. At her hospital bed, she kept a stack of towels she used to wipe the uncontrollable flow of saliva. She couldn't swallow, talk, eat, or drink. Her sole source of nutrition came from a tube inserted into her small intestine through a hole cut into her abdominal cavity.

Maria communicated through her eyes. Sometimes she would glance at the flowers by her bed and seem to marvel at their beauty. Then suddenly she'd become sullen.

At times when her family visited she would lower the towel and begin to speak, only to remember she couldn't. She did this often. After twenty-seven years, it was hard to remember—harder to forget.

Maria would write. The pad of paper and pencil she kept by her bed told what her eyes couldn't. "I'm in pain," she wrote on several occasions, "I want to die."

Her physician and nurses received Maria's notes and witnessed the pain. As did many patients, she pleaded with them to make it stop.

After several weeks, her physician acquiesced. There were family farewells in her hospital room and a minister prayed with her. Then the nurses talked with Maria and said their good-byes. Only her physician, a nonattending physician, and a nurse remained. Her physician laid his hand on her arm. He leaned close to her and said softly, "You are about to go on a journey. I do not know where this journey will take you. But I do know you will never have any more pain." With that he reached over and kissed Maria on the forehead. "Do you need anything else before you go?" he asked her. She motioned for her pad and pencil. She scribbled out her last message and handed it to him. The note said, "Thank you." The procedure began.

The act was done intravenously (as are about half of euthanasia procedures). The physician injected her with a barbiturate that caused her to fall into a deep sleep within three minutes. A second barbiturate put her into a deep coma. The third barbiturate stopped her heart. The process took less than ten minutes.

Many patients choose to die at home or by another method. In any case, euthanasia must be administered by a licensed physician. Barbiturates plus Diazepal (an anti-Parkinson drug) combined with alcohol and water are among the mixtures prepared by the pharmacist at the direction of the physician, to be administered nonintravenously. The physician brings the mixture to the patient. The patient will drink it and usually within minutes will fall asleep. In less than one hour respiration and heart function will cease. There is no pain.

On some occasions the patient retains the material for possible future use rather than drinking it immediately.

HOW ACTIVE EUTHANASIA BECAME LEGAL IN THE NETHERLANDS

Under the Dutch criminal code, active euthanasia is expressly illegal. Only in case law has the procedure been legalized.

The Judicial System in the Netherlands

The Dutch legal system derives from Roman law. It is a civil law–oriented system. Judges in the Netherlands are appointed for life by the Queen and their independence is guaranteed by the Constitution. There is no trial by jury in any case. Unlike common law systems, Dutch law does not rely on case precedent. The Dutch Supreme Court cannot overrule the laws of the Crown and Parliament. The judges' primary latitude is in interpreting the statutory and constitutional law.

The public prosecutor's office is in charge of the prosecution of criminal offenses. It possesses a discretionary freedom of action and has autonomous power in its ability to drop or not prosecute cases if it considers this to be in the public interest. There is no grand jury system. Approximately 80 percent of the alleged criminal offenses that come to the prosecutor's notice are not prosecuted.

All euthanasia cases are referred to the prosecutor (and in special cases to the minister of justice, who heads all the offices of prosecution in the Netherlands). In 1982, 1983, and 1984 twenty-eight out of thirty-six euthanasia cases were never brought to trial. Of these thirty-six cases, four were discussed personally by the prosecutor involved with the minister of justice.

Prosecutors often work closely with the Office of Medical Inspectors, an agency that controls the quality of health care. Its investigation often results in convincing the prosecutor that the act was appropriate according to current ethical medical practice. Then usually no further action is taken by the prosecutor's office.

The Schoonheim Decision

Marie Barendregt was an independent, strong-willed individual who lived an active life until 1976, when she moved to a center for the aged near her home in the Netherlands (Sutorius 1986). At the time she was eighty-nine years old. Her decision to move to the home was based on her realization that the infirmities of old age required that she have assistance in the conduct of her daily affairs. She was finding it difficult to walk—both her vision and hearing were becoming impaired. She reported having dizzy spells.

Four years after her admission to the center she signed a declaration directing her doctor, Dr. Schoonheim, to avoid using extraordinary procedures to keep her alive. On several occasions she had requested the physician to terminate her life by medical means but he had declined.

On one occasion Mrs. Barendregt fell and fractured her hip. She would not consent to surgery unless the physicians would guarantee that she would not survive the surgery. The surgeons refused to operate. She was transferred to a critical care area of the hospital, where her physical condition worsened. She became almost totally bedridden. Walking was impossible and she could not sit up. Her speech became impaired and it was difficult, if not impossible, to understand her.

Mrs. Barendregt was permanently catheterized and totally dependent on the nursing staff for almost all bodily functions, including nourishment, bathing, and evacuation of the bowels. At all times she remained coherent and fully conscious. She continued her requests to her doctor to perform active euthanasia.

At times she was able to communicate with the medical care team and with members of her family. She continuously indicated that she wanted to die and that life was an intolerable burden for her.

Finally she asked her only child, a son, to ensure that she would be medically put to death. She repeated this request to her physician and to the nurses. Several days later, after the physician had discussed the matter fully with his patient and with her son, two independent physicians, and the nursing staff, Dr. Schoonheim agreed to Mrs. Barendregt's request.

Several days later, after she had continuously reaffirmed her position, Mrs. Barendregt's son and daughter-in-law said their farewells to her and she expressed her gratitude to them and to her physician for their compliance with her wish. She spoke to her son and daughter-in-law about arrangements for cremation and named some of her friends to whom she wished to express gratitude for their concerns.

Dr. Schoonheim and his assistant again asked their patient if her wishes were still to die. She confirmed: "If it can be done, please do it at once, doctor, quickly, not one night more." The physicians briefly left the room to enable the family to say one last goodbye.

About fifteen minutes later the physician gave Mrs. Barendregt an injection that put her into an immediate and deep sleep. About ten minutes later she was given another injection that sent her into a deep coma, and about eight minutes later she was given a final injection. Five minutes later there was respiratory arrest and she died.

In all probability little more would ever have been said about Maria Barendregt's case, especially had Dr. Schoonheim issued the usual certificate of death showing that she died from natural causes. Dr. Schoonheim refused to do that. Instead, he advised the medical examiner that her death had been caused by the fatal injections that he had administered.

These acts led to the prosecution of Dr. Schoonheim. The district court acquitted him on the ground that his conduct could not be termed illegal. The rationale of the decision rested on the physician's expressed honest beliefs about his duty to his patient. The court noted that he did not act with criminal intent. The prosecutor appealed.

The Court of Appeals reversed the earlier decision. Dr. Schoonheim was found guilty of violating the Dutch criminal code. The court reasoned that the Homicide Act provided that active euthanasia was a criminal offense in the Netherlands.

Dr. Schoonheim appealed his case to the Dutch Supreme Court. That court quashed the decision of the Court of Appeals. It held that the appellate court should have considered Dr. Schoonheim's defense to the effect that he was subject to a conflict of duties. On the one hand, the physician has a duty as a citizen to follow the law of the land. However, the physician also has a unique duty to his patient, he argued. The defense noted that current ethical medical practice does not require that the patient be kept alive in all instances. Often, relieving the patient from pain and unbearable suffering is a primary duty of the physician to the patient in certain circumstances.

The Supreme Court ruled that the Court of Appeals, giving due consideration to the standards of medical ethics and expertise, should have weighed those conflicting duties and interests. The court reasoned that if Dr. Schoonheim had in fact acted within the current standards of medical ethics, his act could not have been criminal. The court noted that a physician subject to conflicting standards would be guilty of a crime no matter which one he followed. The court remanded the case to the district court of appeals and directed it to consider the merits of the defense. That court, finding that the defendant's act conformed to current ethical current practice, subsequently acquitted Dr. Schoonheim.

The Schoonheim case set the guidelines that courts apply in active euthanasia cases in the Netherlands in determining whether the act is legal or illegal. These guidelines are, first, that there must be clear and convincing evidence of an enduring and well-considered request by the patient. Second, there must be a thorough understanding by the patient of his or her situation based on adequate information. Third, the patient must be in a situation of unbearable, irreversible suffering. Fourth, there must be an absence of reasonable alternatives *from the patient's point of view* (emphasis added). Fifth, the euthanasia must be applied only by a qualified physician after consultation with another physician who concurs in the decision. Finally, due care must be exercised in the review by the physicians of the guidelines and in the performance of the euthanasia itself.

The Schoonheim case places the decision making for euthanasia with the patient and his or her physician. It takes into account the recognition that ethics must go hand in hand with technology and leaves to the medical community the setting of those standards. The latter are always subject to society's approval because of the discretionary power of the public prosecutor and the judicial guidelines. The Schoonheim court was prompted to note the conflict of duties in which a physician may find himself or herself. It might very well be that euthanasia might be justifiable according to current medical practice and appear to be illegal by statute.

The guidelines resulting from case law do not require terminal illness as a prerequisite to active euthanasia. The courts emphasize both the physical and nonphysical aspects of suffering. The courts look at the deterioration of the patient's bodily functions and consider that as a form of pain. The courts consider the issue of death with dignity. For example, in the Schoonheim case the court inquired whether Mrs. Barendregt would no longer be able to die in a dignified way. The courts also require that the euthanasia decision be made only by the patient: Substituted judgment is expressly rejected.

After the Schoonheim case two district courts acquitted physicians in active euthanasia cases using the Schoonheim guidelines. In a subsequent case, one court convicted a physician, but it was clear that the physician had not followed the Schoonheim guidelines. His humane intentions were not successful in defense.

Many argue that, if active euthanasia becomes legal, it will become a matter of daily routine without real and thorough concern for the guidelines. The experience that I have witnessed in the Netherlands leads me to conclude that that is improbable. I have never met a medical doctor in the Netherlands who after performing the act ever appeared indifferent to it. It is a very emotional experience for all concerned and especially for the medical staff and the physician. Medical doctors who have performed the act may remain depressed for days after the action is taken.

Role of the Dutch Voluntary Euthanasia Society

Because of requests to offer help to people wanting active euthanasia but unable to secure the cooperation of their physicians in performing it, an advisory volunteer group was formed in 1975 as part of the Dutch Voluntary Euthanasia Society. It now consists of thirty-five volunteers who work across the country and are supervised by a professional.

The group is usually activated by a phone call initiated by a patient or the patient's family to the society seeking help in the performance of active euthanasia. A volunteer interviews the patient and, in most circumstances, the patient's family. If there is suspicion that the decision for euthanasia is not that of the patient but perhaps is caused by the family or other pressures, the volunteer will insist on talking with the patient on one or more occasions.

Exploratory inquiries are made, such as of the patient's comfort, possible housing problems caused by the patient's illess, problems in care or finance, and concerns about relationships with family and relatives. There are inquiries into the degree of pain and the steps, if any, taken to try to relieve the pain. When the worker is satisfied that all relevant factors have been considered, the patient is encouraged to make or renew a living will.

The volunteer encourages patients to talk with their doctors about their desire for active euthanasia. In many instances, the patient indicates that the attending physician has always been a comfort and may show a fear of alienating the physician. The volunteers then suggest that the patient continue further discussions with the physicians in the hope of reaching a mutually agreeable decision. If not, the society will refer the patient to a physician who will collaborate with the attending physician and help to formulate the appropriateness (or inappropriateness as the case may be) of the patient's decision. Sometimes the patient chooses to dismiss the personal physician and use a physician recommended by the society.

HOW THE CASE LAW DEVELOPED: THE SOCIAL FORCES IN DUTCH SOCIETY

Although the Dutch criminal code contains express language declaring that active euthanasia is a crime, the courts do not interpret those words in the literal sense. There are only seven cases out of approximately 300 reported cases of active euthanasia since 1973 in which Dutch courts have addressed the issue. Nevertheless, the result did not occur suddenly; rather, the courts took a step-by-step approach.

There was much public debate about the subject beginning in the early 1970s. The Dutch community as a whole discussed the legal and ethical questions that the subject raised. Lawyers, judges, medical doctors, clergy, and most responsible governmental, public, and private organizations addressed the subject. Advocates and opponents pressed their views openly in the press, in public debate, and in Parliament. The community felt the need to examine the ethical and legal problems that advanced medical technology raised.

In the Netherlands, medical doctors are rarely, if every, the subject of malpractice actions by their patients. The physician stands in a unique and exalted position. A great deal of public concern arose when some physicians were standing trial as criminal defendants in cases in which active euthanasia was performed and reported by the physician. The influential Royal Medical Association joined forces with patients' rights groups in asserting the use of voluntary active euthanasia in appropriate circumstances.

There is a unique bond between the physician and patient in Holland, based on an unbridled mutual trust. The practice of so-called defensive medicine doesn't exist and the term "liability" is rarely used when discussing the work of the physician.

In the Netherlands, the influence of the church, and most especially the Catholic Church, became less pressing on the subject. In France, by contrast, the church has taken the course of openly questioning the morality of the practice of voluntary active euthanasia. Germany must cope with the taboos created through its history of the Nazi Socialist Party in the 1930s.

In the United States the issue was formulated differently. Those cases that concerned euthanasia were brought usually in the context of living wills or passive euthanasia (e.g., withdrawing extraordinary medical treatment). The concerns of the courts in the United States were whether a living will was valid and whether the competent or comatose patient (by substituted judgment) could direct the withholding or withdrawing of extraordinary measures.

In contrast, the Netherlands is a more homogeneous society and a smaller country. Its citizens have more moderate views with regard to principles of medical ethics concerning the physician-patient relationship. It seems natural then that the Dutch would take up the issue when concerns of terminally ill patients in a state of unbearable suffering are raised.

There have been several hundred cases of active euthanasia in the Netherlands within the last five years. Over 90 percent have never come to trial because after serious investigation by the prosecutors, the decisions indicated that prevailing medical ethics had been followed and that prosecution therefore would not be appropriate.

In all probability more cases of active euthanasia have occurred in that period that have not been reported. Statistics are not accurate because many physicians are still afraid to report the true cause of death (active euthanasia) for fear of prosecution and to avoid the problems that such actions may bring for surviving family members (Admiraal 1986b).

The case law and the public debate that have arisen concerning active euthanasia have led to legislative action. Parliament is now considering two bills that support voluntary active euthanasia. The main text of one of the bills declares that euthanasia shall not be an offense if performed in the context of providing careful assistance to a person who is already dying, enduring unbearable physical or mental suffering, or experiencing suffering as being so. The major difference between this piece of legislation and another one under discussion in Parliament is that in the former the burden would be on the prosecutor to prove that the medical doctor in a given case did not follow the guidelines set down in the earlier case law and did not conform to the ethics of the medical profession. The other bill would place the burden on the physician to prove that there was conformance to those standards.

Two major issues raised by the Dutch cases which are topics of current discussion are: (1) Why did that country resort to active euthanasia? (2) Why could the Dutch not rely on passive euthanasia?

Many physicians fear that excluding active euthanasia as a patient's right and allowing only passive euthanasia might lead to dangerous results. The notion exists that active euthanasia is such an extreme that, in practice, it will be more controlled than passive euthanasia. There is also the argument that pain cannot really be eliminated in all illnesses or even satisfactorily reduced in many. Thus passive euthanasia would not address the issue of unbearable suffering. Active euthanasia as it is performed under case guidelines in the Netherlands is an open act. Many people are involved in it and it must be reported to the prosecutors either before or after it is performed.

There are those who argue that the patient should perform the active euthanasia himself or herself. However, as has been shown in a number of instances, the dying process takes energy and action that many in hopeless situations of terminal illness or unbearable suffering simply cannot, for physical or mental reasons, perform for themselves.

RELATIONSHIPS BETWEEN DUTCH AND U.S. LAW ON EUTHANASIA

Important issues of law, ethics, and public policy have been raised by the Dutch cases. There is a distinct similarity in the rationale of the Dutch courts on the subject of voluntary active euthanasia and the rationale of U.S. courts in cases of passive euthanasia.

Many medical doctors may be willing to assist in carrying out a patient's informed and competent choice of euthanasia, but laws criminalizing active participation in suicide deter doctors from providing such assistance. Consequently, the possibility of criminal prosecution inhibits a free and open exchange of information about euthanasia between doctors and their terminally ill patients. Inadequacy of information about the euthanasia option in the United States prevents the vast majority of terminally ill patients from exercising their right of self-determination and infringes on their privacy rights.

The Constitutional right to privacy, as established by the U.S. Supreme Court in a series of cases culminating in the 1973 decision on abortion, *Roe v. Wade* (1973), protects the individual's fundamental right to self-determination. This protection is particularly important in areas of moral controversy such as abortion, contraception, and euthanasia, where the right to privacy acts to protect private decision making in personal matters.

Courts have extended the right to privacy to include the right of a terminally ill patient to refuse treatment, concluding that the individual patient's interests outweight those of the state. These cases balance an individual's right to self-determination and relief from the "traumatic cost" of prolonged life against such state interests as protecting the sanctity of life. Upholding the right of a terminally ill leukemia patient to refuse chemotherapy treatments, the Massachusetts Supreme Court, in *Superintendent of Belchertown State School v. Saikewicz* (1977), stated,

> The constitutional right to privacy . . . is an expression of the sanctity of individual free choice and self-determination as fundamental constituents of life. The value of life as so perceived is lessened . . . by the failure to allow a competent human being the right of choice.

The New Jersey Supreme Court expanded on this balancing analysis in a 1985 decision upholding a terminally ill patient's right to refuse life-sustaining medical treatment. The court stated that the most important state interest limiting this right is the preservation of life, which embraces the two separate but related concerns of an interest in the life of a particular person and an interest in preserving all life (*In re Conroy* 1985). The state's indirect and abstract interest in preserving the life of a competent patient should generally give way to the patient's much stronger personal interest in directing the course of his or her own life.

These decisions logically extend the *Roe v. Wade* doctrine's protection of a competent individual's right to make decisions about personal and moral matters to that individual's decision to refuse treatment. They reflect judicial recognition of the value of human dignity.

Similarly, courts should apply the *Roe* doctrine to protect a competent, terminally ill patient's request for voluntary active euthanasia. If the right to privacy protects the right to die naturally, it should also protect the competent terminal patient's right to choose a quick and painless death. The difference between a terminal patient's choosing to refuse treatment and choosing a faster means of dying does not offer a basis for a legal distinction. When a competent terminal patient chooses to die, the state interests balanced against that patient's right to privacy are virtually the same regardless of the means chosen. In fact, applying the *Roe* doctrine to decisions made for incompetent patients by others is far more difficult to justify and creates the risk of abuse. Self-determination by definition does not encompass decisions made for an individual by a third party. In contrast, a competent terminal patient's right to choose the time and manner of death fits squarely within the right to privacy doctrine and should be given effect unless there exists a compelling state interest in preserving the patient's life.

In cases in which the terminal patient is unable to end his or her life without another party's assistance, the other party's activities should also come within the constitutional penumbra of protection. Where the Constitution protects an individual's rights, it also protects from criminal sanction second parties whose assistance is necessary in exercising those rights. Constitutional protection extends to third parties whose action is necessary to effectuate the exercise of that right where the individual in question would not be subject to prosecution or the third parties are charged as accessories to an act which could not be a crime. A second party has standing to assert the constitutional rights of another when the second party's intervention is necessary to protect the other party's constitutional rights. Doctors assisting terminal patients in voluntary active euthanasia should be able to defend against prosecution by asserting the patient's constitutional right to self-determination. In many instances, without such assistance, voluntary active euthanasia for terminal patients would be impossible.

The constitutional right to privacy protects a competent terminal patient's right to determine the time and manner of death. Recognition of the right of self-determination is the underlying concept of a community not based on force. Such a community can be termed an ethical community in that it is grounded on rationality and peaceful manipulation rather than force. An ethical community will not allow the use of force to impose certain views on individuals against their wishes. This view undergirds a peaceful accommodation to the fact that there is a pluralism of moral beliefs. Although it may be impossible to agree on what constitutes a good death, each individual should be allowed to make a personal choice as long as the choice does not involve direct violence against others. It should not be presumed that individuals have delegated authority to the state to prevent them from making intensely personal individual choices. The guarantees afforded such individuals by the Constitution compel no other conclusion.

Finally, the reasoning of the Dutch courts is equally applicable to the United States. Current view in this country regarding the physician's duty to his or her patient has been reaffirmed in U.S. law:

Prevailing medical ethical practice does not, without exception demand that all efforts toward life prolongation be made in all circumstance. Rather, as indicated in Quinlan, the prevailing ethical practice seems to recognize that the dying are more often in need of comfort than treatment (*Satz v. Perlmutter*, 1978).

REFERENCES

Admiraal, P. V. 1986a. "Euthanasia Applied at a General Hospital." *The Euthanasia Review* 97(2).
————. 1986b. "Active Voluntary Euthanasia." In A. B. Downing, ed. *Voluntary Euthanasia: Experts Debate the Right to Die.* Atlantic Highlands, NJ: Humanities Press International.
Conroy, In re. 1985. *Atlantic Reporter Second Series* 486:1209.
Roe v. Wade. 1973. *United States Supreme Court Reports* 410:113.
Satz v. Perlmutter. 1978. *Southern Reporter, Second Series* 362:160.
Stitler, D. 1987. "Dying for a Cause." *Rollins Alumni Record* 65(3).
Superintendent of Belcherton State School et al. v. Joseph Saikewicz. 1977. *Massachusetts Reporter* 373:728; *Northeastern Reporter, Second Series* 370:417.
Sutorius, E. 1986. *How Euthanasia Was Legalized in Holland.*

10   Last Rights: The View from a U.S. Courthouse

Arthur S. Berger

This book is like a tour of a foreign country in which guides escort visitors to their favorite sites. Others who have written on the subject of withdrawing or withholding medical treatment without which a patient will die have taken us through their special cultural, moral, ethical, theological, philosophical, or medical vantage points. Some have shown the subject from the vantage points of courthouses in India, Britain, and the Netherlands. In this part of our itinerary, readers will accompany me to the top of a U.S. courthouse to get a sweeping overview of the legal points of interest that must not be missed before life-death decisions regarding the medical treatment of a patient in the United States are made.

Never favorite topics for us, death and dying are now the vogue because of the remarkable strides in medical knowledge and technology. Feeding tubes to supply nutrition and hydration, drugs to kill pain, dialysis machines for kidneys that don't work, fibrillators to restore the heartbeat, and respirators to help breathing can be used to keep people alive who would have died just a few years ago. Kept alive, yes, but, for many, under conditions that are degrading and dehumanizing.

Polls have been taken on the question of whether the wishes of incurably ill adults of sound mind ought to govern all health care decisions, even decisions to refuse treatment without which life cannot be sustained. Eighty-one percent of the people polled by Gallup, 85 percent polled by the Lewis Harris organization, and 90 percent polled in 1986 after the ABC television discussion of "Who Lives, Who Dies, Who Decides?" said "Yes."

The people polled expressed a belief that seems eminently clear and correct in a country that prides itself on the right of self-determination. But what happens to that vaunted right in the real world of hospitals, nursing homes, courtrooms, and legislatures, and why? Our tour takes us to nine basic legal questions and concludes with suggestions for preserving individual autonomy and for dealing with a difficult and confused situation.

A RECENT SCENARIO

The following scenario is taken from an actual case decided in 1986.[1] The scene is laid in the New England Sinai Hospital in Massachusetts but could have taken place in any hospital anywhere in the United States. Paul Brophy, a 49-year-old patient, had been a firefighter and medical technician before his operation for an aneurysm that produced a brain hemorrhage. Following surgery, he entered into a vegetative state in which he remained. He was not able to swallow and so a gastrostomy (or G-) tube was inserted into his stomach to provide him with water and food. His wife, Patricia, remembered that her husband had told her ten years before, when they were talking about the case of Karen Ann Quinlan, "I don't ever want to be on a life-support system. No way do I want to live like that; that is not living." Although he did not talk specifically about whether a feeding tube should be removed, Brophy's brothers, sisters, and adult children confirmed that he would not have wished to be kept alive by a tube. Finally, Patricia Brophy decided that her husband's "life was all over" and asked hospital authorities to remove the G-tube. But Brophy's attending physician, Dr. Lajos Koncz, refused to carry out Mrs. Brophy's request. He believed that he would be willfully causing Brophy's death. The hospital medical and nursing staff agreed with the physician on the ground that compliance with the request would be a harmful act deliberately producing death.

Patricia Brophy asked the probate court to withhold or withdraw from Paul Brophy all treatment, including the feeding tube. The court, finding that Brophy might be maintained for several years by the provision of food and water through the G-tube, chose to ignore Brophy's wishes. It reasoned that the treatment to which the patient was being subjected was not highly invasive or burdensome. The court also pointed out that if Brophy had been terminally ill, the G-tube might have been removed. But he was not. The compelling interest of the state in the preservation of life outweighed Brophy's right to refuse treatment.

On Mrs. Brophy's appeal, the Supreme Judicial Court of Massachusetts on September 11, 1986, held that the right of the patient in this case outweighed the state's interest. Although Brophy had not expressed his wishes in writing and was not terminally ill, he could refuse the artificial feeding tube as he could refuse any other medical treatment.

Artificial feeding was another form of medical treatment and, when used to maintain a patient over several years, was "not only invasive but extraordinary." Its removal would not be the cause of death. It only allowed the disease which prevented Brophy from swallowing to take its natural course. The judgment of the lower court was set aside insofar as it denied removal of the tube. But the high court concurred with the lower court's refusal to force the hospital against its ethical principles to take any affirmative steps to remove the tube. Instead, the hospital need only help in Brophy's transfer to another facility where this could be done. He was transferred to Emerson Hospital in Concord, Massachusetts, where he died eight days later.

While this case is confined to situations in which patients had expressed their preferences to forgo life-sustaining treatment prior to becoming incompetent, it merits attention for several reasons. Some will be mentioned later. This case made significant law in relation to the issue of artificial feeding. The case is significant as well because the ruling by the high court of Massachusetts was a 4–3 decision; three of the judges dissented. The case clearly illustrates how sensitive and difficult the situation is and how unclear the problems are in cases of this kind. Lest it be thought that the Massachusetts case is unique in demonstrating a marked lack of judicial unanimity in this area, twelve other recent major right-to-die court decisions either reversed lower or appellate courts or, in the high courts, were not unanimous.[2]

The *Brophy* case is a springboard for posing several important questions:

Question 1: Does a competent adult who objects to medical treatment have the right to refuse it even if that refusal means death?

Under Anglo-American court decisions from the earliest period of English history, which make up the common law, the principle is settled that individuals have a fundamental right of self-determination. All individuals, therefore, are masters of their bodies and, if of sound mind, have the right to decide what shall be done with their bodies and what medical treatment to authorize or prohibit.[3] The well-known *Quinlan* case, in which a young woman in a persistent vegetative state was kept alive by a respirator because the physicians and hospital refused the pleas of the family to terminate ventilator treatment, was the first in which the question of withholding or withdrawing life-sustaining support from a patient was decided.[4] It was also the first to give another basis, besides the common law, for the right to refuse medical treatment without which a life will be terminated. There is no constitutional right to die given in so many words in the U.S. Constitution. But there is a right of privacy, or what is called the right to be let alone, recognized by the U.S. Supreme Court. Although the Constitution does not expressly confer this right, the Supreme Court has interpreted the First, Fourth, and Fifth Amendments and the Bill of Rights as creating the right. In the *Quinlan* case, the court held that the right of privacy included the right to refuse treatment that one did not want and thereby the right to die. The constitutional right of privacy expressed individual free choice and self-determination as basic constituents of life. The value of life is not lessened by the individual's decision to decline treatment but by the refusal to permit a competent adult the right of choice. Judicial decisions in at least seven jurisdictions—California,[5] Colorado,[6] the District of Columbia,[7] Florida,[8] Hawaii,[9] Massachusetts,[10] and New York[11]—that have ruled that adults of sound mind may refuse life-sustaining medical treatment have all been in line with this reasoning.

Protecting the right of refusal is the common law doctrine of informed consent, which means that prior to agreeing to any touching of one's body, an individual must be given information about the proposed touching. Judicial decisions generally hold that, under this doctrine, it is essential for a physician to obtain consent from a patient before starting any procedure or treatment. For a consent to be valid, the physician must give the patient material information about the course of action proposed, the risks of death or harm the procedure may entail, the alternate therapies, and the problems that may arise during the recovery process. Treatment decisions are for the patient and not the doctor and must be based on the provisions by the physician to the patient of such information. If patients have the legal right to consent to a procedure, it is logical that they also have the right to refuse it.

But it is vital that a patient have the ability to comprehend the information provided and to make a rational decision. The right to refuse medical treatment, therefore, is interwoven with the competence of patients, that is, the mental capacity to understand the nature of their physical problems, to appreciate the information furnished, and to come to a rational decision. There is a presumption in the law that adults are competent until proved incompetent. In the real world of the health care institution, however, where physicians make evaluations of decision-making capacity of patients, there is a tendency to discard the legal presumption. The author's experience as a member of a bioethics committee of a large medical center has shown him that physicians do not hesitate to find reasons for questioning the decision-making capacity of patients who disagree with the course of action proposed by the doctors.

Question 2: Does the right to refuse medical treatment include the right to reject the artificial provision of nutrition and hydration?

The question of artificial feeding and the disturbing prospect of withdrawing from a patient what some see as the basic necessity of life arouse sharp divisions of opinion. In recent years, eight states, including the

Massachusetts court in *Brophy*, have answered "yes" to the question just raised. They hold that the artificial provision of food and water differs little from other forms of artificial life-sustaining treatment, such as artificial breathing furnished by a respirator. It is a burdensome form of medical treatment to fight a fatal disease and extends life artificially. Declining it is not an attempt to commit suicide; it only allows the disease to take its course. All patients, whether competent, incompetent, terminally ill, in a persistent vegetative state, elderly, or young, have the basic right to decline artificial feeding.[12] The Missouri Supreme Court, however, in a decision in *Cruzan v. Harmon* that conflicted with other appellate courts and devastated defenders of the rights of patients, refused a request by parents of a woman in a persistent vegetative state to stop feeding through a G-tube which might maintain her for years. In opposition to *Brophy* and other cases, the holding was that the tube was not invasive or burdensome and was not a medical procedure but the supplying of sustenance, which there is a duty both to provide and to accept.[13] The U.S. Supreme Court never before having addressed the constitutional right of a person to refuse life-sustaining treatment, including artificial feeding, the acceptance by the Court of the family's appeal makes this the first right-to-die case to be heard by the highest court in the land. The Supreme Court has now decided the case (see postscript to this chapter).

The debate over artificial feeding, having spread to the legislatures, has prompted some to adopt living will statutes to ensure that the artificial administration of sustenance is not included in the life-prolonging procedures that may be withheld or withdrawn. The courts have ruled, however, that the right to decline artificial feeding, protected by the federal and state constitutions and the common law, cannot be impaired by these statutes.[14] While a patient has the right to refuse medical treatment and decline artificial feeding, however, a court will not compel a recalcitrant hospital and its staff to withhold food and water contrary to its ethical principles. Instead, the hospital will be authorized to transfer the patient to another facility. If a transfer to another facility will cause undue hardship to patients and their families and the medical institution cannot establish that allowing patients to decline artificial feeding will adversely affect other patients in the institution, however, the institution will be required to accede to the wishes of patients to reject artificial feeding.[15]

Question 3: Can liability be imposed on health care professionals who refuse to honor the wishes of patients to reject life-sustaining treatment?

At a right-to-die conference the author organized in 1988 on behalf of the Florida Endowment for the Humanities, one of the main grievances repeatedly presented by members of the audience was that physicians ignore the wishes of patients, whether expressed in living wills or orally, or the wishes of the families of patients not able to express their wishes, regarding life-prolonging medical treatment. In both the *Quinlan* and *Brophy* cases, in which health care professionals would not honor these wishes, the courts did not go into the liability of medical personnel for forcing unwanted medical treatment on patients. The law seems to indicate clearly, however, that the rights of patients to determine and refuse medical treatment supersedes the beliefs, wishes, or interests of doctors, hospitals, or nursing homes.[16] Health care professionals who refuse to follow the living will of a patient may be held liable.[17] Physicians and hospitals are liable in damages for battery when they maintain patients on life-support systems, including artificial feeding, in the absence of an emergency and after patients have expressed specific wishes that their lives are not to be prolonged by such systems. Damages may be for pain and suffering sustained by patients while the life-support systems were maintained against their consent and for the costs of medical care the patients did not want.[18]

Question 4: Can the interest of the state be used to override the right to refuse life-sustaining treatment exercised by competent adults?

It has been repeatedly affirmed by court decisions that there are several exceptions to this right. One exception is that life is sacred and the state has a compelling interest in preserving it. This interest has two aspects. First, there is the abstract concern to maintain and protect the general respect for the sanctity of all life. Yet the state takes lives in war and by capital punishment when its interests seem to require it. Criminal law has always recognized the taking of life as justified if done in self-defense, and under the common law there is no moral obligation and no legal duty to help someone who is in extreme danger. An individual can be struggling in the water and crying for help, but those watching have no duty to act even if the person drowns in their sight.

Second, there is the specific concern the state may have for the particular life of the individual making the decision to refuse treatment that would save or prolong it. This latter concern can be used to override the decision of a patient whose condition is curable or if it is believed that society will be served by such contributions as the patient may make to it. Generally, however, courts will not intervene to preserve the lives of adult decision makers whose afflictions are not curable and who have chosen to refuse life-sustaining treatment and conclude their lives. The right of self-determination normally will outweigh the interest of the state. In the *Cruzan* case referred to earlier and now before the U.S. Supreme Court, the Missouri Supreme Court held, however, that the state's interest in preserving life is absolute and can intrude upon an individual's right to accept or refuse treatment.

Yet the state has an interest in protecting innocent third parties and the economic and emotional well-being of minors. This may be balanced against the interest of a patient who is competent and wishes to die but is pregnant or has a minor child or children. In one case, for example, a patient's refusal of a blood transfusion was overridden because her responsibility to care for her infant was considered greater than her right to refuse treatment.[19] However, it is very difficult to see how the interests of children can be served by a terminally ill parent. In *In re Rodas*, for instance, the court, in allowing an artificial feeding tube to be discontinued, could not see how two young children could be given any guidance or support by a brain-damaged 34-year-old man who needed nursing care around the clock.[20] In the *Brophy* case, the entire family was in agreement with Patricia Brophy's request to remove her husband's G-tube and let him die. The case, however, suggests a question. If, unlike Brophy, an incurably ill patient is not in a vegetative state but is competent and conscious and a spouse or adult children object to the patient's request that life-sustaining procedures be terminated, will the state intervene to protect them? Does the sorrow or pain that might be caused to adult family members by the death of a loved one give them a legal right to force such a person to be kept alive against his or her wishes? The question has not yet been addressed in any case. When it is, however, it is doubtful that, if families have such rights, they will be allowed to prevail over the rights of patients.

The medical personnel in the *Brophy* case who refused to remove the patient's artificial feeding tube represent a segment of the medical profession that will not abide by a patient's choice to have life-sustaining treatment discontinued. Of all the grounds supporting these refusals, fear of liability may be the strongest. Medical ethics, however, runs a close second.

It is in connection with medical ethics that the state makes its entrance. The state has a long-standing interest in protecting the professional oath and maintaining the ethical standards of the medical profession, which include the right of a doctor to administer medical treatment necessary to preserve a life. The *Brophy* case is significant again because both the lower and appellate courts were careful not to violate the moral and ethical principles of the hospital community and medical profession by not requiring tubal removal by the hospital and its staff; only the removal of the patient was ordered. But the decision also represents what seems to be a judicial trend against permitting the ethical obligations of the medical profession to outweigh the rights of patients to refuse treatment. These rights would be empty of meaning if they were denied because they conflicted with the advice of physicians or the values or practice of the medical profession. Moreover, as one court said, "It is incongruous, if not monstrous, for medical practitioners to assert their right to preserve a life that someone else must live, or, more accurately, endure. . . . We cannot conceive [of inflicting] such an ordeal upon anyone."[21]

Question 5: If patients refuse life-sustaining treatment, are individuals who comply with their wishes by withholding or withdrawing treatment guilty of abetting suicide or committing murder?

The state has an interest in the prevention of suicide by its subjects. The initial issue is whether a competent adult who rejects life-saving medical treatment is commiting suicide. If the answer is yes, then even though suicide is no longer a crime in the United States, it remains a crime to aid or abet a suicide and anyone who helps another commit suicide may be considered a principal to murder. Indeed, in several cases, defendants have been convicted when they encouraged or cooperated with others' efforts to kill themselves.[22] For example, a defendant who was a party to a suicide pact took poison. The other died. The defendant's misfortune was that he did not and therefore was guilty of murder.[23] The analogy is pressed between someone who helps an individual commit suicide and someone who helps a patient to die by removing life-sustaining equipment. In spite of this apparent similarity, there are real differences between suicide and patients' wishes to have their suffering ended. A person in perfect health may commit suicide for various reasons. Life-sustaining equipment is removed from people who are hopelessly ill. People who commit suicide make no requests of anyone because they have the means and ability of taking their own lives. Life-sustaining treatment is always withheld or withdrawn by a second party who has the means and ability to cause death and uses them at a patient's request. Besides these differences, courts, including *Brophy*, add others to exclude the withdrawing or withholding of treatment or equipment from being classified as suicide.[24] The interest of the state is in the prevention of irrational self-killing. The case of a person making a rational decision to reject medical treatment is a very different matter. Death is not caused by declining, withdrawing, or withholding medical procedures, such as artificial feeding. The cause of death is an underlying fatal pathology (for example, in Brophy's case, his inability to swallow) which is allowed to take its course by the rejection or discontinuance of treatment or equipment. In effect, since the rejection of life-sustaining treatment is not suicide but self-determination, an individual who helps in the discontinuance or withholding of treatment is not guilty of the crime of abetting a suicide.

Euthanasia is generally understood to mean an intentional killing motivated by the desire to relieve the victim of a burdensome or painful life. The moral issue is whether "mercy killing" is morally permissible as an act of kindness. The law, however, is clear. Anglo-American courts hold life to be sacred and view as a crime any deliberate killing, regardless of motive, moral justification, or victim's consent. But while it is plain under the common law doctrine of homicide that an affirmative act, such as shooting or administering a lethal dose of morphine, is murder in the first degree, the question of a doctor's omission of medical treatment, for example, by withdrawing or withholding life-sustaining medical procedures at the request of a patient, is not settled. Some legal commentators, and indeed the Morris County, New Jersey, prosecutor who was a party to the *Quinlan* case, maintain that the omission of medical procedures required to sustain the life of a consenting patient constitutes criminal homicide.

Although this may be true in theory, there is a vast difference between criminal law in theory and criminal law in action. For now, it seems, the courts have created an exception to the common law rule. Judicial protection of the right to refuse treatment without which one will die, and judicial approval of the discontinuance or withholding of necessary life-sustaining treatment so that patients can die a "natural death" or "die with dignity," in effect recognize and condone voluntary, passive euthanasia. The problem for the criminal justice system has become even more acute. In spite of the criminal nature of euthanasia, Americans who normally would not violate any law are spurning the criminal statutes by actively assisting in or causing the deaths of incurably ill people. In addition, there is a large number of acquittals by juries, suspended sentences, reprieves, or plain failures to indict. Even when authorities take the rare step of charging physicians with murder for intentionally carrying out the wishes of a patient's family (and without compliance with a state's living will statute) to disconnect equipment and discontinue treatment to sustain the life of a patient, the judicial trend seems to be for courts not to sustain the charges. This flagrant disregard of the criminal justice system suggests that the attitude of the common law of homicide applicable to euthanasia ought to be reviewed. Euthanasia may be killing but it is clearly different from murder because the motive is generally humane and merciful. When it takes the form of withholding or withdrawing life-sustaining treatment in accordance with the wishes of a patient or family, it is not murder but the implementation of the patient's constitutional rights of self-determination and privacy.

Question 6: When patients have not previously given advance instructions and are presently unable to express their wishes about life-sustaining treatment or are mentally disabled to the extent that their judgment is impaired, are their rights to refuse such treatment lost?

In cases of withdrawing or withholding life-sustaining treatment, courts have distinguished between adult patients who are competent to exercise the right to refuse medical treatment and those who are not. Incompetence is not proved by showing that a patient's decision to choose death instead of life-sustaining treatment is unwise, foolish, or in conflict with medical opinion, or by showing that a patient sometimes is forgetful or confused. But if a patient is evaluated as incompetent and has not expressed a preference to forgo medical treatment before becoming incompetent, the question then is whether incompetence entails a loss of the right of refusal. The courts of nine states—New Jersey,[25] New York,[26] Washington,[27] Massachusetts,[28] Arizona,[29] Connecticut,[30] Minnesota,[31] North Dakota,[32] and Ohio[33]—have held that the right to refuse unwanted medical treatment extends to both competent and incompetent adults and is not lost by reason of incompetency. The judiciary and legislatures supply four protective devices to prevent the right from being lost: surrogate decision making, living wills, proxies, and durable powers of attorney.

Question 7: What is surrogate decision making and what standards control it?

To avoid the loss of the right to refuse medical treatment for people who never could or can no longer make meaningful medical decisions, courts have held that third parties or surrogates, such as the family or guardian of an incompetent patient, can exercise their rights and determine the patient's future course of treatment. Where patients are in a persistent vegetative state, fathers,[34] husbands,[35] wives,[36] and designated agents[37] as guardians of the persons of patients have been allowed to express the latters' wishes. The power of surrogate decision making has been extended as well in cases where patients were persistently unconscious,[38] semicomatose,[39] retarded,[40] or incompetent.[41]

How does a surrogate decide? What are the criteria set by the courts for making the "go" or "no go" decision for an incompetent patient?

There are two kinds of criteria. Some courts have adopted the "substituted judgment" criterion.[42] The aim is not to have surrogates decide what is best for a patient, but to decide what the evidence shows patients would have decided if they were competent. The surrogates are to place themselves in the shoes of the patient and make the treatment decisions the patient would have made even if the decisions are different from those the surrogates would have made and even if the decisions are wrong or foolish.

Besides the substituted judgment criterion, there is the criterion of "best interests." This is used when substituted judgment cannot be made and it cannot be determined what a patient's choice would have been, say, in the case of a newborn infant, a retarded person, or one who had never been competent. The courts using this test allow surrogates to make treatment decisions that serve the best interests of the patient.[43] It is assumed that patients will agree with a decision that is in line with their best interests.

The situation regarding minors was clarified by a 1984 case that permitted parents and a physician to discontinue a respirator on which a four-month-old girl in a vegetative state had been maintained. The right to refuse treatment was not diminished by infancy any more than by incompetency.[44]

In New York, however, the state's highest court, running against the judicial tide elsewhere, denies surrogates the power to decide to withdraw or withhold life-sustaining treatment on behalf of patients who, because of incompetency, have been unable to make their wishes known. This was the finding in the case of a man who had always been incompetent and had therefore never been able to express his wishes.[45] But in another case, the high court permitted a respirator to be removed from Brother Fox, a Catholic priest, because considerably before his surgery and vegetative state, he had manifested "clear and convincing evidence" of his opposition to being kept alive on a respirator.[46] The court did not make plain what was meant by "clear and convincing evidence" but a lower New York court has since recognized a living will made before a patient became comatose and terminally ill as a rational decision to refuse medical treatment and as a clear and convincing demonstration of the patient's wishes.[47] What is plain from the high court decision is that, absent such a clear and prior expression of desires, no one can decide for a patient presently unable to decide. It means that for all "silent" patients, those who have never expressed treatment wishes, surrogate decisions cannot be made and life-sustaining treatment cannot be stopped. Their rights to refuse treatment are lost as are those of people who have never been competent to make decisions and whom the New York courts feel obliged to protect.

It is not only in New York that competent adult residents are forewarned to sign clear directives in advance of a condition that may prevent wishes from being expressed. Even in those states in which the law is different, people should sign advance directives in order to be sure that their wishes are carried out in spite of incompetency. One of these directives is the living will.

Question 8: Living wills: What are they and what states have enacted living will statutes?

In the last decade, the difficulty of the issues and the lack of unanimity among the courts have placed more and more pressure on state legislatures to take steps to clarify and protect the right to refuse life-sustaining treatment, and, at the same time, to ensure that the wishes of patients will be carried out by physicians who might otherwise be fearful of civil or criminal liability for acceding to patients' wishes.

Beginning with California in 1976, the states began to yield to this pressure to address the problems, and to date (1990), thirty-eight states and the District of Columbia have passed laws that permit people to refuse medical treatment before they become incapable of speaking for themselves.[48] Besides these laws, the National Conference of Commissioners on Uniform State Laws promulgated legislation known as the Uniform Rights of the Terminally Ill Act because of the lack of uniformity among the living will—also called "death with dignity" or "natural death"—statutes.

Although not identical, these statutes contain the same features. They all affirm the rights of competent adults to prepare and sign directives, duly witnessed as in testamentary documents, which declare that, in the event of a medically confirmed terminal illness or condition, they do not wish life-sustaining treatment or procedures that artificially prolong their lives and that they be permitted to die naturally. The directives may also limit treatment to making patients as comfortable and free from pain as possible. The statutes also protect health care professionals from civil liability and criminal prosecution for acting in accordance with the directives of the patients.

These statutes, however, have several shortcomings. One of the chief complaints patients have is that their living wills are ignored by physicians. Many statutes do not require physicians who receive a copy of a patient's living will to tell the patient that they are not willing for reasons of ethics, conscious, or religious beliefs to comply with it.

Many statutes also do not make it mandatory for physicians or health care facilities to honor the patient's wishes as expressed in a living will. Such statutes impose no penalties on a physician who refuses to follow the declaration. They do not even make noncompliance with the patient's wishes unprofessional conduct. All that most statutes require is that if physicians are not willing to comply with a living will, they take reasonable steps to transfer the patient to another physician. But they do not go further and provide that the transfer must be made to a physician who will be willing to honor the wishes of the patient.

In addition to these shortcomings, virtually all statutes extend the right to refuse medical treatment only to patients who are or will be terminally ill or in a terminal condition, that is, to those who will, as a medical probability, die in a short time no matter what treatment is used or discontinued. These statutes exclude from their protection all people not diagnosed as terminally ill. Further, they raise the question of whether the limitation of the right to refuse life-sustaining procedure implies a legislative declaration that the statutes are the exclusive authority for asserting the right which can be exercised only by terminal patients or their representatives who comply with their provisions. This very argument was made in *Bartling v. Superior Court*, where a nonterminally ill, competent 70-year-old patient executed a living will that did not comply with the California Natural Death Act, signed a durable power of attorney authorizing his wife to make medical decisions, and made a deposition that he wanted his respirator discontinued. The trial court, finding that the patient was not terminally ill, sustained the state's argument. On appeal, however, the California Court of Appeal reversed the decision and held that the right of a competent individual to refuse treatment is a constitutional right that predates any statute and that a statute is not the exclusive method for exercising the right of refusal.[49] *Bartling* illustrates that legislatures can muddy the waters by drafting statutes that try to limit to terminally ill patients the fundamental right to refuse medical treatment and fail to recognize the constitutionally protected rights of, or lay down procedures for, competent adults who are not terminally ill.

A further problem with these statutes is that some may actually undermine even a terminally ill patient's right to refuse medical treatment. Thus the Indiana Living Wills and Life-Prolonging Act of 1985 provides in Section 11 that "a living will declaration ... does not obligate the physician to use, withhold, or withdraw life-prolonging procedures." In other words, the rights of patients are empty because doctors can choose not to implement them. The living will is said by the statute to be "presumptive evidence" only of what a patient wants. The physician is to give it "great weight" but that is all.

Question 9: What other forms of protection are there for competent adults who wish to express their health care decisions prior to being unable to make their own medical decisions?

The living will statutes provide legislative recognition of a document that provides competent adults with the opportunity, in advance of incompetency, clearly and specifically to express informed and rational decisions to reject medical treatment should they become terminally ill. The statutes try to preserve individual autonomy and avoid placing terrible burdens on families. They also try to offer the prospect that adults' wishes will be carried out even if they are unable to express them. But living wills are not the ideal solution because physicians may neglect to carry them out not only because of ethics, conscience, or religious beliefs but because noncomplying physicians may not know a living will exists. If it is not made part of the patient's medical record, they cannot know about it. Another problem with the living will is that one simply cannot foresee and provide instructions for all the medical conditions that may arise or forms of treatment which may be developed in the future. And if the living will was made years ago, and has not been reviewed and updated periodically, there may be a real question about how accurately it reflects a patient's present wishes.

There are two other forms that provide protection in advance of one's inability to make meaningful medical decisions. One is provided expressly or implicitly by the living will statutes of thirteen states under which an agent, proxy, or attorney-in-fact may be designated in the directive to make medical decisions—including whether life-sustaining treatment should be withheld or withdrawn—for patients who are unconscious, incompetent, or otherwise unable to express their wishes.[50] A proxy can make decisions on the spot in situations or for specific conditions not foreseen and, as someone trusted by and familiar with the feelings of a patient, will make decisions in line with what the patient wanted.

In addition to the designation of a proxy in a living will, many living will statutes provide for another protective form. If an individual has not executed a living will, is terminally ill, and is also comatose or incompetent, a written agreement to withhold or withdraw life-prolonging procedures can be made between the attending physician and certain individuals in the following order of priority: a guardian, a person designated by the terminally ill patient, a spouse, an adult child or, if more than one, by the majority of adult children, the parents, or the nearest living relative.

Besides these two procedures, all states and the District of Columbia have statutes that provide a third procedure. They permit a durable power of attorney to be executed which allows an agent to act and make treatment decisions for the principal making the power of attorney. Some states, such as Florida, have Durable Family Power of Attorney statutes that allow the appointment of a spouse, parent, adult child, sibling, niece, or nephew. The aim of such legislation is to help incompetent individuals by allowing family members to handle their affairs and avoiding the necessity of the appointment of a legal guardian.

Ordinary powers of attorney cease when the principal no longer is competent. If the durable power of attorney contains suitable provisions, it will not cease or will begin at the incompetency of the principal. Under ordinary and durable powers of attorney people are permitted to confer on others general powers to act for them in almost every matter. Although some states, including California, Colorado, North Carolina, and Pennsylvania, have enacted durable power of attorney statutes expressly permitting a person appointed by a durable power of attorney to make medical decisions, other states have not. Nevertheless, under the broad provisions of all durable power of attorney statutes, it should be possible to confer on an attorney-in-fact authority to make medical decisions for the conferer when the latter lacks capacity for doing so (Collin et al. 1984).

In comparison to the proxy appointed under the living will statutes, the agent appointed under a durable power of attorney seems to give an individual with a living will additional protection. Under the living will statutes, a living will is not effective until an individual is terminally ill. Many patients, such as Karen Ann Quinlan, are not covered by the statutes. A durable power of attorney would extend treatment decisions to both terminally ill and other patients.

The one problem with the durable power of attorney may be that people do not know an agent they can trust to respect their wishes. The same problem exists, however, with the appointment of a proxy under a living will.

PRIVATE DECISION MAKING

In this panoramic view of the situation, one principal feature stands out. Since the *Quinlan* case in 1976, health care, with its complex and difficult questions, has become as much of a dilemma for legislators and judges as it is for medical ethicists, physicians, philosophers, and theologians.

The legislatures, whose living will statutes needlessly confuse or infringe on the rights of competent adults to refuse procedures, including artificial feeding, have shown that they do not know how to cope with the dilemma. The lack of unanimity among the courts shows that they do not know how to handle it either, and would like to avoid it if possible.

One immediate practical step toward avoiding the terrible strain placed on patients and their families—of unwanted medical expenses (for example, the medical expenses in the Brother Fox case were $87,000) and of the trauma and crushing legal costs of protracted litigation (the legal expenses in the Brother Fox case were more than $50,000)—is greater public education and awareness on the part of the health care community that will preserve both the autonomy of the individual and the integrity of private health care decision making. By "private health care decision making" is meant decisions by the patient or the family of a patient incapable of decision making that are made outside the public process involved in court proceedings. Ideally, such decisions should be made within the physician-patient relationship and with the collaboration and consent of the treating physician. These decisions do not belong to the legislatures or the courts. As the court in the *Quinlan* case said: "We consider that a practice of applying to a court to confirm such decisions would generally be inappropriate."

Amid the rain of laws pouring down from our legislatures, living will statutes are a mere drop. Compared with adjudications made by courts in nonmedical matters, the number of right-to-die controversies is very small. Yet it is surprising that the fraction of living will statutes and even the small number of right-to-die cases are as large as they are, because in hospitals across the country thousands of private decisions to decline life-sustaining treatment are made routinely and jointly by patient, family, and physician (Hilfiker 1983). Prior legislative or judicial approval for doing so is neither required nor desirable.[51] Legislators and judges have become involved only because cases have arisen in which health care institutions and providers have declined to participate in the normal private decision-making process. The refusal may have been grounded on an evaluation by the treating physician that an adult patient lacked decision-making capacity or perhaps because the physician found the views of the family of a patient who could not speak for himself or herself at variance with medical views. The *Quinlan* case is an example. It generated national interest in the right-to-die issue. But what is even more interesting about the case is that it came to court in the first place. Normally, "many, if not most physicians would have routinely acceded to the wishes of the patient's family in a similar situation" (Collester 1976–77) and private decision making would have prevailed. The *Brophy* case, like the *Quinlan* case, represents another failure of private decision making. It became a case only because the attending physician and hospital staff would not accede to the wishes of Brophy and his wife in spite of the fact that most of the New England medical community would have bowed to patients' decisions to forgo artificial nutrition and hydration. The Massachusetts Medical Society, for example, adopted a resolution on July 1985 that recognized the autonomy rights of vegetative or terminally ill individuals who had previously expressed wishes to refuse medical treatment, including artificial feeding, and declared that it is not unethical for physicians to implement their wishes.

Patients and their families are forced into time-consuming, expensive, and burdensome litigation because, as demonstrated in *Quinlan*, the refusal by health care providers to discontinue treating an incompetent patient and to agree with the family on a course of action requires the appointment of a legal guardian. Because of their fears of civil or criminal liability, many health care professionals also insist on legal immunity prior to withholding or withdrawing treatment. Yet these professionals should understand that their fears are unreal. The laws on the books all protect physicians and the risk of liability is minute. Civil and criminal liability exist in cases of withholding or withdrawing life-sustaining treatment only when it is shown that the actions of physicians and hospitals were not in good faith and were intended to harm a patient.[52] Physicians should recognize that living will statutes also protect them from civil liability and criminal prosecution and that these statutes were designed to remove one of the great obstacles to compliance with the wishes of patients who have signed advance directives. Even without such statutes, not one doctor has ever been convicted of murder for withholding or withdrawing life-sustaining procedures. In *Barber v. Superior Court*, the first case to deal with murder charges brought against doctors for withholding or withdrawing these procedures, the court dismissed the charges.[53] In Florida, a tough state when it comes to "mercy killings,"

Peter Rosier, a physician who gave morphine injections and suppositories to his terminally ill wife, was tried in 1988 for first-degree murder and conspiracy to commit murder and was acquitted by the jury (*Miami Herald*, December 2, 1988).

In fact, refusing to honor the wishes of patients to reject treatment and imposing on them unwanted treatment will subject physicians to the very liability they fear.

The physician's concern with medical ethics also drives doctors to the courts to protect their Hippocratic oath, which seems to make any move toward terminating life morally wrong and unethical. But the American Medical Association has made it plain that it is not unethical for physicians to withdraw or withhold life-sustaining medical treatment, including artificially provided hydration and nutrition, if that is the choice of the patient or the surrogate for an incompetent patient, especially one who is terminally ill or comatose (Council on Ethical and Judicial Affairs of the AMA 1986; see excerpt from their opinion at the end of this section).

We who may become the patients of these health care professionals should know that our last rights are: that we have the right to be free from nonconsensual bodily invasions; that we can refuse to submit to medical treatment; that we have a cause of action for damages on the ground of battery against doctors and hospitals for treatment we do not want; and we have the right to discharge paternalistic physicians and replace them with doctors who will accord these rights the respect they deserve. We should also know that we have the right to leave or be removed from uncompromising hospitals or nursing homes to other, more cooperative institutions where our rights will be honored.

If the sampling of people interviewed by the pollsters is representative of all Americans, then 80 to 90 percent of us want to make our own health care decisions. But the grim prospect of future helplessness and loss of capacity to make meaningful decisions as a result of depression, suffering, or medications in the days, weeks, or months before our actual death looms before us all. If we do not wish to lose our power to make medical decisions, it is vital that we make our decisions and make known our wishes before we lose the capacity to do so. Advance directives, proxies, and durable powers of attorney are the means available to us.

The Council of Ethical and Judicial Affairs of the AMA rendered an opinion to this effect on March 15, 1986. In part, it reads as follows:

The social commitment of the physician is to sustain life and relieve suffering. Where the performance of one duty conflicts with another, the choice of the patient, or his family or legal representative if the patient is incompetent to act in his own behalf, should prevail. . . . For humane reasons, with informed consent, a physician may do what is medically necessary to alleviate severe pain, or cease or omit treatment to permit a terminally ill patient whose death is imminent to die.... Even if death is not imminent but a patient's coma is beyond doubt irreversible and there are adequate safeguards to confirm the accuracy of the diagnosis and with the concurrence of those who have responsibility for the care of the patient, it is not unethical to discontinue all means of life prolonging treatment. Life prolonging treatment includes medication and artificially or technologically supplied respiration, nutrition or hydration.

POSTSCRIPT: THE CASE OF NANCY CRUZAN

In order to update the foregoing chapter and supplement or change where necessary any portions of its text, I draw the reader's attention to a landmark decision in the case of *Cruzan v. Missouri* (58 U.S. Law Week 4916, June 25, 1990) made by the highest court in the land after the chapter had gone to press. In the case, the parents of Nancy Cruzan, an incompetent woman in a permanent vegetative state, requested authorization to terminate artificial delivery of food and water. The Missouri State Supreme Court reversed a state trial court and ruled against the parents and co-guardians for the reason that Nancy Cruzan's statements to a roommate a year prior to her incompetency, such as that she would not want to continue her life unless she could live "halfway normally," were not "clear and convincing" evidence of the patient's desire to terminate the feeding. The U.S. Supreme Court granted *certiorari*. References to the case up to this point and under the caption of *Cruzan v. Harmon* appear on pages 133, 134, 148 (fn.2), and 149 (fn.13) in this chapter.

In 1990, the U.S. Supreme Court upheld the Missouri court. Since its decision was by a 5–4 vote, the case further buttresses the chapter's text on p. 131, as it demonstrates the lack of judicial unanimity in the right-to-die field.

The holding of the high court was that the Federal Constitution does not preclude a state, such as Missouri, in a proceeding where guardians seek to terminate life support, from requiring "clear and convincing" evidence of an incompetent's desire to have support withdrawn. This holding, however, implicates several issues. First, under the Constitution, does a competent person have the right to refuse medical treatment? The Supreme Court said that such a right exists. This is consistent with pages 131–32 in this chapter. But where I had analyzed the right in terms of individual autonomy, the right of privacy, and the doctrine of informed consent that state courts had recognized, the U.S. Supreme Court analyzed it in a way never before expressed: as a "liberty interest" to refuse unwanted medical treatment under the Fourteenth Amendment of the Constitution, which prohibits a state from arbitrarily depriving an individual of life, liberty, or property without due process of law.

Whether forced hydration and nutrition can also be refused, the issue raised by Question 2 on page 132 in this chapter, was the second issue in the case. The majority opinion written by Chief Justice Rehnquist assumed, and the concurring opinion of Justice O'Connor asserted, that the "liberty interest" encompassed the refusal of artificially delivered food and water. The conflict between the Missouri court and the *Brophy* line of cases (see page 133 in this chapter) was thus resolved in favor of the latter. Artificial feeding is not distinguishable from other forms of medical procedures.

Third, if there is a constitutional right to refuse treatment, does the Constitution allow the interest of the state in preserving human life to outweigh it? The affirmative holding of the Court does not change the text on page 134 in this chapter that recognized the state's unqualified interest in preserving life as an exception to the neither unfettered nor absolute right to refuse treatment.

The final issue was: If a competent person has a constitutional right to refuse treatment, does an incompetent person such as Nancy Cruzan possess the same right? The Court did not deny the proposition (advanced in the text on page 138 in this chapter) that incompetency does not deprive an incompetent of this right. The Court felt, however, that the real question was not whether an incompetent had the constitutional right to refuse treatment but how such a right could be exercised. In this case, based on Nancy Cruzan's statements to a roommate, her parents as surrogates tried to exercise her right to prevent its loss (see the text on page 138). They asked that her life support be stopped because they thought they knew what course their daughter would have followed. But the Missouri State Supreme Court found the informally expressed statements to be unreliable and insufficient as "clear and convincing" proof of Nancy Cruzan's wishes. This requirement was a strict standard of persuasion, the highest possible in civil cases. In adopting it as a procedure for the "substituted judgment" criterion referred to on page 138 in this chapter, Missouri used the same standard as that used in New York and discussed on page 139 in the chapter.

As already indicated, the high court held that the Constitution permits a state to adopt this standard in order to advance its interest to preserve life and to be certain that the actions of surrogates are consistent with the incompetent's wishes as expressed prior to incompetency.

The holding, of course, does not affect competent patients able to express their wishes or those incompetents who, prior to incompetency, left clear evidence of their desires. But the holding substantially affects Questions 6 and 7 and the text of this chapter on pages 137–138 relating to incompetent patients who have given no advance directions and are unable to make informed choices. It also affects decisions by surrogates and their exercise of the incompetents' rights to refuse medical treatment. The holding serves notice that the constitutional right to refuse treatment, while granted to all, can be exercised by surrogates only in the few cases of those who have the foresight to leave clear proof of their intentions regarding medical treatment. For this reason, the text in the chapter on pages 139–142 regarding living wills, proxies, and durable powers of attorney takes on a special importance.

The Constitution, however, does not require a strict standard of persuasion or prevent states from using a lower standard. The frustrated Cruzan family might, therefore, consider the recommendations in the text of this chapter on page 145. They can, if they wish, remove their daughter from Missouri and the uncompromising hospital where she is a patient and take her to a less hostile state and health care facility where what they believe to be their daughter's wishes will be honored.

The text on pages 143–144 in this chapter remains unaltered by the U.S. Supreme Court ruling, which does not mandate judicial approval for decisions made in a private forum.

NOTES

1. *Brophy v. New England Mt. Sinai Hospital, Inc.*, 398 Mass. 417, 497 N.E. 2d 626 (Massachusetts Supreme Judicial Court, 1986).

2. *Rasmussen v. Fleming*, 741 P.2d 674 (Arizona Supreme Court 1987); *Bouvia v. Superior Court*, 179 Cal. App. 3d 1127, 225 Cal. Rptr. 297 (California Court of Appeal, Second Appellate District, Division Two, 1986) *review denied* (Cal. June 5, 1986); *Bartling v. Superior Court of California*, 163 Cal. App. 3d 186, 209 Cal. Rptr. 220 (California Court of Appeal, 1984; *Barber v. Superior Court of California*, 147 Cal. App. 3d 1006, 195 Cal. Rptr. 484 (California Court of Appeal, 2d District, 1983); *John F. Kennedy Memorial Hospital, Inc. v. The Honorable Donald H. Bludworth*, 452 So. 2d 921 (Florida Supreme Court, 1984); *In re Quinlan*, 70 N.J. 10, 355 A. 2d 647, *certiorari denied sub nom. Garger v. New Jersey*, 429 U.S. 922 (1976) *overruled in part, In re Conroy*, 98 N.J. 321, 486 A. 2d 1209 (1985); *In re Conroy*, 98 N.J. 321, 486 A. 2d 1209 (New Jersey Supreme Court, 1985); *New Mexico ex rel. Smith v. Fort*, No. 14, 768 (New Mexico Supreme Court, 1983); *Delio v. Westchester County Medical Center*, 129 A.D. 2d 1, 516 N.Y.S. 2d 677 (New York Supreme Court, Appellate Division, Second Department, 1987); *Eichner v. Dillon*, 73 A.D. 2d 431, 426 N.Y.S. 2d 517, *reversed sub nom. In re Storar*, 52 N.Y. 2d 363, 420 N.E. 2d 64, 438 N.Y.S.2d 266 (New York Court of Appeals) *certiorari denied* 454 U.S. 858 (1981); *Leach v. Shapiro*, 13 Ohio App. 3d 393, 469 N.E. 2d 1047 (Ohio Court of Appeals for Summit County, 1984); *Cruzan v. Harmon*, 760 S.W. 2d 408 (Missouri Supreme Court, 1988) *certiorari granted* 109 Sup. Ct. Rep. 3240 (1989).

3. *Natanson v. Kline*, 186 Kan. 393, 350 P. 2d 1093 (Kansas Supreme Court, 1960).

4. *In re Quinlan, supra* note 2.

5. *Bouvia v. Superior Court, supra* note 2.

6. *In re Rodas*, No. 86PR139 (Colorado District Court, Mesa County, January 22, 1987).

7. *Tune v. Walter Reed Army Medical Hospital*, 602 F. Supp. 1452 (United States District Court for the District of Columbia, 1985).

8. *Satz v. Perlmutter*, 362 So. 2d 160 (Florida Court of Appeal, 1987) *affirmed* 379 So. 2d 359 (Florida Supreme Court, 1980).

9. *Wilcox v. Hawaii*, Civ. No. 860116 (Hawaii Circuit Court 5th Circuit, June 16, 1986).

10. *Brophy v. New England Mt. Sinai Hospital*, *supra* note 1.

11. *In re Lydia E. Hall Hospital*, 116 Misc. 2d 477, 455 N.Y.S.2d 706 (New York Supreme Court, Nassau County, 1982).

12. *In re Jobes*, 108 N.J. 394, 529 A.2d 434 (New Jersey Supreme Court, 1986); *Bouvia v. Superior Court*, *supra* note 2; *In re Conroy*, *supra* note 2; *In re Peter*, 108 N.J. 365, 529 A.2d 419 (New Jersey Supreme Court 1987); *Brophy v. New England Mt. Sinai Hospital*, *supra* note 1; *Rasmussen v. Fleming*, *supra* note 2; *In re Rodas*, *supra* note 6; *Barber v. Superior Court of California*, *supra* note 2; *Delio v. Westchester County Medical Center*, *supra* note 2; *Corbett v. D'Alessandro*, 487 So. 2d 368 (Florida District Court of Appeal, Second District) *review denied* 492 So.2d 1331 (Florida Supreme Court 1986).

13. *Cruzan v. Harmon*, 760 S.W. 2d 408 (Missouri Supreme Court, 1988) *certiorari granted* 109 Sup. Ct. Rep. 3240 (1989).

14. *Corbett v. D'Alessandro*, *supra* note 12.

15. *In re Rodas*, *supra* note 6.

16. *Bartling v. Superior Court*, *supra* note 2.

17. *John F. Kennedy Memorial Hospital, Inc. v. The Honorable Donald H. Bludworth*, *supra* note 2.

18. *Leach v. Shapiro*, *supra* note 2; *In re Rodas*, *supra* note 6; *Schloendorf v. Society of New York Hospital*, 211 N.Y. 125, 105 N.E. 92 (New York Court of Appeals, 1914).

19. Application of President & Directors of Georgetown College, Inc. 331 F.2d 1000 (District of Columbia Circuit Court) *certiorari denied*. 377 U.S. 478, 84 S. Ct. 1883 (1964).

20. *Supra* note 6.

21. *Bouvia v. Superior Court*, *supra* note 2.

22. *Commonwealth v. Hicks*, 118 Ky. 637, 82 S.W. 265 (1904); *People v. Roberts*, 211 Mich. 187, 178 N.W. 690 (1920).

23. *Barnet v. People*, 204 Ill. 208, 68 N.E. 505 (1903).

24. *In re Conroy*, *supra* note 2; *Satz v. Perlmutter*, *supra* note 2; *Superintendent of Belchertown State School v. Saikewicz*, 373 Mass. 728, 370 N.E. 2d 417 (Massachusetts Supreme Judicial Court, 1977); *In re Colyer*, 99 Wash. 2d 114, 660 P.2d 738 (Washington Supreme Court, 1973).

25. *In re Quinlan*, *supra* note 2.

26. *Delio v. Westchester County Medical Center*, *supra* note 2; *In re Eichner*, 52 N.Y. 2d 363, 420 N.E. 2d 64, 438 N.Y. 2d 266, *cert. den.* 454 U.S. 858 (1981).

27. *In re Colyer*, *supra* note 24.

28. *Superintendent of Belchertown State School v. Saikewicz*, *supra* note 24.

29. *Rasmussen v. Fleming*, *supra* note 2.

30. *Foody v. Manchester Memorial Hospital*, 40 Conn. Supp. 127, 482 A.2d 713 (Connecticut Superior Court, Hartford District, 1984).

31. *In re Torres*, 357 N.W.2d 332 (Minnesota Supreme Court, 1984).

32. *In re Bayer*, No. 4131 (North Dakota Burleigh County Court, February 5, 1987).

33. *Leach v. Shapiro, supra* note 2.

34. *In re Quinlan, supra* note 2.

35. *Corbett v. D'Alessandro, supra* note 12.

36. *Brophy v. New England Mt. Sinai Hospital, supra* note 1.

37. *In re Peter, supra* note 12.

38. *In re Jobes, supra* note 12.

39. *Foody v. Manchester Memorial Hospital, supra* note 30.

40. *Superintendent of Belchertown State School v. Saikewicz, supra* note 24.

41. *John F. Kennedy Memorial Hospital v. The Honorable Donald H. Bludworth, supra* note 2; *Rasmussen v. Fleming, supra* note 2; *In re Conroy, supra* note 2.

42. *In re Quinlan, supra* note 2; *Superintendent of Belchertown State School, supra* note 24; *John F. Kennedy Memorial Hospital v. The Honorable Donald H. Bludworth, supra* note 2.

43. *In re Conroy, supra* note 2; *Rasmussen v. Fleming, supra* note 2.

44. *In re L.H.R.*, 253 Ga. 439, 321 S.E.2d 716 (Georgia Supreme Court, 1984).

45. *In re Storar*, 52 N.Y. 2d 363, 420 N.E.2d 64, 438 N.Y.S. 2d 266 (New York Court of Appeals) *certiorari denied* 454 U.S. 858 (1981).

46. *In re Eichner, supra* note 26.

47. *Saunders v. State*, 129 Misc. 2d. 45, 492 N.Y.S.2d 510 (New York Supreme Court, Nassau County, 1985).

48. Alabama, Alaska, Arizona, Arkansas, California, Colorado, Connecticut, Delaware, Florida, Georgia, Hawaii, Idaho, Illinois, Indiana, Iowa, Kansas, Louisiana, Maine, Maryland, Mississippi, Missouri, Montana, Nevada, New Hampshire, New Mexico, North Carolina, Oklahoma, Oregon, South Carolina, Tennessee, Texas, Utah, Vermont, Virginia, Washington, West Virginia, Wisconsin, and Wyoming.

49. *Bartling v. Supreme Court, supra* note 2.

50. Arkansas, Colorado, Delaware, Florida, Hawaii, Idaho, Indiana, Iowa, Louisiana, Texas, Utah, Virginia, and Wyoming.

51. *In re Torres, supra* note 31; *In re Quinlan, supra* note 2.

52. *John F. Kennedy Memorial Hospital, Inc. v. The Honorable Donald H. Bludworth, supra* note 2; *In re Jobes, supra* note 12.

53. *Supra* note 2.

REFERENCES

Collester, Jr., D. T. 1976–77. "Death, Dying and the Law: A Prosecutorial View of the Quinlan Case." *Rutgers Law Review* 30:304–28.

Collin, F. F., Lombard, J. L., Moses, A. L., and Spitler, H. 1984. *Drafting the Durable Power of Attorney—A Systems Approach.* Lexington, SC: R. P. W. Publishing Co.

Council on Ethical and Judicial Affairs of the AMA. Statement, March 15, 1986.

Hilfiker, D. 1983. "Sounding Board: Allowing the Debilitated to Die." *New England Journal of Medicine* 308 (12): 716–19.

Miami Herald, December 2, 1988. "Doctor is Cleared in Wife's Death."

Appendix A: Right-to-Life and Right-to-Die Organizations

Pro-Life Organizations That Oppose or Disseminate Information on Euthanasia

United States

Ad Hoc Committee in Defense for Life, 1187 National Press Building, Washington, DC 20004.

American Life Lobby, c/o American Family Center, PO Box 1350, Stafford, VA 22554.

Americans United for Life, 2435 S. Dearborn, Suite 1804, Chicago, IL 60604.

Baptists for Life, 2113 Alamo National Building, San Antonio, TX 78205.

Big Bend Right to Life, PO Box 12968, Tallahassee, FL 32317.

Human Life Center, University of Steubenville, Steubenville, OH 43952.

Human Life International, 7845-E Airpark Rd., Gaithersburg, MD 20879.

International Life Services, Inc., 2606 1/2 W. Eighth St., Los Angeles, CA 90057.

Lutherans for Life, 27 N. Syndicate, St. Paul, MN 55104.

Methodists for Life, 12105 Livingston St., Wheaton, MD 20909.

National Conference of Catholic Bishops Pro-Life Affairs Committee, 1312 Massachusetts Ave. NW, Washington, DC 20005.

National Right to Life Committee, 419 Seventh St. NW, Suite 500, Washington, DC 20004.

Pro-Life Action League, 6160 N. Cicero Ave., Chicago, IL 60646.

Protect Life in All Nations, c/o American Life League, 188 Onville Rd., Stafford, VA 22554.

U.S. Coalition for Life, PO Box 315, Export, PA 15632.

Value of Life Committee, 637 Cambridge St., Brighton, MA 02135.

World Federation of Doctors Who Respect Human Life, PO Box 508, Oak Park, IL 60303.

Belgium

World Federation of Doctors Who Respect Human Life, c/o Dr. Philip Schepens, Serruyslaan 76–3, B–8400 Ostend, Belgium.

Canada

Alliance for Life, B1–90 Garry St., Winnipeg, MBR3C, 4H1, Canada.

Right-to-Die Organizations That Support Euthanasia

United States

Americans against Human Suffering, PO Box 11001, Glendale, CA 91206.
Concern for Dying, 250 West 57th St., New York, NY 10107.
The National Hemlock Society, PO Box 11830, Eugene, OR 97440.
Society for the Right to Die, 250 West 57th St., New York, NY 10107.

Australia

South Australia Voluntary Euthanasia Society, PO Box 2151, Kent Town Centre, 5071, S. Australia.
West Australia Voluntary Euthanasia Society, PO Box 7243, Cloisters Square, Perth 6000, W. Australia.
Voluntary Euthanasia Society of New South Wales, PO Box 25, Broadway, New South Wales, 2007.
Voluntary Euthanasia Society of Victoria, PO Box 23, Glen Iris, Victoria 3146, Australia.

Belgium

Association pour le Droit de Mourir dans la Dignité, 15, rue des Prêtres, 1000 Bruxelles, Belgium.
Recht op Waardig Sterven, Somerstraat 45, 2018 Antwerpen, Belgium.

Britain

The Voluntary Euthanasia Society, 13 Prince of Wales Terrace, London W8 5PG, England.
The Voluntary Euthanasia Society of Scotland, 17 Hart Street, Edinburgh EH1 3RO, Scotland.

Canada

Dying with Dignity, 175 St. Clair West, Toronto, Ontario M4V 1P7, Canada.

Colombia

Fundacion Pro-Derecho a Morir Dignamente, A. A. 88900, Bogotá, Colombia.

Denmark

Mit Livstestamente, Sauntes Vaenge, DK2920, Gentofte, Denmark.

France

Association pour le Droit de Mourir dans la Dignité, 103 rue la Fayette, 75010, Paris, France.

Holland

Informatie Centrum Vrijwillige Euthanasie, Zuiderweg 42, 8393 KT Vinkega, Netherlands.
Nederlandse Vereniging voor Vrijwillige Euthanasie, 152 de Lairessestraat Postbus 5331 1007 AH, Amsterdam, Netherlands.

India

The Society for the Right to Die with Dignity, 127 Mahatma Gandhi Road, Bombay 400 023, India.

Israel

The Israeli Voluntary Euthanasia Society, 116 Rotschild Bolv., Tel Aviv, Israel 65271.

Italy

Club dell'Euthanasia, Piazza Firenze, 24, 00186, Rome, Italy.

Japan

Japan Society for Dying with Dignity, Yamazaki Building 302, 2–40–14 Hongou Bunkyo-ku Tokyo 113, Japan.

New Zealand

Voluntary Euthanasia Society, 95 Melrose Road, Island Bay, Wellington 2, New Zealand.
Voluntary Euthanasia Society (Auckland) Inc., PO Box 77029 Mount Albert, Auckland 3, New Zealand.

South Africa

South Africa Voluntary Euthanasia Society, PO Box 37141, Overport 4067, Durban, Republic of South Africa.

Spain

Asociacion Derecho a Morir Dignamente, Apartado 9.094, 28080 Madrid, Spain.

Sweden

Ratten Till Var Dod, Box 48001, 10027 Stockholm, Sweden.

Switzerland

EXIT Deutsche Schweiz Vereinigung für Humanes Sterben, Zwinglistr. 14, CH– 2540 Grenchen, Switzerland.
EXIT—A. D. M. D.—Association pour le Droit de Mourir dans la Dignité, Case Postale 100, CH–1222 Vesenaz, Geneva, Switzerland.

Appendix B: Policy Statements of Important and Influential Groups

American Medical Association

The following is a statement of the Council on Ethical and Judicial Affairs, issued March 15, 1986, on ceasing or omitting life-prolonging medical treatment.

The social commitment of the physician is to sustain life and relieve suffering. Where the performance of one duty conflicts with the other, the choice of the patient, or his family or legal representative if the patient is incompetent to act in his behalf, should prevail. In the absence of the patient's choice or an authorized proxy, the physician must act in the best interest of the patient.

For humane reasons, with informed consent, a physician may do what is medically necessary to alleviate severe pain, or cease or omit treatment to permit a terminally ill patient whose death is imminent to die. However, he should not intentionally cause death. In deciding whether the administration of potentially life-prolonging medical treatment is in the best interest of the patient who is incompetent to act in his own behalf, the physician should determine what the possibility is for extending life under humane and comfortable conditions and what are the prior expressed wishes of the patient and attitudes of the family or those who have responsibility for the custody of the patient.

Even if death is not imminent but a patient's coma is beyond doubt irreversible and there are adequate safeguards to confirm the accuracy of the diagnosis and with the concurrence of those who have responsibility for the care of the patient, it is not unethical to discontinue all means of life-prolonging medical treatment.

Life-prolonging medical treatment includes medication and artificially or technologically supplied respiration, nutrition, or hydration. In treating a terminally ill or irreversibly comatose patient, the physician should determine whether the benefits of treatment outweigh its burdens. At all times, the dignity of the patient should be maintained.

American Hospital Association

In its "Patient's Bill of Rights," the American Hospital Association expressed its official position regarding the right to refuse medical treatment.

The patient has the right to refuse treatment to the extent permitted by law and to be informed of the medical consequences of his action.

The Vatican

Below are excerpts from the Declaration on Euthanasia from the Sacred Congregation of the Faith issued by the Vatican on May 5, 1980.

Euthanasia

It is necessary to state firmly once more that nothing and no one can in any way permit the killing of an innocent human being, whether a fetus or an embryo, an infant or an adult, an old person, or one suffering from an incurable disease, or a person who is dying, Furthermore, no one is permitted to ask for this act of killing, either for himself or herself or for another person entrusted to his or her care, nor can he or she consent to it, either explicitly or implicitly. . . .

Withdrawing Treatment

It is also permissible to make do with the normal means that medicine can offer. Therefore one cannot impose on anyone the obligation to have the recourse to a technique which is already in use but which carries a risk or is burdensome. Such a refusal is not the equivalent of suicide; on the contrary, it should be considered as an acceptance of the human condition, or a wish to avoid the application of a medical procedure disproportionate to the results that can be expected, or a desire not to impose excessive expense on the family or the community. . . .

National Conference of Catholic Bishops Pro-Life Affairs Committee

The following is a statement on the Uniform Rights of the Terminally Ill Act issued by the NCCB Pro-Life Affairs Committee with particular regard to living will legislation, artifical nutrition, hydration and other matters.

Introduction

In proposing a Uniform Rights of the Terminally Ill Act for enactment by state legislatures, the National Conference of Commissioners on Uniform State Laws has presented legislators with a new and complex challenge. The Uniform Act is designed to eliminate disparities among state laws on withholding and withdrawing life-sustaining treatment; such laws have been enacted in most of the fifty states over the past decade. Yet some of the provisions of the Uniform Act raise new and significant moral problems, highlighting the need for serious debate on the purpose and risks of legislation on this subject.

As Catholic bishops in the United States we feel a responsibility to contribute to this debate. We are concerned that legislation which is ethically unsound will further compromise the right to life and respect for life in American society. Moreover, we are confident that out Church's moral tradition can be of great assistance in determing the extent to which legislative proposals in this area are consistent with sound moral principles.

In keeping with this tradition we uphold the duty to preserve life while recognizing certain limits to that duty. We absolutely reject euthanasia, by which we mean "an act or an omission which of itself or by intention causes death, in order that all suffering may this way be eliminated" (Vatican *Declaration on Euthanasia*, 1980). We maintain that one is obliged to use "ordinary" means of preserving life—that is, means which can effectively preserve life without imposing grave burdens on the patient—and we see the failure to supply such means as "equivalent to euthanasia" (U.S. Catholic Conference, *Ethical and Religious Directives for Catholic Health Facilities*, 1975, para. 28). But we also recognize and defend a patient's right to refuse "extraordinary" means—that is, means which provide no benefit or which involve too grave a burden. In cases where patients cannot speak for themselves, we urge family members, others qualified to interpret the patient's intentions, and physicians to be guided by these fundamental moral principles.

The task of judging how these principles can best be incorporated into social policy is complex and difficult. For example, various proposals giving legal force to an advance declaration or "living will" have been offered as ways of clarifying a terminally ill patient's legitimate right to refuse extraordinary medical treatment. From one perspective, clarification of this right seems increasingly necessary as physicians, concerned about legal liability, seek guidance concerning their legal rights and responsibilities. Indeed, public support for such legislation is due in large part to a concern that some physicians are resisting even morally appropriate requests for withdrawal of treatment when these requests have no explicit statutory recognition.

Yet the operative provisions of such legislation, and their degree of conformity with Catholic moral teaching, vary widely form state to state. Some "living will" proposals have been formulated and promoted by right-to-die groups which see them as stepping-stones to the eventual legalization of euthanasia. In fact, some existing laws and proposals could be read not merely as stepping-stones but as actually authorizing euthanasia in certain circumstances. Many "living will" statutes reflect a bias toward facilitating *only* the right to *refuse* means for sustaining life, instead of facilitating morally responsible decisions either to provide or to withhold treatment in accord with the wishes and best interests of the patient.

Due to concerns such as these, the Bishops' Committee for Pro-Life Activities has neither endorsed nor encouraged the trend toward enactment of "living will" legislation. Indeed, many people dedicated to the protection of human life have judged these concerns serious enough to warrant outright opposition to some legislative proposals of this kind, and have sought to amend other proposals to reduce their potential for abuse. As more states have debated and enacted a variety of legislative standards on this subject, we have sought to provide guidance by pointing out serious problems which deserve the special attention of legislators.

Our most comprehensive set of criteria for assessing these problems can be found in the *Guidelines for Legislation on Life-Sustaining Treatment* issued by the Bishops' Committee in November 1984. Such criteria should not be taken as implying support for legislation of this kind, but if incorporated into law they can help safegauard the rights of the terminally ill and uphold the value of human life in this complex area.

The Uniform Act: An Analysis

The Uniform Rights of the Terminally Ill Act merits special consideration because it is designed for nationwide enactment and will undoubtedly be considered in many state legislatures. Assessing the proposed Act in the light of Catholic moral principles, we find that it poses at least three serious problems not always encountered in laws of this kind.

1. *The Scope of the Uniform Act.* Like most "living will" laws, the Uniform Act is intended to authorize withdrawal of life-sustaining treatment from patients in the final stage of a terminal condition—that is, patients who will inevitably die soon. But the ambiguity of key terms in the Uniform Act's "definitions" section creates the potential for a much broader application. For example, the Act could be read as authorizing withdrawal of life-sustaining treatment in cases where the patient could live a long time with treatment but will die quickly without it. Patients who have an incurable or irreversible disabling condition might be seen as falling within this broader scope. In such cases, even treatment that is not unduly burdensome and could effectively prolong life may be dismissed as merely "prolonging the process of dying" and hence removed. Such an interpretation would allow withholding of customary and beneficial medical procedures in order to hasten the patient's death. Thus the potential for abuse is greater here than in laws whose scope is clearly limited to patients in the final stage of a terminal condition.

2. *Nutrition and Hydration.* Because human life has inherent value and dignity regardless of its condition, every patient should be provided with measures which can effectively preserve life without involving too grave a burden. Since food and water are necessities of life for all human beings, and can generally be provided without the risks and burdens of more aggressive means for sustaining life, the law should establish a strong presumption in favor of their use.

The Uniform Act states that it will not affect any existing responsibility to provide measures such as nutrition and hydration to promote comfort. But it does not adequately recognize a distinct and more fundamental benefit of such measures—that of sustaining life itself. This is a serious lapse in light of the ambiguous scope of the Uniform Act, which may include cases in which a patient will live a long time with treatment but die quickly without it. For most patients, measures for providing nourishment are morally obligatory even when other treatment can be withdrawn due to its burdensomeness or ineffectiveness.

Negative judgments about the "quality of life" of unconscious or otherwise disabled patients have led some in our society to propose withholding nourishment precisely in order to end these patients' lives. Society must take special care to protect against such discrimination. Laws dealing with medical treatment may have to take account of exceptional circumstances, when even means for providing nourishment may become too ineffective or burdensome to be oblig-atory. But such laws must establish clear safeguards against intentionally has-tening the deaths of vulnerable patients by starvation or dehydration.

3. *Treatment of Pregnant Women.* The Uniform Act explicitly allows a pregnant woman to refuse treatment that could save the life of her unborn child whenever she herself fulfills the conditions of the Uniform Act. The State is thus placed in the position of ratifying and facilitating a decision to end the life of the child. This provision goes beyond even the U.S. Supreme Court's decisions which removed most legal restrictions on abortion. Instead of ignoring the unborn child's independent interest in life, the law should provide for continued treat-ment if it could benefit the child.

Other Problem Areas

Although the above are the most serious flaws in the proposed Uniform Act, it also contains other problem areas which deserve comment:

- The absence of a preamble stating the exact purpose of the Act is a notable deficiency, because such a preamble could assert a presumption in favor of life and thereby help to eliminate ambiguities in the judicial interpretation of the Uniform Act. For example, a preamble could clearly recognize that a patient's right to refuse treatment is limited by certain legitimate state interests, such as interests in preserving life, preventing suicide and homicide, protecting dependent third parties, and maintaining sound ethics in the medical profes-sion.
- The Act fails to define "euthanasia," or to explain whether this word is meant to include euthanasia by omission, thus reducing the effectiveness of its dis-claimer that it does not authorize euthanasia.
- The broad immunities given for withdrawing life-sustaining treatment, and the penalties imposed upon physicians who do not obey a patient's directive, reinforce the Act's bias toward withdrawing treatment and even encourage such withdrawal in doubtful cases.
- The Act does not encourage communication among patient, family and phy-sician, but tends to exclude family members from the decision-making process.
- The vaguely worded directive intended for a patient's signature provides very little information to help the patient appreciate the scope of the power being granted to a physician. For example, the patient is given no warning that his or her directive may authorize withdrawal of food and water, or that it may apply to situations where he or she could live a long time with continued treatment.

Conclusion

The NCCB Committee for Pro-Life Activities has provided this analysis in order to indicate some serious problems raised by much current "living will" legislation and by the proposed *Uniform Rights of the Terminally Ill Act.* We believe that legislators considering such proposals must appreciate the importance of examing them in light of sound moral principles, precisely because these are matters of life and death for some of the most helpless members of our society. Above all, public policy in this area must be based on a positive attitude toward disabled and terminally ill patients, who have a right to live with dignity and with reasonable care the moment of death.

Society for the Right to Die

The following excerpts are from statements of the Society for the Right to Die as to its purpose and program.

The Society works for nationwide recognition of the right to die with dignity. It seeks to protect the individual's right to control treatment decisions at the end of life, including the right to refuse unwanted medical procedures that can only prolong the dying process.

As to its program, the Society works, among other things, to:

- Inform people of their rights under state statutes and the constitutional and common law rights to refuse treatment.
- Work with legislators and the general public in support of "living will" legislation.
- Distribute Living Will Declarations and appropriate documents authorized in each state.
- Offer right-to-die legal counseling as needed by patients, their families, their caregivers, their attorneys....
- Serve as a clearing house for lawyers on right-to-die law.

National Hemlock Society

Statement of the National Hemlock Society regarding active voluntary euthanasia (from *Derek Humphry: Author, Journalist, Communicator, Campaigner*; Humphry is principal founder of the Hemlock Society):

The Society is dedicated to exploring and expounding the options and rights of active voluntary euthanasia for the terminally ill.

It believes that in compassionate and justified cases there is an obligation to help, if asked, a dying person to end his or her life with dignity.

At the present this is against the law and the Hemlock Society wishes to see this rule modified so that a doctor may help without fear of prosecution.

World Federation of Right-to-Die Societies

Submission made to the United Nations by the World Federation of Right-to-Die Societies with respect to the right to die with dignity. The following statement was agreed to in 1988 at the Seventh Biennial Conference of Right-to-Die Societies.

The developments of modern biomedical technology over the last few decades mean that death has increasingly become a matter of deliberate human decision. For almost any life-threatening condition, there is now some medical means (antibiotics, insulin, kidney dialysis, artificial respiration, organ transplantation, blood transfusions, chemo-therapy and so on) which—if employed—will postpone the moment of death. This means that death is no longer the natural event it once was, but has become a matter of human choice. This has profound implications for human rights. The question is this: If death has become a matter of human choice, *who should make that choice?* Who should have the right to decide when and how a patient dies? Currently, suffering, dying people may have their lives pointlessly prolonged, even against their wishes, where legislation does not allow them to choose otherwise.

The World Federation of Right to Die Societies, representing 27 right-to-die societies from 17 countries, is of the firm belief that patients have a right to die with dignity. This right includes the right to refuse life-sustaining treatment and the right to painless dying. Whilst some countries and states have enacted legislation which will protect patients' rights—for example 37 out of 51 jurisdictions in the USA now have "right-to-die" legislation—there are still many countries where patients do not enjoy similar rights.

In 1982 the World Medical Association, in its "Lisbon Declaration of the Rights of the Patient", officially recognised:

—the right to accept or refuse treatment, and
—the right to die with dignity.

The World Federation of Right to Die Societies is convinced that the matter of dying with dignity is such an important human right that the Human Rights Commission of the United Nations Organisation should deal with it. The United Nations Organisation should encourage its member countries to introduce suitably reformed laws which affirm the patient's right to die with dignity.

In considering the right to die with dignity as a Human Right, the following points should be made:

1. Dying with dignity includes the right to painless dying. If effective pain reduction can only be achieved by methods that shorten the expectation of life, this should not preclude their use.

2. Dying with dignity includes the right to know that one is dying. Hence, unless a patient is clearly unwilling to accept that death is near, those caring for the patient should be open in discussing it with him or her. This will give the patient the opportunity of saying farewell to friends and relatives, and of settling his or her affairs.

3. The dying person's wishes concerning death and the dying process must be respected and not restricted. Decisions against the will of the patient, either on the part of the State, physicians or other institutions or persons, are not in accordance with human rights.

4. Medical technology should never be used to prolong a dying person's life against his or her wishes.

5. Dying with dignity means that the patient's intellectual identity is preserved even in the process of dying. Calling upon or rejecting the ministrations of representatives of religious communities or similar organisations must be according to the wishes of the dying person, who must not be subjected to religious observances that have not been specifically requested.

The organisations united in the World Federation of Right to Die Societies hereby request the Human Rights Commission of the United Nations Organisation to incorporate the Right of Dying with Dignity as an appendix to the Charter of Human Rights of 1948, with wording in accordance with above suggestions and requirements.

World Federation of Doctors Who Respect Human Life

The following is a statement of Dr. Philipp Schepens, secretary of the World Federation of Doctors Who Respect Human Life.

Euthanasia, the right to kill, the right to be killed, is a major turnover in human history.... To yield to, and to perform euthanasia, means the negation of 2,400 years of Hippocratic medicine and to go back to pre-hippocratic medicine, where medicine became a social service to the tyran[t], the ruler or the society at large.... [E]uthanasia will put our profession and society upside down. We will be witness to the greatest regression of civilisation.... If we love our fellow-men, if we love our profession, if we love liberty and democracy, we must combat the euthantic [sic] perversion of medicine....

Appendix C: Digest of U.S. Judicial Decisions Relating to the Right to Refuse Life-Prolonging Treatment

Note: The statements in the paragraphs of this Digest are intended to supply general information and are not meant to give legal advice and counsel as to what the law is in a particular state. Readers with specific questions or problems should consult the statutes, case law, and attorneys in their respective states.

RIGHT TO REFUSE LIFE-SUSTAINING TREATMENT

All adult patients, whether or not terminally ill and regardless of age, competence, or incompetence, have a right to refuse life-sustaining treatment which is recognized and protected by state and federal constitutions as part of the right of privacy.

Brophy v. New England Mt. Sinai Hospital, Inc., 398 Mass. 417, 497 N.E. 2d 626 (Massachusetts Supreme Judicial Court, 1986); *Rasmussen v. Fleming*, 741 P.2d 674 (Arizona Supreme Court 1987); *Bouvia v. Superior Court*, 179 Cal. App. 3d 1127, 225 Cal. Rptr. 297 (California Court of Appeal, Second Appellate District, Division Two, 1986) *review denied* (Cal. June 5, 1986); *In re Quinlan*, 70 N.J. 10, 355 A. 2d 647, *certiorari denied sub nom. Garger v. New Jersey*, 429 U.S. 922 (1976); *Delio v. Westchester County Medical Center*, 129 A.D. 2d 1, 516 N.Y.S.2d 677 (New York Supreme Court. Appellate Division, Second Department, 1987); *Eichner v. Dillion*, 73 A.D.2d 431, 431 N.Y.S.2d 517, *reversed sub nom. In re Storar*, 52 N.Y. 2d 363, 420 N.E. 2d 64, 438 N.Y.S.2d 266 (New York Court of Appeals) *certiorari denied* 454 U.S. 858 (1981); *In re Lydia E. Hall Hospital*, 116 Misc. 2d 477, 455 N.Y.S.2d 706 (New York Supreme Court, Nassau County, 1982); *Leach v. Shapiro*, 13 Ohio App. 3d 393, 469 N.E. 2d 1047 (Ohio Court of Appeals for Summit County, 1984); *Natanson v. Kline*, 186 Kan. 393, 350 P. 2d 1093 (Kansas Supreme Court, 1960); *Schloendorf v. Society of New York Hospital*, 211 N.Y. 125, 105 N.E. 92 (New York Court of Appeals, 1914); *Superintendent of Belchertown State School v. Saikewicz*, 373 Mass. 728, 370 N.E. 2d 417 (Massachusetts Supreme Judicial Court, 1977); *In re Colyer*, 99 Wash. 2d 114, 660 P.2d 738 (Washington Supreme Court, 1973); *In re Rodas*, No. 86PR139 (Colorado District Court, Mesa County, January 22, 1987); *Tune v. Walter Reed Army Medical Hospital*, 602 F. Supp. 1452 (United States District Court for the District of Columbia, 1985); *Satz v. Perlmutter*, 363 So. 2d 160 (Florida Court of Appeal, 1987) *affirmed* 379 So. 2d 359 (Florida Supreme Court, 1980); *Wilcox v. Hawaii*, Civ. No. 860116 (Hawaii Circuit Court 5th Circuit, June 16, 1986); *Foody v. Manchester Memorial Hospital*, 40 Conn. Supp. 127, 482 A.2d 713 (Connecticut Superior Court, Hartford District, 1984); *In re Torres*, 357 N.W.2d 332 (Minnesota Supreme Court, 1984); *In re Bayer*, No. 4131 (North Dakota Burleigh County Court, February 5, 1987); *In re L.H.R.*, 253 Ga. 439, 321, S.E.2d 716 (Georgia Supreme Court, 1984).

Most courts hold that the right includes the right to reject the artificial provision of nutrition and hydration which is another form of medical treatment.

Leach v. Shapiro, 13 Ohio App. 3d 393, 469 N.E. 2d 1047 (Ohio Court of Appeals for Summit County, 1984); *In re Rodas*, No. 86PR139 (Colorado District Court, Mesa County, January 22, 1987).

But in Missouri, the Supreme Court there believe that a G-tube is not medical treatment but the provision of sustenance which all have a duty to provide and accept.

Cruzan v. Harmon, 760 S.W. 2d 408 (Missouri Supreme Court, 1988) *certiorari granted* 109 Sup. Ct. Rep. 3240 (1989).

The right to refuse life-sustaining treatment may be exercised by elderly patients in nursing homes or by young or middle-aged patients in hospitals or at home.

In re Conroy, 98, N.J. 321, 486 A. 2d 1209 (New Jersey Supreme Court, 1985) (elderly patient in nursing home); *In re Jobes*, 108 N.J. 394, 529 A.2d 434 (New Jersey Supreme Court, 1986) (young patient in nursing home); *In re Quinlan*, 70 N.J. 10, 355 A. 2d 647, *certiorari denied sub nom. Garger v. New Jersey*, 429 U.S. 922 (1976) (young patient in hospital); *In re Peter*, 108 N.J. 365,529 A.2d 419 (New Jersey Supreme Court, 1987) (patient in her sixties in nursing home); *In re Farrell*, 108 N.J.335, 529 A.2d 404 (New Jersey Supreme Court, 1987) (middle-aged patient at home); *Delio v. Westchester County Medical Center*, 129 A.D. 2d 1, 516 N.Y.S. 2d 677 (New York Supreme Court, Appellate Division, Second Department, 1987) (middle-aged patient in hospital); *Satz v. Perlmutter*, 362 So. 160 (Florida Court of Appeal, 1987) *affirmed* 379 So. 2d 359 (Florida Supreme Court, 1980) (elderly patient in hospital); *Brophy v. New England Mt. Sinai Hospital, Inc.*, 398 Mass. 417, 497 N.E. 2d 626 (Massachusetts Supreme Judicial Court, 1986) (middle-aged patient in hospital); *In re Colyer*, 99 Wash. 2d 114, 660 P.2d 738 (Washington Supreme Court, 1973) (69-year-old patient in hospital).

Any decision to forgo life-sustaining treatment is not a medical one or one whose soundness is to be reviewed by the courts. It is a moral and philosophical decision that belongs solely to the patient.

Bouvia v. Superior Court, 179 Cal. App. 3d 1127, 225 Cal. Rptr. 297 (California Court of Appeal, Second Appellate District, Division Two, 1986) *review denied* (Cal. June 5, 1986).

As a right protected by federal and state constitutions, the right to reject life-sustaining medical treatment cannot be impaired by any statute, such as living will or natural death legislation.

Corbett v. D'Alessandro, 487 So. 2d 368 (Florida District Court of Appeal, Second District) *review denied* 492 So.2d 1331 (Florida Supreme Court 1986); *In re Colyer,* 99 Wash. 2d 114, 660 P.2d 738 (Washington Supreme Court, 1973).

The right is not absolute, however, and is subject to compelling and counter-vailing interests of the state: protection of human life; prevention of suicide; protection of innocent third parties; and protection of the integrity of the medical profession.

Brophy v. New England Mt. Sinai Hospital, Inc., 398 Mass. 417, 497 N.E. 2d 626 (Massachusetts Supreme Judicial Court, 1986); *In re Quinlan,* 70 N.J. 10, 355 A. 2d 647, *certiorari denied sub nom. Garger v. New Jersey,* 429 U.S. 922 (1976); *Superintendent of Belchertown State School v. Saikewicz,* 373 Mass. 728, 370 N.E. 2d 417 (Massachusetts Supreme Judicial Court, 1977); *In re Colyer,* 99 Wash. 2d 114, 660 P.2d 738 (Washington Supreme Court, 1973).

Moreover, the case law in New York also severely limits the right to decline life-sustaining treatment to those patients who, with no hope of recovery, had clearly expressed their wishes that medical treatment not be used to prolong their lives. Where hopelessly ill patients are presently incompetent, there must be clear and convincing evidence that previously, through oral or written statements, they had made a reasoned and informed decision concerning the termination of medical treatment.

In re Storar, 52 N.Y. 2d 363, 420 N.E.2d 64, N.Y.S. 2d 266 (New York Court of Appeals) *certiorari denied* 454 U.S. 858 (1981); *Eichner v. Dillon,* 73 A.D. 2d 431, 431 N.Y.S. 2d 517, *reversed sub nom. In re Storar,* 52 N.Y. 2d 363, 420 N.E. 2d 64, 438 N.Y.S.2d 266 (New York Court of Appeals) *certiorari denied* 454 U.S. 858 (1981); *In re Lydia E. Hall Hospital,* 116 Misc.2d 477, 455 N.Y.S.2d 706 (New York Supreme Court, Nassau County, 1982); *Saunders v. State,* 129 Misc.2d. 45, 492 N.Y.S.2d 510 (New York Supreme Court, Nassau County, 1985).

HOSPITAL POLICY

A hospital's policy against withholding or withdrawing artificial feeding from a patient cannot prevent a patient from declining such feeding. Neither can the hospital require the patient to leave for another hospital willing to allow the artificial feeding to be terminated.

In re Requena, 213 N.J. Super. 475, 517 A.2d 886 (Super. Ct. Ch. Div.) *affirmed* 213 N.J. Super. 443, 517 A.2d 869 (Super. Ct. App. Div. 1986).

JUDICIAL APPROVAL FOR WITHHOLDING OR WITHDRAWING TREATMENT

Judicial approval is not required in the case of a competent patient who expressed a wish not to be maintained on artificial feeding if a hospital is willing to honor the wishes of the patient. Neither is judicial approval necessary or desirable when physician and family agree on behalf of an incompetent patient to terminate life-sustaining treatment, especially since there is no civil or criminal liability for health care professionals who act in good faith.

Wilcox v. Hawaii, Civ. No. 860116 (Hawaii Circuit Court 5th Circuit, June 16, 1986); *In re Torres*, 357 N.W.2d 332 (Minnesota Supreme Court, 1984); *John F. Kennedy Memorial Hospital, Inc. v. The Honorable Donald H. Bludworth*, 452 So. 2d 921 (Florida Supreme Court, 1984); *In re Jobes*, 108 N.J. 394, 529 A.2d 434 (New Jersey Supreme Court, 1986); *In re Farrell*, 108 N.J. 335, 529 A.2d 404 (New Jersey Supreme Court, 1987).

LIABILITY OF HEALTH CARE PROFESSIONALS FOR NOT HONORING PATIENTS' WISHES TO REFUSE LIFE-SUSTAINING TREATMENT

Medical treatment contrary to a patient's wishes constitutes battery. Damages may be imposed on health care professionals for a patient's pain and suffering while unwanted life-sustaining treatment is provided. Liability may exist as well for the costs of unwanted medical care, and, under an appropriate statute, for attorney's fees.

Schloendorf v. Society of New York Hospital, 211 N.Y. 125, 105 N.E. 92 (New York Court of Appeals, 1914); *Bartling v. Superior Court of California*, 163 Cal. App. 3d 186, 209 Cal. Rptr. 220 (California Court of Appeal, 1984); *Leach v. Shapiro*, 13 Ohio App. 3d 393, 469 N.E. 2d 1047 (Ohio Court of Appeals for Summit County, 1984).

ADVANCE DIRECTIVES AND LIVING WILL OR NATURAL DEATH LEGISLATION

A competent adult patient may provide in advance of incompetency whether life-sustaining treatment should be withheld or withdrawn.

Rasmussen v. Fleming, 741 P.2d 674 (Arizona Supreme Court, 1987).

A living will or natural death statute enacted by a state provides a convenient form for an advance directive. The statute, however, only supplements a patient's constitutionally protected right to refuse such treatment and is not the exclusive avenue for exercising that right.

Rasmussen v. Fleming, 741 P.2d 674 (Arizona Supreme Court, 1987); *Barber v. Superior Court of California*, 147 Cal. App. 3d 1006, 195 Cal, Rptr. 484 (California Court of Appeal, 2d District, 1983).

Where a living will statute provides that "life-prolonging procedures" may be withheld or withdrawn, the provision of artificial feeding is included within the meaning of the term because artificial feeding is an artificial means of overcoming the inability of a patient to swallow and be given nourishment and hydration.

Hazelton v. Pawhatan Nursing Home, Inc., No. Ch98287 (Virginia Circuit Court, Fairfax County, August 29, 1986) *appeal denied* Record M. 860814 (Virginia, Sept. 2, 1986); and Va. Cir. Ct. Op. 414 (Aspen, 1987).

In states, such as New York, which do not have living will statutes and which require clear and convincing devidence that now incompetent patients had expressed their wishes prior to becoming incompetent regarding the termination of life-prolonging treatment, a document such as a living will is recognized as expressing a rational decision to refuse such treatment.

Saunders v. State, 129 Misc.2d. 45, 492 N.Y.S.2d 510 (New York Supreme Court, Nassau County, 1985).

SURROGATE HEALTH CARE DECISIONS

Where a patient is not competent or is in a persistent vegetative state and has not given advance instructions, a surrogate may exercise the patient's constitutional right to discontinue life-sustaining treatment.

Brophy v. New England Mt. Sinai Hospital, Inc., 398 Mass. 417, 497 N.E. 2d 626 (Massachusetts Supreme Judicial Court, 1986); *John F. Kennedy Memorial Hospital, Inc. v. The Honorable Donald H. Bludworth*, 452 So. 2d 921 (Florida Supreme Court, 1984); *In re Quinlan*, 70 N.J. 10, 355 A. 2d 647, *certiorari denied sub nom. Garger v. New Jersey*, 429 U.S. 922 (1976); *Rasmussen v. Fleming*, 741 P.2d 674 (Arizona Supreme Court 1987); *Superintendent of Belchertown State School v. Saikewicz*, 373 Mass. 728, 370 N.E. 2d 417 (Massachusetts Supreme Judicial Court, 1977); *In re Jobes*, 108 N.J. 394, 529 A.2d 434 (New Jersey Supreme Court, 1986); *In re Peter*, 108 N.J. 365, 529 A.2d 419 (New Jersey Supreme Court, 1987); *Foody v. Manchester Memorial Hospital*, 40 Conn. Supp. 127, 482 A.2d 713 (Connecticut Superior Court, Hartford District, 1984).

Where a patient is comatose, incompetent or otherwise incapable of making medical decisions and has not made any advance directive or appointed a proxy, some state statutes lay down procedures concerning who can exercise the patient's right to terminate medical treatment. But where no statute lays down such a procedure, one court recommended that any of the individuals in the following order of priority may request discontinuance of treatment under the supervision of the attending physician: (1) the judicially appointed guardian of the person; (2) the person designated in writing by the patient to make the treatment decision; (3) the spouse of the patient; (4) the patient's adult child; (5) the parents of the patient; (6) the patient's nearest living relative. If none of these is available, treatment may be discontinued at the discretion and under the direction of the attending physician.

Rasmussen v. Fleming, 741 P.2d 674 (Arizona Supreme Court, 1987).

However, the Missouri Supreme Court has held that if the surrogate is a judicially appointed guardian, the surrogate cannot consent to the discontinuance of life-sustaining systems maintaining a patient in a persistent vegetative state although not terminally ill. The guardian's power emanates from the state, whose interest in the preservation of life overrides the right of the patient. (This decision has been affirmed by the U.S. Supreme Court.)

Cruzan v. Harmon, 760 S.W. 2d 498 (Missouri Supreme Court, 1988) *certiorari granted* 109 Sup. Ct. Rep. 3240 (1989), *affirmed* No. 88–1503, June 25, 1990.

Appendix D: Table of States Having Living Will Statutes (with statutory citations)

AL—Code 1975, Secs. 22-8A to 22-8A-10.

AK—Stat. 1986 Secs. 18.12.010 to 18.12.100.

AR—Ark. Stat. Ann. 1987 Secs. 82.3801 to 82.3804.

AZ—Rev. Stat. Ann. 1985 Secs. 36-3201 to 36-3210 (Supp. 1986).

CA—Cal. Health & Safety Code. Secs. 7185 to 7195 (Deering Supp. 1987).

CO—Colorado Rev. Stat. Ann. Secs. 15-18-101 to 15-18-113 (Supp. 1986).

CT—1985 Conn. Gen. Stat. Secs. 19a-570 to 19a-575.

DL—16 Del. Code Ann. 1983 Secs. 2501 to 2509.

DC—D.C. Code 1987 Secs. 6-2401 to 6-2430.

FL—1984 Fla. Stat. Ann. Secs. 765.01 to 765.15.

GA—Ga. Code Ann. 1985 Secs. 31-32-1 to 31-32-12.

HI—Haw. Rev. Stat. 1986 Secs. 338:1688-86-1 to 27.

IA—Iowa Code Ann. 1985 Secs. 144A.1 to 144A.11.

ID—Idaho Code Secs. 39-4501 to 39-4508.

IL—Ill. Ann. Stat. Ch. 10 1/2, paras. 701 to 710.

IN—Ind. Code Ann. 1985 Secs. 16-811-1 to 16-8-11-22.

KS—Kansas Stat. Ann. Secs. 65-28, 101 to 65-28, 122.

LA—La. Rev. Stat. Ann. 1987 Secs. 40:1299.58.1 to 40:1299:58:10.

ME—Maine 1986 Rev. Stat. Ann. Tit. 22, Secs. 2921 to 2931.

MD—Maryland 1986 Code, Health—General Ann. Secs. 5-601 to 5-614.

MS—Mississippi Code Ann. 1986 Secs. 41-41-101 to 41-41-121.

MO—Missouri Ann. Stat. 1985 Secs. 459.010 to 459.055.

MT—Montana Code Ann. 1985 Secs. 50-9-101 to 50-9-206.

NV—Nevada Rev. Stat. 1986 Secs. 449.540 to 449.690.

NH—New Hampshire Rev. Stat. Ann. Secs. 137-H:1 to 137-H:16.

NM—New Mexico Stat. Ann. Secs. 24-7-1 to 24-7-10.

NC—North Carolina Gen. Stat. 1985 Secs. 90-320 to 90-323.

OK—Oklahoma Stat. Ann. 1985 Tit. 63 Secs. 3101 to 3111.

OR—Oregon Rev. Stat. 1983 Secs. 97.050 to 97.090.

SC—South Carolina Code Ann. 1986 Secs. 44-77-10 to 44-77-160.

TN—Tennessee Code Ann. 1985 Secs. 32-11-101 to 32-11-110.

TX—Texas Health and Safety Code Ann. 1977. Amended 1985. Secs. 4590h-1 to 4590h-11.

UT—Utah Code Ann. 1985 Secs. 75-2-1101 to 75-2-1118.

VA—Virgina Code Ann. Secs. 54-325.8:1 to 54-325.8:13.

VT—Vermont Stat. Ann. Tit. 18 Secs. 5251 to 5262.

WA—Wash. Rev. Code Ann. Secs. 70.122.010 to 70.122.905.

WI—Wisconsin Stat. Ann. Secs. 154.01 to 154.15.

WV—West Virginia Code 1985 Secs. 16-30-1 to 16-30-10.

WY—Wyoming Stat. Secs. 33-26-144 to 33-26-152.

COMPARISONS OF SIGNIFICANT FEATURES

Note: The comparisons here are intended to supply general information on some important features and are not meant to give legal counsel and advice as to what law is in a particular state. Readers must consult the statutes of their states for special and specific provisions.

Features and States Recognizing:

Declaration must substantially follow the statutory form: AL; AZ; CA; CT; DC; GA; ID; IL; IN; KS; MD; MA; NV; NM; OK; OR; SC; VT; WA; WV; WI; WY.

Declaration may be oral: FL; LA; VA.

Declaration made in another state recognized: AL; AK; HI; ME; MD; MO; MT; NV.

Declaration revocable: AL; AK; AZ; CA; CO; DE; DC; FL; GA; HI; ID; IL; IN; IA; KS; LA; ME; MD; MS; MO; MT; NV; NH; NM; NC; OK; OR; SC; TN; TX; VT; VA; WA; WV; WI; WY.

Declaration not effective during pregnancy: AL; AK; AZ; CA; CO; CT; DE; FL; GA; HI; IL; IN; IA; KS; MD; MO; MT; NV; NH; OK; SC; VT; WA; WV; WI; WY.

Terminal condition required for declaration to be effective: AL; AK; AZ; CA; CO; CT; DE; DC; FL; GA; HI; ID; IN; IA; KS; LA; ME; MD; MS; MO; MT; NV; NH; NM; NC; OK; OR; SC; TN; TX; VT; VA; WA; WV; WI; WY.

No civil or criminal liability for health care providers carrying out declaration: AL; AK; AZ; AR; CA; CO; CT; DE; DC; FL; GA; HI; ID; IL; IN; KS; LA; ME; MD; MS; MO; MT; NV; NH; NM; NC; OK; OR; SC; TN; TX; VT; VA; WA; WV; WI; WY.

Physicians not complying with statute penalized: AK; CA; CO; DC; HI; IN; KS; ME; MO; MT; OK; SC; TN.

Physicians not obligated by declaration to withhold or withdraw procedures: CA; IN; NV.

Artificial feeding not included in life-prolonging procedure which may be withheld or withdrawn: AZ; CO; CT; FL; GA; HI; IL; IA; KS; MD; MT; NH; OK; OR; SC; TN; VT; WI; WY.

Proxy appointment allowed: AK; CO; DE; FL; HI; ID; IN; IA; LA; TX; VT; VA; WY.

Appendix E: Living Will Form

Note: The validity of a living will is determined by the living will ("natural death," "right to die" or "death with dignity") statute of the state in which it is executed. Some statutes may require that a living will conform to their provisions. The form given below is only a sample and suggestive. It may not be valid for use in the reader's state if that state has adopted a living will statute. Readers are advised to be careful in the use of this form and to consult the statutes of their states when preparing a living will. In states that have no living will statutes, a living will, such as the sample form, may be considered a clear and convincing demonstration of one's wishes regarding medical treatment.

ADVANCE DIRECTIVE TO MY PHYSICIANS, HEALTH CARE PROVIDERS, AND FAMILY

I, _____, being of sound mind, willfully and voluntarily execute this directive to express my wish concerning medical treatment if I am no longer able to make decisions concerning such treatment, have an incurable condition caused by injury, disease or illness that will cause me to die within a relatively short time and the use of life-sustaining procedures will serve only to prolong artificially the process of dying. In these circumstances, I direct my attending physician to withhold or withdraw all life-sustaining procedures, including artificial feeding, not necessary to my comfort or to alleviate pain, and to allow me to die naturally. I ask that my attending physician and those concerned with my care honor this directive as an exercise under the circumstances described of my constitutional and common law right to refuse life-sustaining medical treatment. I am mentally and emotionally competent to understand the meaning of this directive.

Dated:
Signed:
Witness:
Witness:

Appendix F: Proxy Form

Note: The validity of a proxy is determined by the statute of the state in which it is executed. Some statutes may require that a proxy conform to their provisions. The form given below is only a sample and suggestive. It may not be valid for use in the reader's state. Readers are advised to be careful in the use of this form and to consult the statutes of their states when preparing a proxy.

HEALTH CARE PROXY APPOINTMENT

In the event that I am no longer able to make decisions concerning my medical treatment, I hereby appoint _____ as my health care proxy to decide whether life-sustaining medical treatment, including artificial feeding, should be withheld or withdrawn. The proxy I have named has been chosen by me as familar with my beliefs, wishes and attitudes and I direct my attending physician and health care providers to follow this proxy's instructions. If the person whom I have appointed proxy is mentally or physically unable to make medical decisions, I appoint _____ as my health care proxy.

Dated:
Signed:
Witness:
Witness:

Appendix G: Durable Power of Attorney Form

Note: All states and the District of Columbia have statutes that permit a durable power of attorney to be created which allows an agent to act and make treatment decisions for the person making the power of attorney. Some statutes allow the appointment of a spouse, parent, adult child, sibling, niece, or nephew. The validity of a durable power of attorney is determined by the statute of the state in which it is executed. Some statutes may require that a durable power of attorney conform to their provisions. The form given below is only a sample and suggestive. It may not be valid for use in the reader's state. Readers are advised to be careful in the use of this form and to consult the statutes of their states when preparing a durable power of attorney.

The form given here confers management powers found in broad powers of attorney. The key paragraphs are the second, which relates to health care decisions, and the third, which makes the instrument a durable power of attorney.

DURABLE POWER OF ATTORNEY

KNOW ALL MEN that I, _____ residing at _____ , do hereby appoint _____ , residing at _____ , my true and lawful attorney, and in my name and stead and for my benefit, to have full power and authority to execute and perform acts and do things of every kind and nature that should be executed, performed or done in the management of my personal life or business affairs, or that, in the opinion of my said attorney, should be executed, performed or done, as fully as I might execute, perform or do them if personally present; and I hereby ratify and confirm all that my said attorney shall execute, perform or do, or cause to be executed, performed or done, by virtue hereof.

This power includes the power and authority to make decisions concerning my medical treatment if I am unable to do so and to direct my attending physician and health care personnel to implement life-sustaining medical treatment or to withdraw or withhold the same from me, including artificial feeding, not necessary to my comfort or to alleviate pain.

This power of attorney is a durable one and shall remain valid and in full force and effect without being affected in any way by the passage of time, by my subsequent incompetence or inability to make, participate in, communicate or understand medical treatment decisions.

IN WITNESS WHEREOF, I have hereunto set my hand and seal this _____ day of _____ , 19 __ .

_____

Witness:
Witness:

STATE OF _____
COUNTY OF _____
On this _____ day of _____ , 19__ , before me personally appeared _____, to me known to be the person described in, and who executed the foregoing Durable Power of Attorney, and he/she acknowledged to me that he/she executed said instrument freely and for the purposes therein mentioned.

(Notary's Seal)

(Notary signature,
registration no. and
date commission expires)

Selected Bibliography and Sources of Information

DEATH AND DYING—GENERAL

Books

Agee, J. *A Death in the Family.* New York: Avon Books, 1959.

Alvarez, A. *The Savage God.* New York: Random House, 1972.

Aries, P. *Western Attitudes Toward Death.* Baltimore: Johns Hopkins University Press, 1974.

de Beauvoir, S. *A Very Easy Death.* New York: G.P. Putnam & Sons, 1966.

Becker, E. *The Denial of Death.* New York: The Free Press, 1973.

Benton, R. G. *Death and Dying.* New York: Van Nostrand Reinhold, 1978.

Berger, A. S. *Evidence of Life After Death: A Casebook for the Tough-Minded.* Springfield, IL: Charles C. Thomas, 1988.

Berger, A. S., Badham, P., Kutscher, A. H., Berger, J., Perry, M., and Beloff, J. (eds.) *Prespectives on Death and Dying: Cross-Cultural and Multi-Disciplinary Views.* Philadelphia: The Charles Press, 1988.

Choron, J. *Death and Modern Man.* New York: Collier Books, 1964.

——. *Death and Western Thought.* New York: Collier Books, 1963.

Ducasse, C. J. *A Critical Examination of the Belief in a Life After Death.* Springfield, IL: Charles C. Thomas, 1961.

Feifel, H. *The Meaning of Death.* New York: McGraw-Hill, 1959.

Feifel, H. (ed.) *New Meaning of Death.* New York: McGraw-Hill, 1977.

Fulton, R. (ed.) *Death and Identity* (rev. ed.). Bowie, MD: The Charles Press, 1976.

Gorer, G. *Death, Grief, and Mourning.* Garden City, NJ: Doubleday and Co., 1965.

Grof, S. and Halifax, J. *The Human Encounter with Death.* New York: E. P. Dutton, 1978.

Grollman, A. (ed.) *Concerning Death: A Practical Guide for the Living.* Boston: Beacon Press, 1974.

Jackson, E. N. *For the Living.* New York: Channel Press, 1965.

Kastenbaum, R. (ed.) *Between Life and Death.* New York: Springer, 1979.

Kastenbaum, R. and Aisenberg, R. *The Psychology of Death.* New York: Springer, 1972.

Kubler-Ross, E. *Death: The Final Stage of Growth.* Englewood Cliffs, NJ: Prentice Hall/Spectrum, 1975.

————. *On Death and Dying.* New York: Macmillan, 1969.

Kutscher, A. H. (ed.) *Death and Bereavement.* Springfield, IL: Charles C. Thomas, 1969.

————. *A Bibliography of Books on Death, Bereavement, Loss and Grief* (1935–68). New York: Health Sciences Publishing, 1969.

————. *But Not to Lose: A Book of Comfort for the Bereaved.* New York: Frederick Fell, 1969.

Pattison, E. M. *The Experience of Dying.* Englewood Cliffs, NJ: Prentice-Hall, 1977.

President's Commission for the Study of Ethical Problems in Medicine and Biomedical and Behavioral Research. *Defining Death: Medical, Legal and Ethical Issues in the Determination of Death.* Washington, DC: U.S. Government Printing Office, 1981, Chaps. 3 and 4.

Rosenthal, T. *How Could I Not Be Among You?* New York: Braziller, 1973.

Shneidman, E. S. *Deaths of Man.* New York: Quadrangle/New York Times Book Co., 1973.

Shneidman, E. S. (ed.) *Death: Current Perspectives.* Palo Alto, CA: Mayfield, 1976.

Toynbee, A. et al. (eds.) *Man's Concern with Death.* New York: McGraw-Hill, 1969.

Unamuno, M. *Tragic Sense of Life.* New York: Dover Publications, 1954.

Weisman, A. *On Dying and Denying.* New York: Behavioral Publications, 1972.

Journals

Archives of the Foundation of Thanatology, The Foundation of Thanatology, 630 West 168th St., New York, NY 10032.

Death Studies, Hemisphere Publishing Corp., 1101 Vermont Ave., N.W. (Suite 200), Washington, DC 20077.

Omega: The International Journal for the Psychological Study of Dying, Bereavement, Suicide and Other Lethal Behaviors. Greenwood Press, Inc., 88 Post Road West, Westport, CT 06880.

THE RIGHT TO REFUSE TREATMENT

Articles

Annas, G. J. 1984–85. "Refusal of Lifesaving Treatment for Minors." *Journal of Family Law* 23:217.

Annas, G. and Glantz, L. H. 1986. "The Right of Elderly Patients to Refuse Life-Sustaining Treatment." *Milbank Quarterly* 64 Supp. 2.

Cantor, N. L. 1973. "A Patient's Decision to Decline Life-Saving Treatment: Bodily Integrity Versus the Preservation of Life." *Rutgers Law Review* 26:28.

Hastings Center. 1987. "Guidelines on the Termination of Life-Sustaining Treatment and the Care of the Dying."

Hirsch, H. L. and Donovan, R. E. 1977. "The Right to Die: Medico-Legal Implications of *In re Quinlan.*" *Rutgers Law Review* 30:267.

Meulders-Klein, M. T. 1983. "The Right Over One's Body: Its Scope and Limits in Comparative Law." *Boston College International & Comparative Law Review* 6:29.

Organ, M. M. 1986. "Withholding Life-Sustaining Treatment from the Incompetent Patient: The Need for Statutory Guidelines." *Loyola University Chicago Law Journal* 17:427.

President's Commission for the Study of Ethical Problems in Medicine and Biomedical and Behavioral Research. 1983. "Deciding to Forgo Life-Sustaining Treatment." Washington, DC: U.S. Government Printing Office.

Swartz, M. 1985. "The Patient Who Refuses Medical Treatment: A Dilemma for Hospitals and Physicians." *American Journal of Law and Medicine* 11:147.

Books

The Physician and the Hopelessly Ill Patient: Legal, Medical and Ethical Guidelines. New York: The Society for the Right to Die, 1985.

Tribe, L. H. *American Constitutional Law.* Mineola, NY: Foundation Press, 1978.

Veatch, R. M. *Death, Dying and the Biological Revolution: Our Last Quest for Responsibility.* New Haven and London: Yale University Press, 1976.

LIVING WILLS

Handbook of Living Will Laws. New York: Society for the Right to Die, 1987.

Handbook of Living Will Laws: 1981–1984. New York: Society for the Right to Die, 1986.

ARTIFICIAL FEEDING

Callahan, D. 1983. "On Feeding the Dying." *Hastings Center Report* 13: 22.

Capron, A. M. 1984. "Ironies and Tensions in Feeding the Dying." *Hastings Center Report* 14:32.

Lo, B. 1984. "Guiding the Hand That Feeds: Caring for the Demented Elderly." *New England Journal of Medicine* 311: 402.

Myers, D. W. 1985. "Legal Aspects of Withdrawing Nourishment from an Incurably Ill Patient." *Archives of Internal Medicine* 145:125.

Wanzer, S. H. et al. 1984. "The Physician's Responsibility Toward Hopelessly Ill Patients." *New England Journal of Medicine* 310:955.

Zerwekh, J. V. 1983. "The Dehydration Question." *Nursing* 83:47.

DURABLE POWERS OF ATTORNEY

Article

Moore, D. L. 1986. "The Durable Power of Attorney as an Alternative to the Improper Use of Conservatorship for Health-Care Decisionmaking." *St. John's Law Review* 60:631.

Book

Collin, F. F., Lombard, J. L., Moses, A. L., and Spitler, H. *Drafting the Durable Power of Attorney—A Systems Approach.* Lexington, SC: R. P. W. Publishing Co., 1980.

EUTHANASIA

Articles

Admiraal, P. V. "Active Voluntary Euthanasia." In Downing, A. B. and Smoker, B. *Voluntary Euthanasia: Experts Debate the Right to Die.* London: Peter Owen, 1986.

Barrington, M. "The Case for Rational Suicide." In Downing, A. B. and Smoker, B. *Voluntary Euthanasia: Experts Debate the Right to Die.* London: Peter Owen, 1986.

Beloff, J. "Do We Have the Right to Die?" In A. S. Berger, P. Badham, A. H. Kutscher, J. Berger, M. Perry, and J. Beloff (eds.) *Perspectives on Death and Dying: Cross-Cultural and Multi-Disciplinary Views.* Philadelphia: The Charles Press, 1988.

Dyck, A. J. "An Alternative to the Ethic of Euthanasia." In R. H. Williams (ed.) *To Live or to Die.* New York: Springer-Verlag, 1973.

Fletcher, J. "Ethics and Euthanasia." In P. F. Weir (ed.) *Ethical Issues in Death and Dying.* New York: Columbia University Press, 1977.

———. 1967. "Prolonging Life." *Washington Law Review* 42:499.

Kamisar, Y. 1958. "Some Non-Religious Views Against Proposed 'Mercy Killing' Legislation." *Minnesota Law Review* 42:969.

Newman, M. E. "Voluntary Active Euthanasia: An Individual's Right to Determine the Time and Manner of Death." In A. S. Berger, P. Badham, A. H. Kutscher, J. Berger, M. Perry, and J. Beloff (eds.) *Perspectives on Death and Dying: Cross-Cultural and Multi-Disciplinary Views.* Philadelphia: The Charles Press, 1988.

Books

Horan, D. J. and Mall, D. *Death, Dying and Euthanasia.* Frederick, MD: Aleitha Books/University Publications of America, 1980.

Humphrey, D. with Wickett, A. *Jean's Way.* New York: Hemlock/Harper & Row, 1987.

———. *The Right to Die: Understanding Euthanasia.* London: Bodley Head, 1986.

Kohl, M. (ed.) *Beneficent Euthanasia.* Buffalo, NY: Prometheus Books, 1975.

Rachels, J. *The End of Life: Euthanasia and Morality.* Oxford: Oxford University Press, 1986.

Russell, O. R. *Freedom to Die: Moral and Legal Aspects of Euthanasia.* New York: Human Sciences Press, 1975.

Weir, P. F. (ed.) *Ethical Issues in Death and Dying.* New York: Columbia University Press, 1977.

Williams, G. L. *Sanctity of Life and the Criminal Law.* London: Faber and Faber, 1958.

Journals, Booklets, and Other Publications

Euthanasia Review. National Hemlock Society. Human Sciences Press, 72 Fifth Ave., New York, NY 10011.

Euthanasia: Modern America's Rendezvous with Death. National Right to Life Committee, Suite 500, 419 7th St. N.W., Washington, DC 20004.

Pro-Life Action League—Action News. Pro-Life Action League, 6160 N. Cicero Ave., Chicago, IL 60646.

Pro-Life News. Alliance for Life, B1–90 Garry St., Winnipeg, MBR3C 4H1, Canada.

Pro-Life Reporter. U.S. Coalition for Life, PO Box 315, Export, PA 15632.

FILMS

Brian's Song. Learning Corporation of America.

Death Be Not Proud. Learning Corporation of America.

How Could I Not Be Among You. Eccentric Circle Cinema Workshop. Box 1481, Evanston, IL 60204.

The Right to Die (with Raquel Welch and Michael Gross). Produced by Ohlmeyer Communications Company and National Television Network. Cultural Information Service, PO Box 786, Madison Square Station, New York, NY 10159.

What Man Shall Live and Not See Death? NAMH, Film Service, PO Box 7316, Alexandria, VA 22307.

VIDEOTAPES

Life, Death and the Dying Patient, Part I and Part II. Elisabeth Kübler-Ross. Elisabeth Kübler-Ross Center, South Route #616, Head Waters, VA 24442.

The Right to Die: The Choice Is Yours. The Society for the Right to Die. 250 W. 57th St., New York, NY 10107.

EDUCATIONAL, MEMBERSHIP, AND RESEARCH ORGANIZATIONS

Americans Against Human Suffering, PO Box 11001, Glendale, CA 91206.

American Civil Liberties Union, 22 E. 40th St., New York, NY 10016.

American Coalition of Citizens with Disabilities, 1012 14th St., N.W., Suite 901, Washington, DC 20005.

American Medical Association, 535 N. Dearborn St., Chicago, IL 60610.

Center for Death Education and Research, 1167 Social Science Building, University of Minnesota, 267 19th Ave. S., Minneapolis, MN 55455.

Concern for Dying, 250 West 57th St., New York, NY 10107.

Disability Rights Education and Defense Fund, 2212 6th St., Berkeley, CA 94710.

Forum for Death Education and Counseling, 2211 Arthur Ave., Lakewood, OH 44107.
Foundation of Thanatology, 630 West 168 St., New York, NY 10032.
The Hastings Center, 255 Elm St., Briarcliff Manor, NY 10510.
International Institute for the Study of Death, PO Box 8565, Pembroke Pines, FL 33084.
The Kennedy Institute for Ethics, Paulton Hall, 37th and P Sts. N.W., Georgetown University, Washington, DC 20057.
The National Hemlock Society, PO Box 11830, Eugene, OR 97440.
Society for the Right to Die, 250 West 57th St., New York, NY 10107.
The Value of Life Committee, 637 Cambridge St., Brighton, MA 02135.

Index

About the Editors and Contributors

ARTHUR S. BERGER, J.D., an author and attorney, is Director of the International Institute for the Study of Death. He is also a member of a medical center bioethics committee and Vice President for Cross-Cultural Affairs of the Foundation of Thanatology.

JOYCE BERGER, M.A., is Administrator of the International Institute for the Study of Death and co-editor of *Perspectives on Death and Dying*. She has been involved in many projects relating to the study of death and dying.

M. ADIL AL ASEER, Ph.D., is Imam and Director at the Islamic Center of Tampa Bay, Tampa, Florida.

MARY ROSE BARRINGTON is an author, solicitor of the Supreme Court of the Judicature of England, and former chairperson of the Voluntary Euthanasia Society (England).

SHIGERU KATO is Professor of Philosophy and Religion at the Tokyo University of Art and Design.

HELENE A. LUTZ, M.A., M.Div., is a Bioethics Fellow at Washington Hospital Center.

JAMES J. McCARTNEY, O.S.A., Ph.D., teaches at the Department of Philosophy, Villanova University.

MARVIN E. NEWMAN, J.D., is Professor of Legal Studies at Rollins College.

DAVID V. SCHAPIRA, M.B.Ch.B., is chief of the Cancer Prevention

Program, H. Lee Moffit Center, and Associate Professor of Medicine at the University of South Florida College of Medicine.

DAYA SHANKER is an advocate of the High Court.

KWASI WIREDU, Ph.D., teaches in the Department of Philosophy, University of South Florida, as a specialist in African philosophy.